The English Flora: Or A Catalogue Of Trees, Shrubs, Plants And Fruits, Natives As Well As Exotics

Richard Weston

THE ENGLISH FLORA:

OR, A

CATALOGUE

OF

Trees, Shrubs, Plants *and* Fruits,

NATIVES as well as EXOTICS,

Cultivated, for Ufe or Ornament, in the

Englifh Nurferies, Greenhoufes and Stoves,

Arranged according to the Linnæan Syftem;

WITH

The LATIN Trivial, and common ENGLISH Names,

And an *Englifh* Index referring to the *Latin* Names.

ALSO,

A General Catalogue of SEEDS,

FOR THE

Kitchen-Garden, Flower-Garden, Grafs-Lands, &c.

USUALLY RAISED FOR SALE,

AND

Thofe annually imported from AMERICA.

Hic ver purpureum, varios hic flumina circum
Fundit humus flores. VIRG. Ecl, 9.

By RICHARD WESTON, Efq;

AUTHOR OF THE UNIVERSAL BOTANIST, &c.

LONDON:

Printed for the AUTHOR:

And Sold by J. MILLAN, *Whitehall*; ROBSON and Co. *New Bond-Street*;
T. CARNAN, *St. Paul's Church-Yard*; E. and C. DILLY, in the *Poultry*;

And by all the NURSERYMEN and SEEDSMEN in *England*.

MDCCLXXV.

[Price 3s. 6d. in boards, 4s. 6d. bound.]

TO

THE RIGHT HONOURABLE

J O H N,

E A R L of B U T E,

LORD MOUNT-STUART,

KNIGHT OF THE MOST NOBLE ORDER OF THE GARTER,

RANGER OF RICHMOND PARK,

A GOVERNOR OF THE CHARTER-HOUSE,

ONE OF THE TRUSTEES OF THE BRITISH MUSEUM,

CHANCELLOR OF THE

MARISCHAL COLLEGE AT ABERDEEN,

AND

ONE OF HIS MAJESTY'S MOST HONOURABLE

PRIVY COUNCIL.

My Lord,

THE great encouragement, Botany has received from the Nobility of this kingdom, entitles us to boaſt a ſupe-riority, in this uſeful and entertaining

ſcience,

DEDICATION.

fcience, over all the other countries of
Europe united, by the noble collections
of Plants in the refpective Gardens of
England, which will do immortal ho-
nour to the good tafte and zeal of the
Cultivators.

To the credit of YOUR LORDSHIP's
NAME, it is univerfally allowed, that no
one has contributed more than You, to
give England this flattering afcendency,
in an art that equally contributes to
accomplifh the Member of Society and
the Gentleman ; and fhould more of
the Nobility be difpofed to follow YOUR
LORDSHIP's laudable example, in an
extenfive Culture of Plants both curious and ufeful, Great-Britain might
fhortly claim the exclufive honour of
uniting, in her Gardens, the native
beauties of every part of the globe.

The

DEDICATION.

The motive of my ambition in inscribing this little work to YOUR LORDSHIP is very obvious. It is to have an opportunity of paying you that homage, which I cannot but look upon as the duty of every writer on my subject, to pay a Nobleman, who has bestowed so much attention upon it. Possibly, YOUR LORDSHIP may not think this undertaking totally unuseful, as I have comprised in a small compass, a Catalogue of the Vegetable Beauties contained in our Gardens; and, should the present taste of arranging the Plants at Kew be followed, the plan will be greatly facilitated by exhibiting at one view, all the Varieties that can be collected.

I am, MY LORD,

With the most profound Respect,

Your Lordship's

most humble and obedient Servant,

Richard Weston.

London, Dec. 13, 1775.

INTRODUCTION.

THE great variety of curious Plants now cultivated in the Englifh Nurferies and Gardens, and which are annually increafing in number, requires that there fhould be one general Catalogue of them, to inform thofe Gentlemen, who are making Collections of Plants, what the United Nurferies of England contain ; for it cannot be fuppofed that any one Nurfery, however copious, can have every Plant which is cultivated : befides, this will certainly create an ambition, both in Gentlemen and Nurferymen, to increafe their collections.

This Catalogue, it is prefumed, will be of ufe to every Gentleman, who has a large collection of Plants, as it will enable him with a very little trouble, by marking in his Book, to form a Catalogue of all the Plants which

he

he has; nor will it be an unuſeful companion to thoſe, who viſit Kew and Chelſea Gardens, ſince the Plants are there arranged after the Linnæan ſyſtem; and this will give the Engliſh names.

To the Nurſerymen, it will ſave the trouble and expence of printing Catalogues of what they have to ſell; for, although this United Catalogue will undoubtedly contain more Varieties than are in any one Nurſery, yet in two or three books kept for their own uſe, to ſhew their cuſtomers, they can eaſily croſs out thoſe varieties which they do not cultivate; but at the ſame time it will inform Gentlemen of ſuch varieties, and perhaps induce them to purchaſe the Plants.

To the Seedſmen, it will be of ſimilar uſe and convenience as to the Nurſerymen, to ſhew what Seeds are uſually raiſed for ſale.

As every one now arranges his Plants by the Linnæan names, it was judged proper to add the Claſs and Order each Plant belongs to, with the Latin trivial, beſides the common
Engliſh

INTRODUCTION.

English names, to make the trivial names of Linnæus familiar to the young Botanist, and be of more general utility.

A mark † is affixed to those Plants which have been but lately introduced into England, or such as are not at present plentiful enough to be sold, to save both Gentlemen and Nurserymen, the trouble of enquiring after them.

The correspondence of any Gentleman, Nurseryman, or Seedsman, who will be so obliging as to communicate to the Author, an account of any varieties in their collection, not inserted here, will be esteemed a very particular favour; as an Appendix shall be published of such, when they amount to a sufficient number, and given *gratis* to the purchasers of this Catalogue.

* * * * *

In the mean time, while the work has been printing, the Author has discovered several Plants, omitted by him: he has therefore inserted them at the end of the work, to save the trouble to any of his correspondents concerning them,

them, until the Appendix is printed, when they will be more fully inferted.

It has been very difficult to afcertain properly the cultivated varieties of feveral of the Kitchen-Garden Plants, particularly the Peas and Beans, the fame fort frequently paffing under different names : however imperfect, therefore, that part may appear to fome, it has not been for want of care or attention, but only on account of the difficulty of felecting the proper ones, for fear of inferting the fame fort twice under a different name.

The Appendix is intended to be publifhed in June, and given *gratis* ; the Author therefore requefts, that thofe who have difcovered any omiffions will be fo obliging as to communicate them to him before that time, and to omit binding of their books till they receive the Appendix.

An ANNUAL SUPPLEMENT is alfo intended to be publifhed, giving an account of any new Plants introduced into England, with a Botanical Defcription of them : the correfpondence, there-

fore,

INTRODUCTION.

fore, of any Gentleman, Nurferyman, Seedfman, or Gardener, giving an account of fuch, and where they can be procured, will be efteemed a particular favour; and if a Drawing be fent, it fhall be paid for with great pleafure, by directing to the Author, to the care of Mr. MILLAN, Bookfeller, at Whitehall.

ERRATA,

CONTENTS of the WORK.

CHAP. I.

HARDY TREES and SHRUBS,

Cultivated in the open Ground.

---

1. ACER.

MAPLE-TREE,——(In French)—ERABLE.

Lin. Gen. Plant. 1155.   Polygamia Monoecia.   Claffis 23. Ordo 1.

1. campeftre.	Small Maple.
2. creticum.	Cretan Maple.
3. monfpeffulanum.	Montpelier Maple.
4. Negundo.	Virginian Afh-leaved Maple.
5. Opalus.	Italian Maple, or Opalus.
6. penfylvanicum.	Penfylvanian Maple.
7. Platanoides. - - 1.	Plane-tree-leaved Norway Maple.
8. *Plat. laciniatum.* - 2.	Jagged-leaved Norway Maple.
9. *Plat. variegatum.* - 3.	Variegated Norway Maple.
10. Pfeudo-Platanus. - 1.	Sycamore or Greater Maple.
11. *Pf. Plat. variegatus* 2.	Variegated Sycamore.
12. rubrum. - - - 1.	Scarlet-flowering Virginian Maple.
13. *pallidè rubrum* - 2.	Sir Charles Wager's Maple.
14. faccharinum.	American Sugar Maple.
15. tataricum.	Tartarian Maple.

2. ÆSCULUS.

HORSE-CHESNUT-TREE,——(Fr.)—Maronier d'Inde.

L. G. Pl. 462.   Heptandria Monogynia.   Cl. 7. Ord. 1.

1. Hippocaftanum.	Horfe-Chefnut-tree.
2. *Hip. albo-variegatum.*	White-ftriped Horfe-Chefnut-tree.
3. *Hip. luteo-variegatum.*	Yellow-ftriped Horfe-Chefnut-tree.
4. *Hip. flavum.*	Yellow-floweringHorfe-Chefnut-tree
5. Pavia.	Scarlet-floweringHorfe-Chefnut tree.

B

3. AMORPHA.

BASTARD INDIGO,——(Fr.)—

L. G. Pl. 861.　　　Diadelphia Decandria.　　　Cl. 17. Ord. 7.
1. fruticofa.　　　　Baftard Indigo.

4. AMYGDALUS.

ALMOND-TREE,——(Fr.)—Amandier.

L. G. Pl. 619.　　　Icofandria Monogynia.　　　Cl. 12. Ord. 1.,

1. communis - -   1. Common Bitter Almond-tree.
2. *dulcis.* - - - 2. Sweet Almond-tree.
3. *alba.* - - - - 3. White-flowering Almond-tree.
†4. orientalis.　　　Silvery-leaved Eaftern Almond-tree.
5. nana. - - - 1. Dwarf Almond-tree.
6. *nana plena.* - - 2. Double-flowering Dwarf Almond.
†7. Amygdalo-Perfica.　Peach-bearing Almond-tree.
†8. chinenfis.　　　　Chinefe Almond-tree.

AMYGDALUS-PERSICA.

PEACH-TREE,——(Fr.)—Pecher.

1. vulgaris. - - 1. Peach-tree.
2. *plena.* - - - 2. Double-flowering Peach-tree.
3. *nana.* - - - 3. Dwarf Orleans Peach-tree.

5. ANDROMEDA.

ANDROMEDA,——(Fr.)—

L. G. Pl. 549.　　　Decandria Monogynia.　　　Cl. 10. Ord. 1.

1. arborea.　　　　Tree Andromeda.
2. axillaris.　　　　Axillary-flowered Andromeda.
3. calyculata.　　　Calyculated Andromeda.
4. daboecia.　　　　Irifh Whorts, or Cantabrian And.
5. ferruginea.　　　Iron-coloured Andromeda.
6. globulifera.　　　Globular Andromeda.
7. lucida.　　　　Shining-leaved Andromeda.
8. mariana.　　　　Ovate-leaved Andromeda.
9. myrtifolia.　　　Myrtle-leaved Andromeda.
10. paniculata.　　　Paniculated Andromeda.
11. pilulifera.　　　Pill-fhaped Andromeda.
12. Polifolia.　　　　Rofemary-leaved Andromeda.
13. racemofa.　　　　Branching Andromeda.

6. ANNONA.

ANNONA, or CUSTARD-APPLE,——(Fr.)—

L. G. Pl. 693.   Polyandria Polygynia.   Cl. 13. Ord. 7.
  1. triloba.   Carolina Annona, or Papaw-tree.
  2. glabra.   Smooth Annona.

7. ARALIA.

ARALIA, or BERRY-BEARING ANGELICA,——(Fr.)—

L. G. Pl. 386.   Pentandria Pentagynia.   Cl. 5. Ord. 5.
  1. arborefcens.   Tree Aralia.
  2. nudicaulis.   Naked-ftalked Aralia.
  3. fpinofa.   Prickly Aralia, or Angelica-tree.

8. ARBUTUS.

STRAWBERRY-TREE, or ARBUTUS, (Fr.) Arboufier.

L. G. Pl. 552.   Decandria Monogynia.   Cl. 10. Ord. 1.
  1. Unedo. - - - 1.   Arbutus or Strawberry-tree.
  2. *Unedo duplex.* - - 2.   Double-flowering Arbutus.
  3. *Unedo rubra.* - - 3.   Red-flowering Arbutus.
 †4. *Unedo bacciflava.* - 4.   Yellow-berried Arbutus.
  5. Andrachne.   EafternStrawberry-tree or Andrachne
  6. Uva Urfi.   Bear-berry.
  7. alpina.   Alpine Arbutus.

9. ARISTOLOCHIA.

BIRTHWORT,——(Fr.)—Ariftoloche.

L. G. Pl. 1022.   Gynandria Hexandria.   Cl. 20. Ord. 5.
  1. arborefcens.   Tree Birth-wort.

10. ARTEMISIA-ABROTANUM.

SOUTHERNWOOD,——(Fr.)—Auronne.

L. G. Pl. 945.   Syngenefia Polygamia Superflua. Cl. 19. Ord. 2.
  1. Abrotanum.   Southernwood.
  2. humile.   Dwarf Southernwood.

ARTEMISIA-ABSINTHIUM.

WORMWOOD,——(Fr.)—Abfinte.

  1. arborefcens.   Tree Wormwood.

B 2

11. ASCYRUM.

SAINT PETER's WORT.

L. G. Pl. 903.   Polyadelphia Polyandria.   Cl. 18. Ord. 3.
1. Crux Andreæ.   St. Peter's Wort.

12. ASTRAGALUS-TRAGACANTHA.

GOAT's-THORN, (Fr.) Barbe-Renarde.

L. G. Pl. 892.   Diadelphia Decandria.   Cl. 17. Ord. 3.
1. Tragacantha   Goat's-thorn.

13. ATRIPLEX.

SEA PURSLANE-TREE, (Fr.) Pourpier de Mer.

L. G. Pl. 1153.   Polygamia Monoecia.   Cl. 6. Ord. 2.
1. Halimus.   Sea Purslane-tree.

14. AZALEA.

AZALEA.

L. G. Pl. 212.   Pentandria Monogynia.   Cl. 5. Ord. 1.
1. nudiflora - - 1. Red Azalea.
2. *nudiflora serotina* - 2. Late Red Azalea.
3. viscosa - - - 1. White Azalea.
4. *viscosa serotina* - 2. Late White Azalea.
5. procumbens. Alpine Azalea.

15. BACCHARIS.

PLOUGHMAN's SPIKENARD and GROUNDSEL-TREE, (Fr.) Bacchante.

L. G. Pl. 949.   Syngenesia Polygamia Superflua.   Cl. 19. Ord. 2.
1. Halimifolia.   Groundsel-tree.

16. BERBERIS.

BERBERRY-TREE,——(Fr.)—Epine-vinette.

L. G. Pl. 442.   Hexandria Monogynia.   Cl. 6. Ord. 1.
1. vulgaris. - - - 1. Berberry-tree.
2. *vulg. enuclea.* - - 2. Stoneless Berberry-tree.
3. *vulg. alba.* - - 3. White-fruited Berberry-tree.
4. canadensis. Canadian Berberry-tree.

17. BETULA.

BIRCH-TREE,——(Fr.)—Aune.

L. G. Pl. 1052.	Monoecia Tetrandria.	Cl. 21. Ord. 4.
1. alba.	Birch-tree.	
2. canadenfis.	Canadian Birch-tree.	
3. lenta.	Poplar-leaved Virginian Birch-tree.	
4. nana.	Dwarf Birch-tree.	
5. nigra.	Black Virginian Birch-tree.	

BETULA-ALNUS,

ALDER-TREE,——(Fr.)

1. Alnus.	Alder-tree.
2. glutinofa.	Turkey Alder-tree.
3. incana.	Hoary-leaved Alder-tree.

18. BIGNONIA.

TRUMPET-FLOWER or SCARLET JESSAMINE, (Fr.) Bignonia.

L. G. Pl. 759.	Didynamia Angiofpermia.		CL. 14. Ord. 1.
1. Catalpa,			Trumpet-flower or Catalpa,
2. radicans.	-	1.	Afh-leaved Bignonia.
3. radicans minor.	-	2.	Small-flowered Bignonia.
4. fempervirens.			Evergreen Bignonia.
5. Unguis Cati.			Four-leaved Bignonia.

19. BUXUS.

BOX-TREE,——(Fr.)—Buis.

L. G. Pl. 1053.	Monoecia Tetrandria.		Cl. 21. Ord. 4.
1. arborefcens	-	1.	Box-tree.
2. aureo-variegata	-	2.	Gold-ftriped Box-tree.
3. argentata	-	3.	Silver-edged Box-tree.
4. aurata	-	4.	Gold-edged Box-tree.
5. angufifolia	-	5.	Narrow-leaved Box-tree.
6. angufifolia-aurata		6.	Gold-edged narrow-leaved Box-tree.
7. aureo-notata	-	7.	Gold-tipped Box-tree.
8. fuffruticofa	-	8.	Dwarf Box,
9. fuffrut. variegata	-	9.	Striped Dwarf Box.
10. myrtifolia	-	10.	Myrtle-leaved Box-tree.

B 3

20. CALYCANTHUS.

L. G. Pl. 639.   Icofandria Polygynia.   Cl. 21. Ord. 5.

1. florida   -   -   -   1. Carolinian Allfpice.
2. *florida nana*   -   -   2. Dwarf Carolinian Allfpice.

21. CARPINUS.

HORNBEAM,——(Fr.)—Charme.

L. G. Pl. 1073.   Monoecia Polyandria.   Cl. 21. Ord. 8.

1. Betulus   -   -   -   1. Hornbeam.
2. *Bet. aureo-variegata* 2. Gold-ftriped Hornbeam,
3. orientalis.   Eaftern Hornbeam.
4. Oftrya.   Hop Hornbeam.
5. virginiana.   Virginian Hornbeam,

22. CASSINE.

CASHIOBERRY BUSH, or SOUTH-SEA TEA-TREE.

L. G. Pl. 371.   Pentandria Trigynia.   Cl. 5. Ord. 3.

1. Peragua.   South-Sea Tea-tree.

23. CEANOTHUS.

CEANOTHUS, or NEW-JERSEY TEA-TREE.

L. G. Pl. 267.   Pentandria Monogynia.   Cl. 5. Ord. 1.

1. Americana.   New-Jerfey Tea-tree or Ceanothus.

24. CELASTRUS.

STAFF-TREE, or CELASTRUS.

L. G. Pl. 270.   Pentandria Monogynia.   Cl. 5. Ord. 1.

1. fcandens.   Climbing Staff-tree.
2. bullatus.   Round-leaved Staff-tree.

25. CELTIS.

LOTE, or NETTLE-TREE,——(Fr.)—Micoulier.

L. G. Pl. 1143.   Polygamia Monoecia.   Cl. 23. Ord. 1.

1. auftralis.   European black-fruited Nettle-tree.
2. occidentalis.   American purple-fruited Nettle-tree.
3. orientalis.   Eaftern yellow-fruited Nettle-tree.

26. CEPHALANTHUS.

AMERICAN BUTTON-WOOD-TREE,——(Fr,)—

L. G. Pl. 113.   Tetrandria Monogynia.   Cl. 4. Ord. 1.
1. occidentalis.   American Button-wood-tree.

27. CERCIS.

JUDAS-TREE,——(Fr.)—Guainier.

L. G. Pl. 510.   Decandria Monogynia.   Cl. 10. Ord. 1.

1. canadensis.   Canadian Judas-tree.
2. Siliquastrum - - 1.   European Judas-tree.
3. *Siliquastrum album* 2.   White-flowered Judas-tree.

28. CHIONANTHUS.

FRINGE, or SNOWDROP-TREE.

L. G. Pl. 21.   Diandria Monogynia.   Cl. 2. Ord. 1.

1. virginica.   Fringe, or Snowdrop-tree.

29. CISTUS.

CISTUS, or ROCK ROSE,——(Fr.)—Cifte.

L. G. Pl. 673.   Polyandria Monogynia.   Cl. 13. Ord. 1.

1. albidus.   White-leaved Cistus.
2. appenninus,   German Dwarf Cistus.
3. brevifolius.   Small-leaved Cistus.
4. cordifolius.   Heart-shaped-leaved Cistus.
5. creticus,   Cretan Cistus.
6. crispus.   Curled-leaved Cistus.
7. halimifolius - - 1.   Sea-Purslane-leaved Cistus.
8. *halimifolius angustus* 2,   Narrow Sea-Purslane-leaved Cistus.
9. Helianthemum.   Dwarf Cistus.
10. hispanicus.   Spanish Cistus.
11. incanus - - - 1,   Hoary-leaved Cistus.
12. *incanus.longifolius* 2.   Long-hoary-leaved Cistus,
13. ladaniferus. - - 1.   Laudanum-bearing Cistus.
14. *ladaniferus maculatus* 2.   Spotted Laudanum-bearing Cistus.
15. laurifolius.   Laurel-leaved Cistus.
16. libanotis.   Spanish narrow-leaved Cistus.
17. lusitanicus.   Portugal Cistus,
18. monspeliensis - - 1.   Montpelier Cistus

B 4

19. *monfpelienfis oleæfol.*	2.	Montpelier Olive-leaved Ciftus.
20. pilofus,		Hairy-leaved Ciftus.
21. populifolius.		Poplar-leaved Ciftus.
22. falicifolius	1.	Willow-leaved Ciftus.
23. *falicifolius maculatus*	2.	Spotted-flowered Willow-leavedCift.
24. falvifolius,		Sage-leaved Ciftus.

30. CLEMATIS.

Virgin's Bower, Climber or Traveller's Joy, (F.)Clematite.

| L. G. Pl. 696. | Polyandria Polygynia. | Cl. 13. Qrd. 7. |

1. canadenfis.		Canadian Virgin's Bower.
2. crifpa,		Curled Virgin's Bower.
3. orientalis.		Eaftern Virgin's Bower.
4. fibirica,		Siberian Virgin's Bower.
5. Viorna.		Carolinian Virgin's Bower.
6. Vitalba.		Wild Traveller's Joy.
7. Viticella	1.	Blue or Purple Virgin's Bower.
8. *Viticella rubra*	2.	Red Virgin's Bower.
9. *Viticella plena*	3.	Douple Purple Virgin's Bower.

31. CLETHRA.

Clethra,——(Fr.)——

| L. G. Pl. 553. | Decandria Monogynia. | Cl. 10. Ord. 1. |

| 1. alnifolia | 1. | Clethra, |
| 2. *alnifolia anguftifolia* | 2. | Narrow-leaved Clethra, |

32. CNEORUM.

Widow-Wail,——(Fr.)——

| L. G. Pl. 48. | Triandria Monogynia. | Cl. 3. Ord. 1. |
| 1. tricoccum, | Widow-Wail. | |

33. COLUTEA.

Bladder Sena,——(Fr.)—Baguenaudier.

| L. G. Pl. 880. | Diadelphia Decandria. | Cl. 17. Ord. 3. |

1. arborefcens.		Bladder Sena,
2. arboref. integerrima.		Entire-leaved Bladder Sena,
3. Iftria.		Yellow-flowered Bladder Sena,
4. orientalis.		Oriental or Pocock's Bladder Sena,

34. CORIARIA.

MYRTLE-LEAVED SUMACH,——(Fr.)——

L. G. Pl. 1129.   Dioecia Decandria.   Cl. 22. Ord. 9

1. myrtifolia.   Myrtle-leaved Sumach.

35. CORNUS.

CORNELIAN CHERRY, or DOGWOOD,——(Fr.)——Cournouiller.

L. G. Pl. 149.   Tetrandria Monogynia.   Cl. 4. Ord. 1.

1. mascula - ⊢ - 1. Cornelian Cherry.
2. *mascula alba* - - 2. White-fruited Cornelian Cherry.
3. alba. Newfoundland Dogwood.
4. amomum. Blue-berried American Dogwood.
5. angustifolia. Narrow-leaved American Dogwood.
6. florida. Virginian red-twigged Dogwood.
7. nova-belgica. New-Holland Dogwood.
8. sanguinea - - 1. English Dogwood, or Cornel-tree.
9. *sanguinea variegata* 2. Striped-leaved Cornel-tree.

36. CORONILLA.

CORONILLA, or JOINTED-PODDED COLUTEA.

L. G. Pl. 883.   Diadelphia Decandria.   Cl. 17. Ord. 4.

1. hispanica. Jointed-podded Colutea.
2. Emerus. Scorpion Sena.

37. CORYLUS.

HAZEL, or NUT-TREE,——(Fr.)

L. G. Pl. 1074.   Monoecia Polyandria.   Cl. 21. Ord. 8.

1. avellana - - - 1. Hazel or Nut-tree.
2. *avellana sativa* - 2. Filbert-tree.
3. Colurna. Byzantine Nut-tree.
4. cornuta. Amerian Cuckold Nut-tree.
5. transylvanica. Transylvanian Nut-tree.

38. CRATÆGUS.

WILD SERVICE-TREE,——(Fr.)——Alizier.

L. G. Pl. 622.   Icosandria Digynia.   Cl. 12. Ord. 2.

1. Aria. White Bean-tree, or White leaf-tree.
2. Azarolus. Azarole.

3. coccinea.	Virginian Cockfpur Hawthorn.
4. dulcis.	Sweet-fruited Hawthorn.
5. Crus galli.	Virginian Pear-leaved Azarole.
6. flava.	Yellow Pear-fhaped Hawthorn.
7. Oxyacantha - - 1.	Hawthorn, or Whitethorn.
8. *Oxyac. plena* - - 2.	Double-flowering Hawthorn.
9. *Oxyac. bacciflava* - 3.	Yellow-berried Hawthorn.
10. *Oxyac. biflora* - - 4.	Glaftonbury Hawthorn.
11. penfylvanica.	Penfylvanian Hawthorn.
12. prunifolia.	Plum-leaved Hawthorn.
13. pyrifolia.	Pear-leaved Hawthorn.
14. falicifolia.	Willow-leaved Hawthorn.
15. tomentofa.	Goofeberry-leaved Virginian Hawth,
16. torminalis.	Englifh Wild Service-tree.
17. viridis.	Maple-leaved Virginian Hawthorn.

39. CUPRESSUS.

CYPRESS-TREE,——(Fr.)—Cyprès.

L. G. Pl. 1079.   Monoecia Monadelphia.   Cl. 21. Ord. 9.

1. difticha.	Deciduous Virginian Cyprefs.
2. horifontalis.	Spreading or Horifontal Cyprefs,
3. lufitanica.	Portugal Cyprefs, or Goa Cedar,
4. fempervirens.	Upright Italian Cyprefs.
5. Thyoides.	Dwarf Maryland Cyprefs.

40. CYTISUS.

CYTISUS, or BASE TREFOIL-TREE,——(Fr.)—Cytife.

L. G. Pl. 877.   Diadelphia Decandria.   Cl. 17. Ord. 3.

1. auftriacus.	Auftrian or Tartarian Cytifus.
2. glutinofus.	Glutinous-leaved Cytifus.
3. hirfutus.	Hairy Evergreen Cytifus.
4. nigricans.	Smooth black Cytifus.
5. feffilifolius.	Seffile-leaved Cytifus.
6. fupinus.	Trailing Cytifus.
7. tataricus.	Tartarian or Siberian Cytifus.

CYTISUS LABURNUM.

LABURNUM,——(Fr.)—

1. latifolium - - 1.	Broad-leaved Laburnum.
†2. *lat. variegatum* - 2.	Variegated Broad-leaved Laburnum.
3. *lat. breviflorum* - 3.	Scotch Short-flowered Laburnum.
4. anguftifolium.	Long-fpiked Narrow-leaved Labu

41. DAPHNE.

SPURGE LAUREL, or MEZEREON,——(Fr.)—Garou.

L. G. Pl. 485.　　　Octandria Monogynia.　　　Cl. 8. Ord. 1.

1. alpina.	Alpine Woolly-leaved Daphne.
2. Cneorum.	Narrow-leaved Daphne.
3. Laureola.	Evergreen Spurge Laurel.
†4. *Laur. variegata* - 1.	Variegated Evergreen Spurge Laurel.
5. Mezereum - .- 2.	Purple Mezereon, or Spurge Olive.
6. *album* - - - 3.	White Mezereon.
7. *rubefcens* - - - 4.	Pale-red Mezereon.
8. *rubrum* - - - 5.	Red Mezereon.
9. *variegatum* - - 6.	Yellow-ftriped-leaved Mezereon.
10. *autumnale* - - 7.	Autumnal Purple-flowering Mezer.
11. Tarton-Raira.	Silvery-leaved Daphne.

42. DIOSPYROS.

DATE PLUM,——(Fr.)—

L. G. Pl. 1161.　　　Polygamia Dioecia.　　　Cl. 23. Ord. 2.

1. Lotus.	Indian Date Plum.
2. Virginiana.	Virginian Pifhamin Plum.

43. DIRCA.

LEATHERWOOD,——(Fr.)—

L. G. Pl. 486.　　　Octandria Monogynia.　　　Cl. 8. Ord. 1.

1. paluftris.	Virginian Marfh Leatherwood.

44. DRYAS.

DRYAS,———(Fr.)——

L. G. Pl. 637.　　　Icofandria Polygynia.　　　Cl. 12. Ord. 5.

1. octopetala.	Dryas.

45. ELÆAGNUS.

WILD OLIVE-TREE,——(Fr.)—Olivier Sauvage.

L. G. Pl. 159.　　　Tetrandria Monogynia.　　　Cl. 4. Ord. 1.

1. anguftifolia.	Narrow-leaved Wild Olive-tree.
2. latifolia.	Broad-leaved Wild Olive-tree.

46. EMPETRUM.

CROW-BERRY,——(Fr.)——

L. G. Pl. 1100.   Dioecia Tetrandria.   Cl. 22. Ord. 4.

1. nigrum.   Crow-berry.

47. EPHEDRA.

SHRUBBY HORSE-TAIL.——(Fr.)——

L. G. Pl. 1136.   Dioecia Monadelphia.   Cl. 22. Ord. 4.

1. diftachya.   Shrubby Horfe-tail.
2. monoftachya.   Dwarf Shrubby Horfe-tail.

48. EPIGÆA.

EPIGÆA, or TRAILING ARBUTUS,——(Fr.)——

L. G. Pl. 550.   Decandria Monogynia.   Cl. 10. Ord. 1.

1. repens.   Trailing Arbutus.

49. ERICA.

HEATH,——(Fr.)—Bruyere.

L. G. Pl. 484.   Octandria Monogynia.   Cl. 8. Ord. 1.

1. arborea.   Great White Heath.
2. ciliaris.   Rough-leaved Englifh Heath.
3. cinerea.   Fine-leaved Englifh Heath.
4. vulgaris - - - 1.   Common Englifh Heath or Ling.
5. *vulg. alba* - - 2.   White-flowering Englifh Heath.
6. lufitanica.   Portugal upright red Heath.
7. multiflora.   Fir-leaved Englifh Heath.
8. multiflora alba.   White Fir-leaved Englifh Heath.
9. paniculata.   Ethiopian Heath.
10. tetralix - - - 1.   Crofs-leaved Englifh Heath.
11. *tetralix alba* - - 2.   White Crofs-leaved Englifh Heath.

50. EUONYMUS.

SPINDLE-TREE,——(Fr.)—Fufain.

L. G. Pl. 271.   Pentandria Monogynia.   Cl. 5. Ord. 1.

1. europæus - - 1.   Red-capfuled Spindle-tree.
2. *eur. albus* - - 2.   White-capfuled Spindle-tree.

3. *eur. latifolius* - - 3.   Broad-leaved Spindle-tree.
4. *eur. lat. variegatus* 4.   Variegated Broad-leaved Spindle-tr.
5. americanus.   American Evergreen Spindle-tree.
6. longifolius.   Carolina long-leaved Spindle-tree.
7. verrucofus.   Warty Spindle-tree.

51. FAGUS.

BEECH-TREE,——(Fr.)—Hêtre.

L. G. Pl. 1072.   Monoecia Polyandria.   Cl. 21. Ord. 8.

1. sylvatica - - - 1.   Beech-tree.
2. *sylv. luteo-variegata* 2.   Yellow-striped Beech-tree.
3. *sylv. albo-variegata* 3.   White-striped Beech-tree.
4. *sylv. atro-purpurea* 4.   American Purple-leaved Beech.

FAGUS-CASTANEA.

CHESNUT-TREE,——(Fr.)—Chateigner.

1. Caftanea fativa - 1.   Chefnut-tree.
2. *Caft. aureo-variegata* 2.   Gold-ftriped Chefnut-tree.
3. dentata.   American large-fruited Chef.
4. pumila.   Dwarf Chefnut-tree, or Chinquepin.

52. FICUS.

FIG-TREE,——(Fr.)—Figuier.

L. G. Pl. 1168.   Polygamia Monoecia.   Cl. 23. Ord. 1.

1. Carica.   Fig-tree, For whofe Varieties fee the Fruit Catalogue.

53. FOTHERGILLA.

FOTHERGILLA.

L. G. Pl.   Cl.   Ord.

1. fpeciofa.   Fothergilla.

54. FRAXINUS.

ASH-TREE,——(Fr.)—Frêne.

L. G. Pl. 1160.   Polygamia Dioecia.   Cl. 23. Ord. 2.

1. excelfior - - - 1.   Afh-tree.
†2. *excel.argenteo-varieg.*2.   Silver-ftriped Afh-tree.

†3. excel. *aureo-variegata*.　　Gold-ftriped Afh-tree.
4. Ornus.　　Dwarf Afh-tree.
5. paniculata.　　Virginian Flowering Afh-tree.
6. americana.　　Carolinian Broad-keyed Red Afh.
7. Calabrienfis.　　Calabrian Manna Afh-tree.
8. alba.　　New-England White Afh-tree.
9. nigra.　　American Black Afh-tree.
10. penfylvanica.　　Penfylvanian Afh-tree.

55. GAULTHERIA.

GAULTHERIA.

| L. G. Pl. 551. | Decandria Monogynia. | Cl. 10. Ord. 1. |
| 1. procumbens. | Canadian Gaultheria. | |

56. GENISTA.

BROOM,——(Fr.) Genêt.

L. G. Pl. 859.	Diadelphia-Decandria.	Cl. 17. Ord. 3.
1. anglica.	Dwarf Englifh Broom.	
2. candicans.	Montpelier Broom, or Cytifus.	
3. florida.	Spanifh Dyer's Broom.	
4. pilofa.	Branching Broom.	
5. fagittalis.	Jointed Dwarf Broom.	
6. tinctoria. - - 1.	Dyer's Broom.	
7. *tinctoria italica*. - 2.	Lucca Broom.	

57. GINKGO.

MAIDENHAIR-TREE,——(Fr.)—

| L. G. Pl. | | Cl.   Ord. |
| 1. biloba. | Japanefe Ginkgo, or Maidenhair-tree. | |

58. GLEDITSIA.

TRIPLE-THORNED ACACIA,——(Fr.)—

L. G. Pl. 1159.	Polygamia Dioecia.	Cl. 23. Ord. 2.
1. fpinofa.	Triple-thorned Acacia.	
2. inermis.	Water Acacia.	
3. orientalis.	Eaftern Acacia.	

59. GLYCINE.

CAROLINIAN KIDNEY-BEAN-TREE,——(Fr.)—

L. G. Pl. 868. Diadelphia Decandria. Cl. 17. Ord. 3.

1. frutefcens. Carolinian Kidney-bean-tree.
2. Apios. Virginian Kidney-bean-tree.

60. GUILANDINA.

BONDUC, or NICKAR-TREE,——(Fr.)—

L. G. Pl. 517. Decandria Monogynia. Cl. 10. Ord. 1.

1. dioica mafula. Male Bonduc, or Nickar-tree.
2. dioica fœminea. Female Bonduc, or Nickar-tree.

61. HALESIA.

HALESIA,——(Fr.)—

L. G. Pl. 596. Dodecandria Monogynia. Cl. 11. Ord. 1.

1. tetraptera. Carolinian Quadrangular-fruited Halefia.

62. HAMAMELIS.

WITCH HAZEL,——(Fr.)—

L. G. Pl. 169. Tetrandria Digynia. Cl. 4. Ord. 2.

1. virginiana. Virginian Witch Hazel.

63. HEDERA.

IVY,——(Fr.)—

L. G. Pl. 283. Pentandria Monogynia. Cl. 5. Ord. 1.

1. Helix. - - - 1. Ivy.
2. *argenteo-variegata.* 2. Silver-ftriped Ivy.
3. *aureo-variegata.* - 3. Gold-ftriped Ivy.
4. quinquefolia. Virginian Creeper, or Ivy.

64. HIBISCUS.

ÆTHÆA FRUTEX, or SYRIAN MALLOW,——(Fr.)—

L. G. Pl. 846. Monadelphia Polyandria. Cl. 16. Ord. 3.

1. Syriacus. - - - 1. Red Althæa.
2. *albus.* - - - - 2. White Althæa.

3. *albus et ruber.* -	3.	Red and White Althæa.
4. *flavus.* - - -	4.	Yellow Althæa.
5. *purpureus.* - -	5.	Purple Althæa.
6. *pallidè purpureus.*	6.	Pale Purple Althæa.
7. *albo-variegatus.* -	7.	Silver-ftriped-leaved Althæa.
8. *luteo-variegatus.*	8.	Gold-bloatched-leaved Althæa.

65. HIPPOPHAE.

SEA BUCKTHORN, or SALLOW-THORN,——(Fr.)—

L. G. Pl. 1136. Dioecia Tetrandria. Cl. 22. Ord. 4.

1. canadenfis. Canadian Sea Buckthorn.
2. Rhamnoides. Sea Buckthorn.

66. HYDRANGEA.

HYDRANGEA,——(Fr.)—

L. G. Pl. 557. Decandria Digynia. Cl. 10. Ord. 2.

1. arborefcens. Virginian Hydrangea.

67. HYPERICUM.

SAINT JOHN's WORT,——(Fr.) Millepertuis.

L. G. Pl. 902. Polyadelphia Polyandria. Cl. 14. Ord. 1.

1. Androfæmum. Tutfan.
2. canarienfe. Canary St. John's Wort.
3. hircinum. Stinking St. John's Wort.
4. *hircinum nanum.* Dwarf Stinking St. John's Wort.
5. inodorum. Scentlefs St. John's Wort.
6. kalmianum. American fweet-fmelling St. J. W.
7. olympicum. Eaftern St. John's Wort.
8. prolificum. Proliferous St. John's Wort.

68. JASMINUM.

JESSAMINE-TREE,——(Fr.) Jafmin.

L. G. Pl. 17. Diandria Monogynia. Cl. 2. Ord. 1.

1. fruticans. Yellow Jeffamine.
2. humile. Italian Yellow Jeffamine.
3. officinale. - - 1. White Jeffamine.

4. off. *aureo-variegat.* 2. Gold-ftriped Jeſſamine.
5. off.*argenteo-varieg.* 3. Silver-ftriped Jeſſamine.

69. ILEX.

HOLLY-TREE,——(Fr.) Houx.

L. G. Pl. 172.   Tetrandria Tetragynia.   Cl. 4. Ord. 3.

1. Aquifolium viride.   Common Green Holly.
2. *glabrum,*   Smooth-leaved Green Holly.
3. *ferriforme,*   Saw-leaved Green Holly.
4. *baccialbum.*   White-berried Green Holly.
5. *bacciflavum,*   Yellow-berried Green Holly,
6. *baccifl. variegatum.*   Bloatched-leaved ditto.
7. *echinatum* - - 1.   Green Hedge-hog Holly.
8. *ech. argenteum* - 2.   Silver-edged Hedge-hog Holly.
9. *ech. aureum* - - 3.   Gold-edged Hedge-hog Holly.
10. *ech.aureo-variegatum* 4.   Gold-bloatched Hedge-hog Holly.

The following Varieties are all with variegated Leaves.

11. Aſlett's Holly.
12. Bagſhot's Holly,
13. Bench's Holly.
14. Blind's cream Holly,
15. Bowen's Holly,
16. Box-leaved Holly.
17. Bradley's long-leaved Hol.
18. Bradley's beft Holly.
19. Bradley's yellow Holly.
20. Bridgman's Holly.
21. Britiſh Holly.
22. Broderick's Holly.
23. Brownrig's Holly.
24. Capel's mottled Holly.
25. Cheney's Holly.
26. Chimney-fweepers' Holly.
27. Chohole Holly.
28. Eale's Holly.
29. Ellis's Holly,
30. Franklin's Holly,
31. Fuller's cream Holly.

32. Glafs's Holly.
33. Glory of the Eaft Holly.
34. Glory of the Weft Holly.
35. Gray's Holly.
36. Hertfordſhire white Holly.
37. Langton Holly.
38. Longſtaff's Holly.
39. Mafon's copper-col. Holly.
40. Milkmaid Holly.
41. Painted-Lady Holly.
42. Partridge's Holly.
43. Phyllis Holly.
44. Pritchet's Holly.
45. Rench's Holly.
46. Union Holly.
47. Wells's Holly.
48. Whitmill's Holly.
49. Wife's Holly.
50. White-bloatched Holly.
51. Yellow-bloatched Holly.

52. caroliniana. - - - 1, Carolinian, or Dahoon Holly.
53. *carol. anguſtifolia.* - - 2. Narrow-leaved Dahoon Holly.

C

70. ITEA.

ITEA,————(Fr.)———

L. G. Pl. 275.   Pentandria Monogynia.   Cl. 5. Ord. 1.

1. virginica.   Virginian Itea.
2. *virginica angustifolia.*   Narrow-leaved Virginian Itea.

71. IVA.

FALSE JESUIT'S BARK-TREE,————(Fr.)———

L. G. Pl. 1059.   Monoecia Pentandria.   Cl. 21. Ord. 5.

1. frutescens.   False Jesuit's Bark-tree.

72. JUGLANS.

WALNUT-TREE,————(Fr.)—Noyer.

L. G. Pl. 1071.   Monoecia Polyandria.   Cl. 21. Ord. 8.

1. regia.   Walnut-tree.
2. alba.   Hickery-Nut-tree.
3. minor.   Small Hickery-Nut-tree.
4. ovata.   Shag-bark'd Hickery-Nut-tree.
5. minima.   Pignut-tree.
6. cinerea.   Pensylvanian Walnut-tree.
7. nigra.   Black Virginian Walnut-tree.
8. *nigra oblonga* - - 1.   Oblong Black Virginian Walnut-tr.
9. *oblonga alba* - - 2.   Oblong White Virginian Walnut-tr.
10. illinea.   Illinois Walnut-tree.

73. JUNIPERUS.

JUNIPER-TREE,————(Fr.)—Genevrier.

L. G. Pl. 1134.   Dioecia Monadelphia.   Cl. 22. Ord. 12.

1. communis.   Juniper.
2. orientalis.   Eastern Juniper.
3. suecica.   Swedish Juniper.
4. Oxycedrus.   Spanish Juniper.
5. bermudiana.   Bermudian Cedar.
6. caroliniana.   White Carolinian Cedar.
7. lycia.   Lycian Large-berried Cedar.
8. phœnicea.   Phenician Cedar.
†9. thurifera.   Spanish Cedar.
10. virginiana.   Virginian Red Cedar.

JUNIPERUS-SABINA.

SAVIN,——(Fr.)——

1. Sabina - - - 1. Savin.
2. *Sabina variegata* - 2. Striped Savin.
3. lufitanica 　 Upright Portugal Savin.

74. KALMIA.

KALMIA,——(Fr.)——

L. G. Pl. 545. 　 Decandria Monogynia. 　 Cl. 10. Ord. 1.

1. anguftifolia. 　 Narrow-leaved Kalmia.
2. latifolia. 　 Broad-leaved Kalmia.
3. polifolia. 　 Polium-leaved Kalmia.

75. LAVANDULA.

LAVENDER,——(Fr.)—Lavande.

L. G. Pl. 711. 　 Didynamia Gymnofpermia. 　 Cl. 14. Ord. 1.

1. Spica. 　 Lavender.
2. anguftifolia. 　 Narrow-leaved Lavender.
3. latifolia. 　 Broad-leaved Lavender.

LAVANDULA-STŒCHAS.

FRENCH LAVENDER, or STŒCHAS.

1. Stœchas officinalis. 　 French Lavender.

76. LAURUS.

BAY-TREE,——(Fr.)—Laurier.

L. G. Pl. 503. 　 Enneandria Monogynia. 　 Cl. 19. Ord. 1.

1. nobilis. 　 Bay-tree.
2. *nobilis latifolia.* 　 Broad-leaved Bay-tree.
3. *nob. tenuifolia.* 　 Narrow-leaved Bay-tree.
4. *nob. undulata.* 　 Waved-leaved Bay-tree.
†5. *nob. plena.* 　 Double-flowering Bay-tree.
†6. *nob. variegata.* 　 Striped-leaved Bay-tree.
7. Benzoïn 　 Benjamin-tree.
8. Borbonia. 　 Blue-berried Carolinian Bay.
9. Saffafras. 　 Saffafras-tree.

C 2

77. LEDUM.

MARSH CISTUS, or WILD ROSEMARY.——(Fr,)—

L. G. Pl. 546.   Decandria Monogynia.   Cl. 10. Ord. 1.

1. paluftre - - - 1. Marfh Ciftus.
2. *paluftre minus* - 2. Small Marfh Ciftus.
3. thymæfolium.   Thyme-leaved Ciftus.
4. Viffikapucca.   Labrador-tea.

78. LIGUSTRUM.

PRIVET,——(Fr.)—Troene.

L. G. Pl. 18.   Diandria Monogynia.   Cl. 2. Ord. 1,

1. vulgare.   Privet.
2. *aureo-variegatum.*   Gold-bloatched Privet,
3. *argenteo-variegatum.*   Silver-ftriped Privet.
4. italicum.   Evergreen Italian Privet.

79. LIQUIDAMBAR.

LIQUIDAMBER, or STORAX-TREE,——(Fr.)—

L. G. Pl. 1076.   Monoecia Polyandria.   Cl. 21. Ord. 8,

1. Styraciflua.   Virginian Liquidamber, or Storax-tr.
2. afplenifolia.   Canadian Spleenwort-leaved Liquid.
†3. orientalis.   Eaftern Liquidamber.

80. LIRIODENDRON.

TULIP-TREE,——(Fr.)—Tulipier.

L. G. Pl. 689.   Polyandria Polygynia.   Cl. 13. Ord. 7.

1. Tulipifera.   Virginian Tulip-tree.

81. LONICERA.

HONEYSUCKLE, or WOODBINE,——(Fr.)—Chevre-feuille.

L. G. Pl. 233.   Pentandria Monogynia.   Cl. 5. Ord. 1.

1. cœrulea - - - 1. Blue-berried Upright Honeyfuckle.
2. *nigra* - - - - 2. Black-berried Upright Honeyfuckle.
3. *rubra* - - - 3. Red-berried Upright Honeyfuckle.
4. tatarica.   Tartarian Upright Honeyfuckle.
5. Xylofteum.   Fly Honeyfuckle.

LONICERA-PERICLYMENUM.

1. Periclymenum alb.	1.	White Englifh Honeyfuckle.
2. *rubrum* - - -	2.	Red Honeyfuckle.
3. *variegatum* - -	3.	Yellow-ftriped-leaved Honeyfuckle.
4. *quercinum* - -	4.	Oak-leaved Honeyfuckle.
5. *quercinum variegat.*	5.	Striped Oak-leaved Honeyfuckle.
6. *germanicum* - -	1.	Dutch Red Honeyfuckle.
7. *longiflorens* - -	2.	Long-flowering Honeyfuckle.
8. *ferotinum* - -	3.	Late-flowering Honeyfuckle.
9. *fempervirens* - -	4.	Evergreen Honeyfuckle.
10. album - - -	1.	Early White Italian Honeyfuckle.
11. *flavum* - - -	2.	Early Yellow Italian Honeyfuckle.
12. *rubrum* - - -	3.	Early Red Italian Honeyfuckle.
13. *rubrum ferotinum* -	4.	Late Red Italian Honeyfuckle.
14. virginianum - -	1.	Virginian Scarlet Trumpet Honeyf.
15. *carolinianum* - -	2.	Carolina, or fmaller ditto.
16. fempervirens.		Evergreen Scarlet Trumpet Honeyf.
17. glaucum.		Minorca Evergreen Scarlet T. H.

LONICERA-DIERVILLA.

1. Diervilla.	Yellow Diervilla.

LONICERA-SYMPHORICARPOS.

1. Symphoricarpos	St. Peter's Wort.

82. LOTUS.

BIRD'S-FOOT,——(Fr.)—LOTIER.

L. G. Pl. 897.	Diadelphia Decandria.	Cl. 17. Ord. 3.
1. hirfutus.	Tall hairy Bird's-foot Trefoil.	
2. rectus.	Upright Bird's-foot Trefoil.	

83. LYCIUM.

BOX-THORN,——(Fr.)——

L. G. Pl. 262.	Pentandria Monogynia.	Cl. 5. Ord. 1.
1. barbarum.	Willow-leaved Boxthorn.	

C 3

84. MAGNOLIA.

MAGNOLIA, or LAUREL-LEAVED TULIP-TREE.
(Fr.)—Laurier Tulipier.

L. G. Pl. 690.   Polyandria Polygynia.   Cl. 13. Ord. 7.

1. acuminata.		Blue Deciduous Magnolia.
2. glauca.		Small-leaved Magnolia.
3. grandiflora	- - 1.	Evergreen Magnolia.
4. *grand. angustifolia*	2.	Narrow-leaved Evergreen Magnolia.
5. tripetala.		Umbrella-tree.

85. MARRUBIUM.

BASTARD DITTANY, or HOREHOUND.

L. G. Pl. 721.   Didynamia Gymnospermia.   Cl. 14. Ord. 1.

1. acetabulosum.   Bastard Dittany.

86. MESPILUS.

MEDLAR-TREE,————(Fr.)————

L. G. Pl. 625.   Icosandria Pentagynia.   Cl. 12. Ord. 4.

1. Amelanchier.		Amelanchier.
2. arbutifolia.		Arbutus-leaved Medlar.
3. canadensis.		Snowy Canadian Medlar.
4. Chamæ-mespilus.		Dwarf M. or Lady Hardwick's Shrub.
5. cordata.		Heart-shaped-leaved Medlar.
6. Cotoneaster.		Bastard Quince-tree.
7. *Cotoneaster minor.*		Small Bastard Quince-tree.
8. germanica	- - 1.	German, or Dutch Medlar-tree.
9. *germanica laurifolia*	2.	Bay-leaved German Medlar-tree.
10. humilis.		Dwarf Medlar-tree.
11. orientalis.		Dwarf Cherry of Mount Ida.
12. Pyracantha.		Evergreen Thorn, or Pyracantha.

87. MORUS.

MULBERRY-TREE,————(Fr.)—Meurier.

L. G. Pl. 1055.   Monoecia Tetrandria.   Cl. 21. Ord. 4.

1. nigra	- - - 1.	Black Mulberry.
2. *alba*	- - - 2.	White Mulberry.
3. *rubra*	- - - 3.	Red Mulberry.
4. italica.		Italian Mulberry.
5. papyrifera.		Chinese Mulberry.

HARDY TREES AND SHRUBS. 23

88. MYRICA.

CANDLE-BERRY MYRTLE,——(Fr.)—

L. G. Pl. 1107.   Dioecia Pentandria.   Cl. 22. Ord. 5.
1. cerifera.   Candle-berry Myrtle.
2. carolinenſis   CarolinianBroad-leaved C. M.
3. Gale.   Sweet Willow, or Dutch Myrtle.

89. NYSSA.

TUPELO-TREE,——(Fr.)—

L. G. Pl. 1163.   Polygamia Dioecia.   Cl. 23. Ord. 2.
1. aquatica.   Aquatic Tupelo.
2. uniflora.   Single-flowered Tupelo.

90. OLEA.

OLIVE-TREE,——(Fr.)—Olivier.

L. G. Pl. 20.   Diandria Monogynia.   Cl. 2. Ord. 1.
1. europæa.   Olive-tree.

91. ONONIS.

REST-HARROW,——(Fr.)—

L. G. Pl. 863.   Diadelphia Decandria.   Cl. 17. Ord. 3.
1. fruticoſa.   Shrubby Reſt-Harrow.

92. PASSIFLORA.

PASSION-FLOWER,——(Fr.)—Fleur de Paſſion.

L. G. Pl. 1021.   Gynandria Pentandria.   Cl. 20. Ord. 4.
1. cœrulea.   Paſſion-Flower.

93. PERIPLOCA.

VIRGINIAN SILK,——(Fr.)

L. G. Pl. 303.   Pentandria Digynia.   Cl. 5. Ord. 2.
1. græca.   Virginian Silk.

94. PHILADELPHUS.

SYRINGA, or MOCK ORANGE,——(Fr.)—

L. G. Pl. 19.   Icoſandria Monogynia.   Cl. 12. Ord. 1.
1. coronarius - - 1. Syringa, or Mock Orange.
†2. cor. plenus - - 2. Double Syringa.

C 4

3. *cor. variegatus* - 3. Striped-leaved Syringa.
4. *cor. humilis* - - 4. Dwarf Syringa.
5. *inodorus* - - - 5. Scentlefs Carolinian Syringa.

95. PHILLYREA.

PHILLYREA, or MOCK PRIVET,——(Fr.)—Filarie.

L. G. Pl. 19.   Diandria Monogynia.   Cl. 2. Ord. 1.

1. latifolia.   Broad-leaved Phillyrea.
2. fpinofa.   Prickly, or Ilex-leaved Phillyrea.
3. media.   Oval fmooth-leaved Phillyrea.
4. liguftrifolia.   Privet-leaved Phillyrea.
5. oleæfolia.   Olive-leaved Phillyrea.
6. anguftifolia.   Narrow-leaved Phillyrea.
7. rofmarinifolia.   Rófemary-leaved Phillyrea.
8. argenteo-variegata. Silver-ftriped Phillyrea.
9. aureo-variegata.   Gold-ftriped Phillyrea.

96. PHLOMIS.

JERUSALEM SAGE-TREE.——(Fr.)—

L. G. Pl. 723.   Didynamia Gymnofpermia.   Cl. 14. Ord. 1.
1. fruticofa - - - 1. Broad-leaved Sage-tree.
2. *anguftifolia* - - 2. Narrow-leaved Sage-tree.
3. purpurea.   Purple-flowered Sage-tree.

97. PHYTOLACA.

AMERICAN NIGHTSHADE,——(Fr.)—

L. G. Pl. 588.   Decandria Decagynia.   Cl. 10. Ord. 5.
1. dioica.   Amer. Nightfh. or Virginian Poke.

98. PINUS.

PINE-TREE,——(Fr.)—Pin.

L. G. Pl. 1077.   Monoecia Monadelphia.   Cl. 21. Ord. 9.
1. Cembra.   Aphernoufli Pine.
2. echinata.   Prickly-coned Pine.
3. halepenfis.   Aleppo Pine.
4. paluftris.   Swamp Pine.
5. Pinea.   Stone Pine.
6. rigida.   Three-leaved Virginian Pine.
7. rubra.   Scotch Pine.
8. Strobus.   New-England, or Weymouth Pine.

9. fylveftris.   Pineafter, or Wild Pine.
10. tatarica.   Tartarian Pine.
11. Tæda.   Frankincenfe Pine.
12. virginiana.   Two-leaved Virginian, or JerfeyPine.

PINUS-LARIX.

LARCH-TREE,——(Fr)—Meleze.

1. rubra.   Red Larch.
2. alba.   White Larch.
3. nigra.   Black Larch.
4. chinenfis.   Chinefe, or Siberian Larch.
5. Cedrus.   Cedar of Lebanon.

PINUS-ABIES.

FIR-TREE,——(Fr.)—Sapin.

1. alba.   Yew-leaved Silver Fir-tree.
2. americana.   Hemlock Spruce Fir-tree.
3. Balfamea.   Balm of Gilead Fir-tree.
4. canadenfis - - 1.   Newfoundland White Spruce Fir-tr.
5. *can. nigricans* - 2.   Newfoundland Black Spruce Fir-tr.
6. *can. rubefcens* - 3.   Newfoundland Red Spruce Fir-tree.
7. orientalis.   Eaftern Fir-tree.
8. Picea - - - 1.   Norway Spruce Fir, or Pitch-tree.
9. *Picea longa* - - 2.   Long-coned Cornifh Fir-tree.

99. PISTACHIA.

PISTACIA NUT, or TURPENTINE TREE,——(Fr.) Terebinte.

L. G. Pl. 1108.   Dioecia Tetrandria.   Cl. 22. Ord. 4.

1. Terebinthus.   Turpentine-tree.
2. trifolia.   Three-leaved Turpentine-tree.
3. vera.   Piftachia-Nut-tree.

100. PLATANUS.

PLANE-TREE,——(Fr.)—Platane.

L. G. Pl. 1075.   Monoecia Polyandria.   Cl. 21. Ord. 8.

1. hifpanica.   Spanifh Plane-tree.
2. occidentalis.   Occidental, or Virginian Plane-tree.
3. orientalis.   Oriental Plane-tree.

101. POPULUS.

POPLAR-TREE,——(Fr.) Peuplier.

L. G. Pl. 1123.   Dioecia Octandria.   Cl. 22. Ord. 7.

1. alba   -   -   -   1. White Poplar, or Abele-tree.
2. *alba minor*   -   -   2. Small-leaved White Poplar-tree.
3. balfamifera.   Carolinian Poplar-tree.
4. heterophylla   -   1. Virginian Poplar-tree.
†5. *heteroph. athenienfis* 2. Athenian Poplar-tree.
6. italica.   Italian, or Lombardy Poplar-tree.
7. nigra!   Black Poplar-tree.
8. Tacamahacca.   Tacamahacca.
9. tremula.   Trembling Poplar, or Afpen-tree.

102. POTENTILLA.

SHRUBBY CINQUEFOIL.

L. G. Pl. 634.   Icofandria Polygynia.   Cl. 12. Ord. 5.

1. fruticofa.   Shrubby Cinquefoil.

103. PRINOS.

WINTER-BERRY,——(Fr.)

L. G. Pl. 441.   Hexandria Monogynia.   Cl. 6. Ord. 1.

1. verticillatus.   Virginian Winter-berry.
2. glaber.   Evergreen Winter-berry, Yappon, or
                              South-Sea Tea Shrub.

104. PRUNUS.

PLUM-TREE,——(Fr.) Prunier.

L. G. Pl. 620.   Icofandria Monogynia.   Cl. 12. Ord. 1.

1. fylveftris   -   -   1. Wild Plum-tree.
2. fativa   -   -   2. Plum-tree, (for whofe Varieties fee
                              the Fruit Catalogue.)
3. *argenteo-variegata*   3. Silver-ftriped Plum-tree.
4. *aureo-variegata* -   4. Gold-bloatched Plum-tree.
5. *plena*   -   -   5. Double-flowering Plum-tree.

6. infititia.   Bullace-tree.
7. fpinofa.   Black-thorn, or Sloe-tree.
8. virginica.   Virginian Cherry-Plum-tree.

PRUNUS-ARMENIACA.

ApricOT-TREE,————(Fr.)——Abricotier.

1. Armeniaca - - 1. Apricot-tree, (for whofe Varieties fee the Fruit Catalogue.)
2. *Armeniaca variegata* 2. Silver-ftriped Apricot-tree.

PRUNUS-CERASUS.

CHERRY-TREE,————(Fr.)——Cerifier.

1. fylveftris - - - 1. Wild Black Cherry-tree.
†2. *fylv. plena* - - 2. Double-flowering Wild Cherry-tree.
3. *fativa* - - - 3. Cherry-tree, (for whofe varieties fee the Fruit Catalogue.)
4. *fativa-plena* - - 4. Double-flowering Kentifh Cherry.
5. canadenfis.   Canadian Bird Cherry-tree.
6. mahaleb.   Perfumed Cherry-tree.
†7. femperflorens.   Monthly, or All-Saints Cherry.

PRUNUS-LAURO-CERASUS.

LAUREL-TREE,——(Fr.)—Laurier-Cerife.

1. Lauro-Cerafus - 1. Laurel.
2. *L.C. argenteo-varieg.* 2. Silver-ftriped Laurel.
3. *L.C. aureo-variegata* 3. Gold-ftriped Laurel.
4. lufitanica.   Portugal Laurel.

105. PTELEA.

SHRUB-TREFOIL,——(Fr.)—

L.G. Pl. 152.   Tetrandria Monogynia.   Cl. 4. Ord. 1.

1. trifoliata.   Carolina Shrub Trefoil, or Ptelea.

106. PUNICA.

POMEGRANATE-TREE,——(Fr.)—Grenadier.

L. G. Pl. 618.   Icofandria Monogynia.   Cl. 12. Ord. 1.

1. Granatum - - 1. Pomegranate-tree.
†2. *Granatum plenum* - 2. Double-flowering Pomegranate.
3. nana - - - - 1. Dwarf Pomegranate.
4. *nana plena* - - 2. Double-flowering Dwarf Pomegr.

107. PYROLA.

WINTERGREEN,——(Fr.)—Pyrole.

L. G. Pl. 554.   Decandria Monogynia.   Cl. 10. Ord. 1.

1. maculata.   Spotted Maryland Pyrola.
2. rotundifolia.   Round-leaved Pyrola.
3. umbellata.   Arbutus-flowered Pyrola.

108. PYRUS.

PEAR-TREE,——(Fr.)—Poirier.

L. G. Pl. 626.   Icofandria Pentagynia.   Cl. 12. Ord. 4.

1. fylveftris - - - 1. Wild Pear-tree.
2. *fativa* - - - 2. Pear-tree, (for whofe Varieties fee
                       the Fruit Catalogue.)
3. *fativa duplex* - - 3. Double-flowering Pear-tree.
4. *fativa biflorens* - 4. Twice-flowering Pear-tree.

PYRUS-MALUS.

APPLE-TREE,——(Fr.)—Pomier.

1. fylveftris - - - 1. Crab, or Wild Apple-tree.
2. *fativa* - - - 2. Apple-tree, (for whofe Varieties fee
                       the Fruit Catalogue.)
3. *fativa-duplex* - - 3. Double-flowering Apple-tree.
4. *fativa-fugax* - - 4. Fig-Apple-tree.
5. baccata.   Siberian Crab-tree.
6. coronaria.   Virginian fweet-fcented Crab-tree.
7. fempervirens.   Carolinian Evergreen Crab-tree.
8. paradifiaca.   Paradife Apple-tree.

PYRUS-CYDONIA.

QUINCE-TREE,——(Fr.)—Coignaffier.

1. fylveftris - - 1. Wild Quince-tree.
2. fativa - - - 2. Quince-tree, (for whofe Varieties fee the Fruit Catalogue.)

109. QUERCUS.

OAK-TREE,——(Fr.)—Chêne.

L. G. Pl. 1070,   Monoecia Polyandria.   Cl. 21. Ord. 8.

1. Robur - - - 1. Common Englifh Oak-tree.
2. Rob.argenteo-varieg. 2. Silver-ftriped Oak-tree.
3. Rob. breve - - 3, Short-foot-ftalked Oak-tree.
4. Ægilops. Prickly-cupped Spanifh Oak-tr.
5. alba. White Virginian Oak-tree,
6. carolinienfis. Carolinian Oak-tree.
7. Cerris. Turkey Oak-tree.
8. ferruginea. Iron Oak-tree.
9. montana. Red Mountain Oak-tree.
10. nigra. Black Oak-tree.
11. Phellos - - - 1. Willow-leaved Oak-tree.
12. Phellos brevifolia - 2. Short-willow-leaved Oak-tree.
13. Phellos heterophylla 3. Various-willow-leaved Oak-tree.
14. Phellos longifolia - 4. Long-willow-leaved Oak-tree.
15. Prinus. Virginian Chefnut-leaved Oak-tree.
16, rubra. Scarlet Oak-tree.

QUERCUS-ILEX.

ILEX, or EVERGREEN OAK-TREE,——(Fr.)—Chêne-vert.

1. Ilex. Ilex, or Evergreen Oak.
2. anguftifolia. Narrow-leaved Ilex.
3. gramuntia. Montpelier Holly-leaved Ilex.
4. lanata. Montpelier Woolly-leaved Ilex.
5. rotundifolia. Round-leaved Ilex.
6. Coccifera - - 1. Prickly-leaved Kermes Oak-tree.
7. Coccifera echinata - 2. Prickly-cupped Kermes Oak-tree.

QUERCUS-SUBER.

CORK-TREE,——(Fr.)—Liege.

1. Suber latifolia - 1. Broad-leaved Cork-tree.
2. *Suber anguſtifolia* - 2. Narrow-leaved Cork-tree.

110. RHAMNUS.

BUCKTHORN, or PURGING THORN,——(Fr.)—Nerprun.

L. G. Pl. 265.   Pentandria Monogynia.   Cl. 5. Ord. 1.

1. catharticus maſculus 1. Male Buckthorn, or Purging Thorn.
2. *cathart. fœmineus* - 2. Female Buckthorn, or Purging Thorn.
3. lineatus. Supple Jack.
4. lycioides. Dwarf Rhamnus.

RHAMNUS-ALATERNUS.

ALATERNUS, or EVERGREEN PRIVET,——(Fr.)—Alaterne.

1. communis - - 1. Alaternus.
2. *aureo-variegatus* - 2. Gold-ſtriped Alaternus.
3. *argenteo-variegatus* 3. Silver-ſtriped Alaternus.
4. *aureo-maculatus* - 4. Gold-bloatched Alaternus.
5. laciniatus - - 1. Jagged-leaved Alaternus.
6. *lac. argenteo-variegat.*2. Silver-ſtriped Jagged Alaternus.
7. *lac. aureo-variegatus* 3. Gold-ſtriped Jagged Alaternus.

RHAMNUS-FRANGULA.

BERRY-BEARING ALDER,——(Fr.)—

1. communis. Black Berry-bearing Alder.
2. alpina. Alpine Berry-bearing Alder.

RHAMNUS-PALIURUS.

CHRIST's-THORN,——(Fr.)—

1. palæſtinus. Paleſtine Buckthorn, or Chriſt's Th.

111. RHODODENDRON.

RHODODENDRON, or DWARF ROSE BAY.

L. G. Pl. 548.   Decandria Monogynia.   Cl. 10. Ord. 1.

1. maximum - - 1. Large American Rhododendron.
†2. *max. rubrum* - 2. Red-flowered Rhododendron.
3. ferrugineum.   Alpine Rhododendron.

112. RHODORA.

RHODORA, or ROSE BAY,——(Fr.)—

L. G. Pl. 547.   Decandria Monogynia.   Cl. 10. Ord. 1.

1. canadenſis,   Canadian Rhodora.

113. RHUS.

SUMACH-TREE,——(Fr.)—

L. G. Pl. 369.   Pentandria Trigynia.   Cl. 5. Ord. 3.

1. Copallinum.   Lentiſcus-leaved Sumach-tree.
2. Coriaria.   Myrtle-leaved Sumach-tree.
3. Cotinus.   Venetian Sumach-tree.
4. glabrum.   Scarlet Sumach-tree.
5. Metopium.   Five-leaved Poiſon-tree.
6. radicans.   Creeping Poiſon Oak.
7. ſinenſe.   Lac-tree.
8. Toxicodendron   Three-leaved Poiſon-tree.
9. typhinum.   Stag's-Horn Sumach-tree.
10. Vernix.   Varniſh-tree.

114. RIBES.

CURRANT-TREE,——(Fr.)—

L. G. Pl. 281.   Pentandria Monogynia.   Cl. 5. Ord. 1.

1. rubrum - - - 1. Currant-tree.
2. *rubrum variegatum* 2. Striped-leaved Currant-tree.
3. nigrum.   Black Currant-tree.
4. Groſſularia.   Gooſeberry-tree.

115. ROBINIA.

L. G. Pl. 879.   Diadelphia Decandria.   Cl. 17. Ord. 3.

1. Caragana.   Siberian Caragana.
2. frutescens.   Shrubby Caragana.
3. hispida.   Scarlet-flowered Acacia.
4. Pseudo-Acacia.   False Acacia.
5. pygmæa.   Four-leaved Acacia.

116. ROSA.

ROSE-TREE,——(Fr.)—Rosier.

L. G. Pl. 631,   Icosandria Polygynia.   Cl. 12. Ord 5.

1. alba - - - - 1. Semidouble White Rose.
2. *alba plena* - - 2. Double White Rose.
3. *alba major duplex* 3. Large Semidouble White Rose.
4. *alba major plena* - 4. Large Double White Rose.

5. alpina - - - 1. Alpine Rose.

*6. arvensis - - - 1. White Dog-Rose.
7. *arvensis variegata* 2. Striped-leaved White Dog-Rose.

8. belgica - - - 1. Red Belgic Rose.
9. *belgica incarnata* - 2. Blush Belgic Rose.

10. burgundensis - 1. Blush Burgundy Rose.
11. *burgundensis humilis* 2. Dwarf Blush Burgundy Rose.
12. *burgundensis kermesina* 3. Crimson Burgundy Rose.

*13. canina - - - 1. Red Dog-Rose.

14. centifolia - - 1. Hundred-leaved Rose.
15. *centifolia incarnata* 2. Blush Hundred-leaved Rose.
16. *centifolia kermesina* 3. British, or Singleton's hd.-leaved R.

17. chinensis - - 1. Chinese Rose.

18. cinnamomea - - 1. Cinnamon Rose.
19. *cinnamomea plena* - 2. Double Cinnamon Rose.

20. damascena - - 1. Damask Rose.
21. *damascena plena* - 2. Double Damask Rose.
22. *damascena alba* - 3. White Damask Rose.
23. *damascena incarnata* 4. Blush Damask Rose.
24. *damascena provincialis* 5. Damask Provence Rose.
25. *damascena versicolor* 6. York and Lancaster Rose.

26. *Eglanteria	-	-	1.	Sweet-Briar.
27. *Eglanteria duplex*			2.	Semidouble Sweet-Briar.
28. *Eglanteria plena*			3.	Double Sweet-Briar.
29. *Eglant. sempervirens*			4.	Evergreen Sweet-Briar.
30. *Eglanteria variegata*			5.	Striped-leaved Sweet-Briar.
31. *Eglanteria incarnata*			6.	Double Blush Sweet-Briar.
32. *Eglanteria coccinea*			7.	Double Scarlet Sweet-Briar.

| 33. florida | - | - | - | 1. | Florida Rose. |

| 34. francofurtensis | - | 1. | Franckfort, or Purple Rose. |

35. gallica	-	-	-	1.	Semidouble Red Rose.
36. *gallica plena*	-	-	2.	Double Red Rose.
37. *gallica Rosa Mundi*	3.	Rosa Mundi Rose.

38. holoserica	-	-	1.	Single Velvet Rose.
39. *holoserica duplex*	-	2.	Semidouble Velvet Rose.
40. *holoserica plena*	-	3.	Double Velvet Rose.

| 41. incarnata | - | - | 1. | Maiden's Blush Rose. |
| 42. *incarnata major* | - | 2. | Great Maiden's Blush Rose. |

| 43. inermis | - | - | - | 1. | Thornless Rose. |

| 44. labradora | - | - | 1. | Labrador Rose. |

45. lutea	-	-	-	1.	Single Yellow Rose.
46. *lutea plena*	-	-	2.	Double Yellow Rose.
47. *lutea austriaca*	-	3.	Yellow Austrian Rose.
48. *lutea bicolor*	-	-	4.	Red and Yellow Austrian Rose.

| 49. marmorea | - | - | 1. | Semidouble Marbled Rose. |
| 50. *marmorea plena* | - | 2. | Double Marbled Rose. |

51. menstrua	-	-	1.	Red Monthly Rose.
52. *menstrua alba*	-	-	2.	White Monthly Rose.
53. *menstrua incarnata*	3.	Blush Monthly Rose.
54. *menstrua variegata*	4.	Striped Monthly Rose.

| 55. moschata | - | - | 1. | Musk Rose. |
| 56. *moschata plena* | - | - | 2. | Double Musk Rose. |

| 57. muscosa | - | - | - | 1. | Moss Provence Rose. |
| 58. *muscosa variegata* | 2. | Striped-leaved Moss Provence Rose. |

| 59. pendula | - | - | - | 1. | Pendulous-fruited Rose. |

D

60. penfylvanica - - 1. Penfylvanian Rofe.
61. *penfylvanica plena* 2. Double Penfylvanian Rofe.

62. pimpinellifolia - 1. Burnet-leaved Rofe.

63. portlandica - - 1. Portland Crimfon Monthly Rofe.

64. provincialis - - 1. Provence Rofe.
65. *provincialis plena* 2. Double Provence Rofe.
66. *provincialis prolifera* 3. Childing Provence Rofe.
67. *provincialis variegata* 4. Striped Provence Rofe.
68. *provincialis alba* - 5. White Provence, or Belladonna Rofe.
69. *provincialis incarnata* 6. Blufh, or Imperial Provence Rofe.

70. regia - - - 1. Great Royal Rofe.

71. fanguinea - - 1. Red-ftalked American Rofe.

72. fempervirens - 1. Evergreen Rofe.

73. *fpinofiffima - - 1. White Scotch Rofe.
74. *fpinofiffima flava* 2. Pale Yellow Scotch Rofe.
75. *fpinofiffima rofea* 3. Red Scotch Rofe.
76. *fpinofiff. variegata* 4. Striped Scotch Rofe.

77. ftebonenfis - - 1. Stebon Rofe.

78. *villofa - - - 1. Apple Rofe.
79. *villofa duplex* - 2. Semidouble Apple Rofe.
80. *villofa plena* - - 3. Double Apple Rofe.

⁎ A more copious Catalogue of Rofes *really exifting* in the curious Gardens in England could have been given; but all thefe are to be readily found in the different Nurferies, although not in any one.

The fix Rofes marked with Afterifms are the native Rofes of England.

ROSES

Arranged Alphabetically by their Englifh Names, with Reference to the Latin.

1. Alpine Rofe   Rofa Alpina. 5.

2. *Apple Rofe - - - - 1. villofa. 78.
3. *Semidouble Apple Rofe* - - 2. *villofa duplex.* 79.
4. *Double Apple Rofe* - - - 3. *villofa plena.* 80.

5. Auftrian Rofe - - - 1. lutea auftriaca. 47.
6. *Red and Yellow Auftrian R.* 2. *lutea bicolor.* 48.

7. Belgic Rofe - - - - 1. belgica. 8.
8. *Blufh Belgic Rofe* - - - 2. *belgica incarnata.* 9.

9. Burgundy Rofe - - - 1. burgundenfis. 10.
10. *Dwarf Blufh Burgundy Rofe* 2. *burgundenfis humilis.* 11.
11. *Crimfon Burgundy Rofe* - 3. *burgundenfis kermefina.* 12.

12. Burnèt-leaved Rofe - - 1. pimpinellifolia. 62.

13. Chinefe Rofe - - - 1. chinenfis. 17.

14. Cinnamon Rofe - - - 1. cinnamomea. 18.
15. *Double Cinnamon Rofe* - - 2. *cinnamomea plena.* 19.

16. Damafk Rofe - - - - 1. damafcena. 20.
17. *Double Damafk Rofe* - - 2. *damafcena plena.* .21.
18. *White Damafk Rofe* - - 3. *damafcena alba.* 22.
19. *Blufh Damafk Rofe* - - 4. *damafcena incarnata.* 23.
20. *Damafk Provence Rofe* - - 5. *damafcena provincialis.* 24.

21.*Dog-Rofe (white) - - 1. arvenfis. 6.
22. *Striped-leaved white Dog-Rofe* 2. *arvenfis variegata.* 7.

23.*Dog-Rofe (red) - - - 1. canina. 13.

24. Evergreen Rofe - - - 1. fempervirens. 72.

25. Florida Rofe - - - - 1. florida. 33.

26. Franckfort Rofe - - - 1. francofurtenfis. 34.

27. Hundred-leaved Rofe - - 1. centifolia. 14.
28. *Blufh Hundred-leaved Rofe* - 2. *centifolia incarnata.* 15.
29. *Singleton's Hundred-leaved Rofe* 3. *centifolia kermefina.* 16.

30. Labrador Rofe - - - 1. labradora. 44.

31. Maiden's Blufh Rofe - - 1. incarnata. 41.
32. *Great Maiden's Blufh Rofe* - 2. *incarnata major.* 42.

33. Marbled Rofe - - - . 1. marmorea. 49.
34. *Double Marbled Rofe* - - 2. *marmorea plena.* 50.

35. Monthly Rofe - - - 1. menftrua. 51.
36. *White Monthly Rofe* - - 2. *menftrua alba.* 52.
37. *Blufh Monthly Rofe* - - 3. *menftrua incarnata.* 53.
38. *Striped Monthly Rofe* - - 4. *menftrua variegata.* 54.

39. Mofs Provence Rofe - - 1. mufcofa. 57.
40. *Striped-leaved MofsProvence R.* 2. *mufcofa variegata.* 58.

41. Musk Rose. - - - - 1. moschata. 55.
42. *Double Musk Rose.* - - 2. *moschata plena.* 56.

43. Pendulous-fruited Rose - 1. pendula. 59.

44. Pensylvanian Rose - - 1. pensylvanica. 60.
45. *Double Pensylvanian Rose* - 2. *pensylvanica plena.* 61.

46. Portland Rose - - - 1. portlandica. 63.

47. Provence Rose - - - - 1. provincialis. 64.
48. *Double Provence Rose* - - 2. *provincialis plena.* 65.
49. *Childing Provence Rose* - - 3. *provincialis prolifera.* 66.
50. *Striped Provence Rose* - - 4. *provincialis variegata.* 67.
51. *White, or Belladonna Provence R.* 5. *provincialis alba.* 68.
52. *Blush, or Imperial Provence R.* 6. *provincialis incarnata.* 69.

53. Red Rose - - - - - 1. gallica. 35.
54. *Double Red Rose* - - - 2. *gallica plena.* 36.

55. Red-stalked American Rose 1. sanguinea. 71.

56. Rosa Mundi Rose - - - 1. gallica Rosa Mundi. 37.

57. Royal Rose - - - - 1. regia. 70.

58. *Scotch Rose - - - - 1. spinosissima. 73.
59. *Pale Yellow Scotch Rose* - 2. *spinosissima flava.* 74.
60. *Red Scotch Rose* - - - 3. *spinosissima rosea.* 75.
61. *Striped Scotch Rose* - - 4. *spinosissima variegata.* 76.

62. Stebon Rose - - - - 1. stebonensis. 77.

63. *Sweet-Briar - - - - 1. Eglanteria. 26.
64. *Semidouble Sweet-Briar* - 2. *Eglanteria duplex.* 27.
65. *Double Sweet-Briar* - - 3. *Eglanteria plena.* 28.
66. *Evergreen Sweet-Briar* - 4. *Eglanteria sempervirens.* 29.
67. *Striped-leaved Sweet-Briar* - 5. *Eglanteria variegata.* 30.
68. *Double Blush Sweet-Briar* - 6. *Eglanteria incarnata.* 31.
69. *Double Scarlet Sweet-Briar* 7. *Eglanteria coccinea.* 32.

70. Thornless Rose - - - 1. inermis. 43.

71. Velvet Rose - - - - 1. holoseriea. 38.
72. *Semidouble Velvet Rose* - - 2. *holoserica duplex.* 39.
73. *Double Velvet Rose* - - - 3. *holoserica plena.* 40.

74. Yellow Rose - - - - 1. lutea. 45.
75. *Double Yellow Rose* - - 2. *lutea plena.* 46.

76. York and Lancafter Rofe - 1. damafcena verficolor. 25.

77. White Rofe - - - - 1. alba. 1.
78. *Double White Rofe* - - 2. *alba plena.* 2.
79. *Large Semidouble White Rofe* 3. *alba major duplex.* 3.
80. *Large Double White Rofe* - 4. *alba major plena.* 4.

115. ROSMARINUS.

Rosemary,——(Fr.)—Rofmarin.

L. G. Pl. 38.   Diandria Monogynia.   Cl. 2. Ord. 1,

1. officinalis - - 1. Rofemary.
2. *offic.argenteo-varieg.* 2. Silver-ftriped Rofemary.
3. *offic.aureo-variegatus* 3. Gold-ftriped Rofemary.

116. RUBUS.

Raspberry,——(Fr.)—Ronce.

L. G. Pl. 632.   Icofandria Polygynia.   Cl. 12. Ord. 5.

1. idæus - - - 1. Rafpberry.
2. *idæus albus* - - 2. White Rafpberry.
3. *idæus plenus* - - 3. Double-flowering Rafpberry.
4. *idæus biflorens* - 4. Twice-flowering Rafpberry.
5. *idæus variegatus* - 5. Striped-leaved Rafpberry.
6. canadenfis.   Canadian Rafpberry.
7. fruticofus - - 1. Bramble.
8. *fruticofus inermis* - 2. Pricklefs Bramble.
9. *fruticofus plenus* - 3. Double-flowered Bramble.
10. hifpidus.   Hifpid-ftalked Rafpberry.
11. odoratus.   Sweet-flowered Virginian Rafpberry.

117. RUSCUS.

Butcher's-Broom,——(Fr.)—Houx-Frelon.

L. G. Pl. 1139.   Dioecia Syngenefia.   Cl. 22. Ord. 13.

1. aculeatus.   Butcher's Broom, or Knee Holly.
2. androgynus.   Broad-leaved Alexandrian Laurel,
3. Hypogloffum.   Horfe-Tongue Laurel.
4. Hypophyllum.   Broad-leaved Butcher's Broom.
5. racemofus.   Alexandrian Laurel.

D 3

118. RUTA.

RUE,——(Fr.)—Rue.

L. G. Pl. 523.   Decandria Monogynia.   Cl. 10. Ord. 1.

1. graveolens   -   - 1. Rue.
2. *graveolens tenuifolia* 2. Small-leaved Rue.
3. *graveolens variegata* 3. Striped-leaved Rue.
4. linifolia.   Spanish Rue.

119. SALICORNIA.

GLASS-WORT, or SALT-WORT,——(Fr.)—

L. G. Pl. 10.   Monandria Monogynia.   Cl. 1. Ord. 1.

1. fruticosa.   Shrubby Evergreen Glasswort.

120. SALIX.

WILLOW-TREE,——(Fr.)—Saule.

L. G, Pl. 1098.   Dioecia Diandria.   Cl. 22. Ord. 2.

1. alba.   White Willow.
2. amygdalina.   Almond-leaved Willow.
3. arenaria.   Sand Willow.
4. babylonica.   Babylonian, or Weeping Willow.
5. caprea   -   -   - 1. Sallow.
6. *caprea variegata* - 2. Striped-leaved Sallow.
7. fragilis.   Crack, or Brittle Willow.
8. fusca.   Brown Willow.
9. glauca.   Glaucous-leaved Tough Willow.
10. hermaphroditica.   Shining Willow.
11. Helix.   Rose, or Yellow Dwarf Willow.
12. lanata.   Lapland Woolly-leaved Willow.
13. pentandra.   Sweet Willow.
14. purpurea.   Norfolk Purple Willow.
15. reiculata.   Round-leaved Willow.
16. rosmarinifolia.   Rosemary-leaved Willow.
17. rubra.   Red Willow.
18. triandra.   Triandrous White-barked Willow.
19. vimenalis.   Ozier.
20. vitellina.   Yellow Willow.

121. SALVIA.

SAGE,——(Fr.)—Sauge.

L. G. Pl. 39.   Octandria Monogynia.   Cl. 8. Ord. 1.

1. officinalis - - 1. Green Sage.
2. *offic. luteo-variegata* 2. Yellow and Green-ftriped Sage.
3. *offic. albo-variegata* 3. White and Green-ftriped Sage.
4. *offic. rubra* - - 4. Red Sage.
5. *offic. rubra-variegata* 5. Variegated Red Sage.
6. auriculata - - 1. Sage of Virtue, or Tea Sage.
7. *aur.-variegata* - 2. Striped Sage of Virtue.
8. *aur. alba* - - 3. White-flowered Sage of Virtue.

122. SAMBUCUS.

ELDER-TREE,——(Fr.)—Saureau.

L. G. Pl. 372.   Pentandria Trigynia.   Cl. 5. Ord. 3.

1. nigra - - - - 1. Elder-tree.
2. *viridis.* - - - 2. Green-berried Elder-tree.
3. *alba* -- - - - 3. White-berried Elder-tree.
4. *laciniata* - - - 4. Parfley-leaved Elder-tree.
5. *argenteo-variegata* 5. Silver-ftriped Elder-tree.
6. *aureo-punctata* - 6. Silver-dufted Elder-tree.
7. *aureo-variegata* - 7. Gold-ftriped Elder-tree.
8. canadenfis. Canadian Elder-tree.
9. racemofa. Mountain Red-berried Elder-tree.

123. SANTOLINA.

LAVENDER-COTTON,—(Fr.)—Petit Cyprès, Garde-Robe.

L. G. Pl. 942.   Syngenefia Polygamia Æqualis.   Cl. 19. Ord 1.

1. Chamæ Cypariffus. Lavender Cotton.
2. rofmarinifolia. Rofemary-leaved Lavender Cotton.

124. SATUREJA.

SAVORY,——(Fr.)—Sarriette.

L. G. Pl. 707.   Didynamia Gymnofpermia.   Cl. 14. Ord. 1.

1. montana. Winter Savory.

D 4

125. SIDEROXYLON.

IRONWOOD,——(Fr.)—

L. G. Pl. 264.	Pentandria Monogynia.	Cl. 5. Ord. 1,
1. lycioides.	Canadian thorny Ironwood.	

126. SMILAX.

ROUGH BINDWEED,——(Fr.)—

L. G. Pl. 1120.	Dioecia Hexandria.	Cl. 22. Ord. 6,
1. aspera.	Rough Bindweed.	
2. laurifolia,	Bay-leaved Rough Bindweed,	
3. rotundifolia,	Rough-leaved Smilax.	
4. Sarsaparilla,	Ivy-leaved, or Sarsaparilla.	
5. tamnoides,	Briony-leaved Smilax,	

127. SOLANUM.

NIGHTSHADE,——(Fr,)—Morelle.

L. G. Pl. 251.	Pentandria Monogynia.	Cl. 5. Ord. 1,
1. Dulcamara - -	1. Woody Nightshade.	
2. *argenteo-variegata*	2. Silver-striped Woody Nightshade,	
3. *aureo-variegata* -	3. Gold-striped Woody Nightshade,	

128. SORBUS.

SERVICE-TREE,——(Fr.)—Sorbier,

L. G. Pl. 623.	Icosandria Trigynia.	Cl. 12. Ord. 3,
1. Aucuparia.	Mountain Ash, or Wild Service,	
2. domestica - -	1. Service-tree, or Sorb.	
3. *domestica pyrifolia* -	2. Pear-leaved Service-tree,	

129. SPARTIUM.

BROOM,——(Fr.)—

L. G. Pl. 858.	Diadelphia Decandria.	Cl. 17. Ord. 3.
1. junceum - - -	1. Spanish Broom.	
2. *junceum plenum* -	2. Double Spanish Broom.	
3. monospermum -	1. Single-seeded Broom.	

4. *monospermum album* 2. White Single-seeded Broom.
5. radiatum. Starry Broom.
6, scoparium, English Broom.

130. SPIRÆA.

SPIRÆA,——(Fr.)—

L. G. Pl. 630. Icosandria Pentagynia. Cl. 12. Ord. 4.

1. crenata. White-flowered Spiræa.
2. hypericifolia. Hypericum-leaved Spiræa.
3. opulifolia. Gelder-Rose-leaved Spiræa,
4. salicifolia, Willow-leaved Spiræa.
5, tomentosa, Downy-leaved Red Spiræa.

131, STAPHYLÆA.

BLADDER-NUT-TREE,——(Fr.)—Nez-coupez.

L. G. Pl. 374. Pentandria Trigynia. Cl. 5. Ord. 3.

1. pinnata, Bladder-Nut-tree.
2, trifoliata, Virginian Three-leaved Bl. Nut-tr.

132. STEWARTIA.

L. G. Pl. 847. Monadelphia Polyandria. Cl. 16. Ord. 8.

1, Malacodendron. Virginian Stewartia.

133. STYRAX.

STORAX-TREE,

L. G. Pl. 595. Dodecandria Monogynia. Cl. 11. Ord. 1.

1. officinale, Syrian Storax-tree.

134. SYRINGA.

LILAC,——(Fr.)—

L. G. Pl. 22. Diandria Monogynia. Cl. 2. Ord. 1.

1. vulgaris alba - - 1. White Lilac.
2. *vulg. aureo-variegat.* 2. Gold-bloatched Lilac.
3. *vulg.argenteo-varieg.* 3. Silver-bloatched Lilac.
4. *vulg. cœrulea* - - 4. Blue Lilac.

5. *vulg. purpurea* - 5. Purple Lilac.
6. perfica - - - 1. Perfian Lilac
7. *perfica alba* - - 2. White Perfian Lilac.
8. *perfica laciniata* - 3. Cut-leaved Perfian Lilac.

135. TAMARIX.
TAMARISK,——(Fr.)—Tamaris.

L. G. Pl. 375. · · Pentandria Trigynia. · Cl. 5. Ord. 3,

1. gallica. French Tamarifk.
2. germanica. German Tamarifk,

136. TAXUS.
YEW-TREE.——(Fr.)—If.

L. G. Pl. 1135. Dioecia Monadelphia. Cl. 22. Ord. 12,

1. baccata. Yew-tree.
2. noxifera. Japanefe Yew-tree.

137. TEUCRIUM.
TREE-GERMANDER,——(Fr.)—

L. G. Pl. 706. Didynamia Gymnofpermia. Cl. 14. Ord. 1,

1. flavum. Tree Germander.
2. lucidum. Shining-leaved Tree Germander.
3. Marum. Syrian Maftich, or Marum.

138. THEA.
TEA-TREE,——(Fr.)—Thèe.

L. G. Pl. 668. Polyandria Monogynia. Cl. 13. Ord. 1.

1. Bohea. Bohea Tea-tree.
2. viridis. Green Tea-tree.

139. THUJA.
ARBOR VITÆ,——(Fr.)—Arbre de Vie.

L. G. Pl. 1078. Monoecia Monadelphia. Cl. 21. Ord. 9,

1. occidentalis - - 1. Common Arbor Vitæ.
2. *occid. variegata* - 2. Striped-leaved Arbor Vitæ.
3. *occid. odorata* - 3. American Sweet-fcented Arbor Vit.
4. orientalis. Chinefe Arbor Vitæ.

140. THYMUS.

THYME,——(Fr.)—Thim.

L. G. Pl. 727.   Didynamia Gymnofpermia.   Cl. 14. Ord. 1.

1.	vulgaris - - -	1.	Broad-leaved Thyme.
2.	*vulgaris variegatus*	2.	Striped Broad-leaved Thyme.
3.	*vulgaris tenuifolius*	3.	Narrow-leaved Thyme.
4.	cephalotus		Portugal Thyme.
5.	maftichinus.		Maftich Thyme.
6.	Zygis.		Narrow-leaved Upright Thyme.

THYMUS-SERPILLUM.

WILD THYME, or MOTHER OF THYME,——(Fr.)—Serpolet.

1.	Serpyllum - -	1.	Wild Thyme.
2.	*Serp. argenteo-varig.*	2.	Silver-ftriped Thyme.
3.	*Serp. citratum* -	3.	Lemon Thyme.
4.	*Serp. hirfutum* - -	4.	Hairy Mother of Thyme.

141. TILIA.

LIME-TREE,——(Fr.)—Tilleul,

L. G. Pl. 660.   Polyandria Monogynia.   Cl. 13. O.d. 1.

1.	europæa - - -	1.	L me, or Linden-tree.
2.	*europæa rubra* -	2.	Red-twigged Lime-tree.
3.	*europæa variegata*	3.	Striped Lime-tree.
4.	americana.		American Black Lime-tree.
5.	caroliniana.		Carolinian Lime-tree.

142. VACCINIUM,

WHORTLE-BERRY,——(Fr.)—Airelle, ou Mirtil.

L. G. Pl. 483.   Octandria Monogynia.   Cl. 8. Ord. 1.

1.	album.	White Vaccinium.
2.	amœnum.	
3.	elevatum.	
4.	frondofum.	Frondofe Vaccinium.
5.	myrtillus.	Bilberry, or Black Whorts.
6.	oxycoccos.	Cranberry, MofsBerry, or MoorBerry.
7.	tenellum.	

8. turgefcens.
9. venuftum.
10. virgatum.
11. vitis idæa.   Red Whorts, or Whortle Berry.
12. uliginofum.   Great Bilberry.

143. VIBURNUM.

PLIANT MEALY-TREE, or WAY-FARING-TREE,
(Fr.)—Viorne.

L. G. Pl. 370.   Pentandria Trigynia.   Cl. 5. Ord. 3.

1. Lantana - - - 1. Common Viburnum.
2. *Lant. variegata* - 2. Striped Viburnum.
3. *Lant. ovata* - - 3. Ovate-leaved Viburnum.
4. acerifolium.   American Gelder-Rofe.
5. dentatum.   Dentated-leaved Viburnum.
6. Lentago.   Canadian Viburnum.
7. nudum.   American Tinus, or Viburnum.
8. prunifolium.   Plum-leaved, or Virginian Black Haw.
9. pyrifolium.   Pear-leaved Viburnum.
10. fempervirens.   Evergreen Viburnum.
11. Caffinoides.   Caffioberry-bufh, or South-Sea Tea.

VIBURNUM-OPULUS.

MARSH ELDER, or GELDER-ROSE,——(Fr.)—Obier.

1. Opulus - - - 1. Gelder Rofe.
2. *opulus variegatus* - 2. Striped Gelder Rofe.
3. *opulus plenus* - - 3. Double Gelder Rofe.

VIBURNUM-TINUS,

LAURUSTINUS,——(Fr.)—Tinus,

1. Tinus anguftifolia 1, Narrow-leaved Lauruftinus.
2. *ang. argenteo-varieg.* 2. Silver-ftriped Narrow-leaved L.
3. *ang. aureo-variegata* 3. Gold-ftriped Broad-leaved Lauruft.
4. *latifolia* - - - 4. Broad-leaved Lauruftinus.
5. *lat. argenteo-varieg.* 5. Silver-ftriped Broad-leaved L.
6. *lat. aureo-variegata* 6. Gold-ftriped Broad-leaved L.
7. *hirfuta* - - - 7. Hairy-leaved Lauruftinus.
8. *fplendens* - - - 8. Shining-leaved Lauruftinus.

144. VINCA.

PERIWINKLE,——(Fr.)—Pervence.

L. G. Pl. 304.   Pentandria Monogynia.   Cl. 5. Ord. 1.

1. minor -   -   -   1. Blue Periwinkle.
2. *alba* -   -   -   - 2. White Periwinkle.
3. *purpurea*   -   -   3. Purple Periwinkle.
4. *purpurea plena*   -   4. Double purple Periwinkle.
5. *argenteo-variegata*   5. Silver-ftriped White Periwinkle.
6. *aureo-variegata* - 6. Gold-ftriped White Periwinkle.
7. major.   Large Green blue-flowered P.

145. VISCUM.

MISSELTOE,——(Fr.)——

L. G. Pl. 1105.   Dioecia Tetrandria.   Cl. 22. Ord. 4.

1. album.   Miffeltoe.

146. VITEX.

AGNUS CASTUS, or CHASTE-TREE,——(Fr.)—

L. G. Pl. 790.   Didynamia Angiofpermia.   Cl. 14. Ord. 2.

1. Agnus Caftus   -   1. Narrow-leaved. Chafte-tree.
2. *alba* -   -   -   - 2. White Narrow-leaved Chafte-tree.
3. latifolia -   -   - 1. Broad-leaved Chafte-tree.
4. *latifolia alba*   -   - 2. White, Broad-leaved Chafte-tree.

147. VITIS.

VINE,——(Fr.)—Vigne.

L. G. Pl. 284.   Decandria Monogynia.   Cl. 5. Ord. 1.

1. vinifera -   -   -   1. Vine (for whofe Varieties fee the Fruit Catalogue.)
2. *vin. variegata*   -   2. Striped-leaved Vine.
3. *vin. laciniata* -   - 3. Canadian Parfley-leaved Vine.
4. arborea.   Winged-leaved Vine.
5. vulpina.   Virginian Fox Vine.

148. ULEX.

FURZE, WHINS or GORSE,——(Fr.)——Genet epineux.

L. G. Pl. 881.   Diadelphia Decandria.   Cl. 17. Ord. 3.

1. europæus   -   -   1. Furze.
2. *europæus albus*   -   2. White-flowering Furze.
3. *europæus humilis*   -   3. Dwarf Furze.

149. ULMUS.

ELM-TREE,——(Fr.)—Orme.

L. G. Pl. 316.   Pentandria Digynia.   Cl. 5. Ord. 2.

1. campeſtris   -   -   1. Broad-rough-leaved Engliſh Elm.
2. *argenteo-variegata*   2. Silver-ſtriped.
3. *aureo-variegata*   -   3. Gold-ſtriped.
4. anguſtifolia   -   -   1. Narrow-rough-leaved Corniſh Elm.
5. *argenteo-variegata*   2. Silver-ſtriped.
6. *aureo-variegata*   -   3. Gold-ſtriped.
7. glabra   -   -   -   1. Wych Elm.
8. *argenteo-variega a*   2. Silver-ſtriped.
9. *aureo-variegata*   -   3. Gold-ſtriped.
10. latifolia   -   -   -   1. Broad-leaved Wych Elm.
11. *argenteo-variegata*   2. Silver-ſtriped.
12. *aureo-variegata*   -   3. Gold-ſtriped.
13. belgica   -   -   -   1. Dutch Elm.
14. *anguſtifolia*   -   -   2. Narrow-leaved Dutch Elm.
15. *argenteo-variegata*   3. Silver-ſtriped.
16. *aureo-variegata*   -   4. Gold-ſtriped.

150. YUCCA.

YUCCA, or ADAM's NEEDLE,——(Fr.)—

L. G. Pl. 429.   Hexandria Monogynia.   Cl. 6. Ord. 1.

1. filamentoſa   Virginian Thready-leaved Yucca.
2. glorioſa.   Canadian Yucca.

151. ZANTHOXYLON.

TOOTHACH-TREE,——(Fr.)—

L. G. Pl. 1109.   Dioecia Pentandria.   Cl. 22. Ord. 5.

1. Clava Herculis.   Toothach-tree.
2. fraxinifolium.   Aſh-leaved Toothach-tree.

CHAP. II.

HERBACEOUS PLANTS.

1. ACANTHUS.

BEAR'S-BREECH,——(Fr.)—Acante.

Lin. Gen. Plant. 793. Dydinamia Angiofpermia. Claffis 14. Ordo 2.

1. mollis.   Smooth-leaved Bear's-Breech.
2. fpinofus.   Prickly Bear's-Breech.

2. ACHILLEA.

MILFOIL, YARROW, and SNEEZEWORT,—(Fr.) Mille-feuille.

L. G. Pl. 971.   Syngenefia Polygamia Superflua.   Cl. 19. Ord. 8.

1. millefolium - - 1.	Milfoil, or Yarrow.
2. *Millefal. purpureum* 2.	Purple Milfoil.
3. *Millefol. variegatum* 3.	Variegated Milfoil.
4. abrotanifolia.	Southernwood-leaved Yarrow.
5. Ageratum.	Sweet Maudlin.
6. alpina.	Alpine Milfoil.
7. Clavennæ.	Silver-leaved Milfoil.
8. falcata.	Eaftern Milfoil.
9. macrophylla.	Long-leaved Milfoil.
10. nobilis.	Noble Milfoil.
11. Ptarmica - - 1.	Sneezewort.
12. *Ptarmica plena* - 2.	Double Sneezewort.
13. pubefcens.	Downy Milfoil.
14. fantolina.	Lavender-Cotton-leaved Milfoil.
15. tomentofa.	Yellow Milfoil.

3. ACONITUM.

ACONITE, WOLF's-BANE, or MONKSHOOD,—(Fr.)—Aconit.

L. G. Pl. 682.   Polyandria Trigynia.   Cl. 13. Ord. 3.

1. Anthora - -	1. Wholfome Wolf's-bane.
2. *Anthora alba* - -	2. White Wholfome Wolf's-bane.
3. cammarum.	Greater Monk's-hood.
4. Lycoctonum.	Yellow Poifonous Aconite.
5. Napellus.	Early Blue Wolf's-bane.
6. orientale.	White Oriental Wolf's-bane.
7. pyrenaicum.	Fennel-leaved Wolf's-bane.
8. variegatum.	Variegated Wolf's-bane.
9. uncinatum.	American Wolf's-bane.

4. ACORUS.

SWEET-SMELLING FLAG, or RUSH.

L. G. Pl. 434.   Hexandria Monogynia.   Cl. 6. Ord. 1.

1. calamus   Sweet Rush.

5. ACTÆA.

HERB CHRISTOPHER.

L. G. Pl. 644.   Polyandria Monogynia.   Cl. 13. Ord. 1.

1. alba.	White-berried Herb Chriftopher.
2. racemofa.	Branching Herb Chriftopher.
3. fpicata.	Spiked Herb Chriftopher.

6. ADONIS.

BIRD's EYE, or PHEASANT's EYE.

L. G. Pl. 698.   Polyandria Polygynia.   Cl. 13. Ord. 7.

1. vernalis.   Perennial Adonis, or Bird's Eye.

7. ADOXA.

TUBEROUS MOSCHATEL.

L. G. Pl. 501.   Octandria Tetragynia.   Cl. 8. Ord. 4.

1. mofchatellina.   Tuberous Mofchatel.

8. AGERATUM.

BASTARD HEMP AGRIMONY.

L. G. Pl. 667. Syngenefia Polygamia Æqualis. Cl. 19. Ord. 1.
a. altiffimum. Perennial Baftard Hemp Agrimony.

9. AGRIMONIA.

AGRIMONY,——(Fr.)—Agrimoine.

L. G. Pl. 607. Dodecandria Digynia. Cl. 11. Ord. 2.

1. Eupatoria. Agrimony.
2. odorata. Sweet-fcented Agrimony.
3. repens. Creeping Agrimony.

10. AGROSTEMMA.

CORN-CAMPION, COCKLE, or ROSE-CAMPION.

L. G. Pl. 607. Decandia Pentagynia. Cl. 10. Ord. 4.

1. Coronaria alba - 1. White Rofe-Campion.
2. Coronaria rubra - 2. Red Rofe-Campion.
3. Coronaria plena - 3. Double Red Rofe-Campion.
4. Coronaria bicolor - 4. Red and White Rofe-Campion.

11. AJUGA.

BUGLE,——(Fr.)—Bugle.

L. G. Pl. 705. Didynamia Gymnofpermia. Cl. 14. Ord. 1.

1. orientalis. Eaftern Bugle.
2. pyramidalis. Pyramidal Bugle.
3. reptans. Creeping Bugle.

12. ALCEA.

HOLLYHOCK.

L. G. Pl. 840. Monadelphia Polyandria. Cl. 16. Ord. 5.

1. Alcea rofea - - 1. White Hollyhock.
2. incarnata - - 2. Flefh-coloured Hollyhock.
3. rubra - - 3. Red Hollyhock.
4. atro-rubens - - 4. Deep-red Hollyhock.

E

5. *purpurea* - - - 5. Purple Hollyhock.
6. *fulphurea* - - - 6. Pale Yellow Hollyhock.
7. *lutea* - - - - 7. Yellow Hollyhock.
8. ficifolia. Fig-leaved Hollyhock.

N. B. Of these Varieties there are both single and double-flowered.

13. ALCHEMILLA.

LADIES MANTLE,——(Fr.)—Pied de Lion.

L. G. Pl. 165.　　　Tetrandria Monogynia.　　Cl. 4. Ord. 1.

1. alpina.　　　　　Alpine Ladies Mantle.
2. pentaphylla.　　 Five-leaved Ladies Mantle.
3. vulgaris - - - 1. Ladies Mantle.
4. *vulgaris hirfata* - 2. Hairy Ladies Mantle.

14. ALETRIS.

ALETRIS.

L. G. Pl. 428.　　　Hexandria Monogynia.　　Cl. 6. Ord. 1.

1. Uvaria,　　　　　Uvaria Aletris, or Aloe.

15. ALLIUM.

GARLIC,——(Fr.)—Ail.

L. G. Pl. 409.　　　Hexandria Monogynia.　　Cl. 6. Ord. 1.

1. arenarium.　　　Bulb-bearing Garlic.
2. canadenfe.　　　Canadian Garlic.
3. Chamæ-Moly.　　Dwarf Moly.
4. flavum.　　　　 Yellow-flowering Garlic.
5. Moly.　　　　　Yellow Moly.
6. rofeum.　　　　Starry-flowered Garlic.
7. fativum.　　　　Garlic.
8. Scorodoprafum.　Rocambole.
9. fenefcens.　　　Narciffus-leaved Garlic.
10. Sphærocephalon.　Cives.
11. fubhirfutum.　　Umbellated White Garlic.
12. victoriale.　　　Broad-leaved Garlic.
13. urfinum.　　　Wild Garlic.

ALLIUM-CEPA.

ONION,——(Fr.)—Oignon.

1. Cepa - - - - 1. Onion.
2. *Cepa alba* - - - 2. White Onion.
3. *Cepa rubra* - - 3. Red Onion.
4. afcalonicum - - 1. Scallion, or Efcallion.
5. *afcalonicum* - - 2. Efcalot, or Shallot.
6. Schænoprafum - 1. Cives.
7. *Schænoprafum* - 2. Welfh Onion.

ALLIUM-PORRUM.

LEEK,——(Fr.)—Poireau.

1. Porrum - - - 1. Leek.
2. *Porrum latifolium* 2. Broad-leaved, or London Leek.

16. ALTHÆA.

MARSH-MALLOW,——(Fr.)—Guimauve.

L. G. Pl. 839.   Monadelphia Polyandria.   Cl. 16. Ord. 4.

1. cannabina.   Hemp-leaved Marfh-Mallow.
2. officinalis.   Marfh-Mallow.

17. ALYSSUM.

MADWORT,——(Fr.)—Alyffon.

L. G. Pl. 805.   Tetradynamia Siliculofa.   Cl. 15. Ord. 1.

1. creticum.   Cretan Madwort.
2. halimifolium.   Sea-Purflane-leaved Sweet Madwort.
3. hyperboreum.   Northern Purple Madwort.
4. incanum.   Hairy Madwort.
5. montanum.   Mountain Madwort.
6. faxatile.   Yellow Madwort.
7. utriculatum.   Bladder-podded Madwort.

18. AMARYLLIS.

AMARYLLIS, or LILY-DAFFODIL,——(Fr.)—Lis-Narciffe.

L. G. Pl. 400.   Hexandria Monogynia.   Cl 6. Ord. 1.

1. lutea.   Autumnal Narciffus, or Amaryllis.
2. regina.   Belladonna Lily.

E 2

3. farnienfis.   Japanefe, or Guernfey Lily.
4. vernalis.   Spring Yellow Amaryllis.

19. A M M I.

Bishop's-Weed.

L. G. Pl. 334.   Polyandria Digynia.   Cl. 5. Ord. 2,
1. glaucifolium.   Bifhop's-Weed.

20. ANCHUSA.

Bugloss,——(Fr.)—Buglofe.

L. G. Pl. 182.   Pentandria Monogynia.   Cl. 5. Ord. 1.

1. orientalis.   Eaftern Buglofs.
2. fempervirens.   Evergreen Buglofs.

21. ANDRYALA.

Downy Sowthistle.

L. G. Pl. 915.   Syngenefia Polygamia Æqualis.   Cl. 19. Ord. 1.

1. lanata.   Downy Sowthiftle.

22. ANEMONE.

Anemone, or Wind-flower,——(Fr.)—Anemone.

L. G. Pl. 694.   Polyandria Polygynia.   Cl. 13. Ord. 7.

1. apennina.   Blue Apennine Anemone.
2. coronaria.   Garden Anemone.
3. dichotoma.   Forked-ftalked Anemone.
4. hortenfis.   Broad-leaved Garden Anemone.
5. narciffiflora.   Narciffus-flowered Anemone.
6. nemorofa   - - 1.   Blue Wood Anemone.
7. *nemorofa plena* - 2.   Double Blue Wood Anemone.
8. fylveftris.   White Wood Anemone.
9. thalictroides.   Goat's-Rue-leaved Anemone.
10. virginiana.   Virginian Anemone.

ANEMONE-HEPATICA.

Hepatica, or Liverwort.

1. alba.   White Hepatica.
2. cærulea - - - 1.   Blue Hepatica.

3. *cærulea plena* - - 2. Double Blue Hepatica,
4. rubra - - - - 1. Red Hepatica.
5. *rubra plena* - - 2. Double Red Hepatica.

ANEMONE-PULSATILLA.

PASQUE-FLOWER,——(Fr.)—Coquelourde.

1. vulgaris. Pasque-flower.

23. ANETHUM.

DILL,——(Fr.)—Anet.

L. G. Pl. 364. Pentandria Digynia. Cl. 5. Ord. 2.
1. graveolens. Dill.

ANETHUM-FOENICULUM.

FENNEL,——(Fr.)—Fenouil.

1. vulgare. Fennel.
2. azoricum, Finochio,

24. ANGELICA.

ANGELICA,——(Fr.)—Angelique.

L. G. Pl. 347. Pentandria Digynia. Cl. 5. Ord. 2.
1. Archangelica. Angelica.
2. atropurpurea. Purple Angelica.

25. ANTHEMIS.

CAMOMILE,——(Fr.)—Camomile.

L. G. Pl. 970. Syngenesia Polygamia Superflua. Cl. 19. Ord. 2,
1. anthemis - - - 1. Camomile.
2. *anthemis plena* - 2. Double Camomile.
3. Pyrethrum. Spanish Pellitory.
4. tinctoria. Ox-eye.

E 3

26. ANTHERICUM.

SPIDERWORT.

L. G. Pl. 422.   Hexandria Monogynia.   Cl. 6. Ord. 1.

1. frutefcens.   Yellow Cape Spiderwort.
2. Liliago.   Spiderwort.
3. Liliaftrum.   Savoy Spiderwort.
4. offifragum.   Marfh Afphodel.
5. ramofum.   Branching Spiderwort.

27. ANTIRRHINUM.

SNAPDRAGON,——(Fr.)—Mufle de Veau.

L. G. Pl. 750.   Didynamia Angiofpermia.   Cl. 14. Ord. 2.

1. geniftifolium.   Genifta-leaved Toad-flax.
2. Linaria.   Toad-flax.
3. majus   - - - 1. Snapdragon.
4. majus album   - - 2. White Snapdragon.
5. majus flavum - - 3. Yellow Snapdragon.
6. majus rubrum   - 4. Red Snapdragon.
7. majus variegatum - 5. Striped-leaved Snapdragon.
8. monfpeffulanum.   Montpelier Toad-flax.

28. APIUM.

PARSLEY,——(Fr.)—Perfil.

L. G. Pl. 367.   Pentandria Digynia.   Cl. 5. Ord. 2.

1. Petrofelinum   - 1. Parfley.
2. Petrofelinum crifpum 2. Curled-leaved Parfley.
3. latifolium.   Large-rooted Parfley.
4. dulce.   Celery.
5. rapaceum.   Celeriac.

29. APOCYNUM.

DOGSBANE,——(Fr.)—Apocin.

L. G. Pl. 305.   Pentandria Digynia.   Cl. 5. Ord. 2.

1. androfæmifolium.   Tutfan-leaved Dogfbane.
2. cannabinum.   Canadian Dogfbane.

30. A QUILEGIA.

COLUMBINE,——(Fr.)—Ancholie.

L. G. Pl. 684.   Polygamia Pentagynia.   Cl. 13. O rd.

1. alpina.   Alpine Columbine.
2. canadenfis.   Canadian Columbine.
3. vulgaris - - - 1.   Wild Blue Columbine.
4. *vulgaris multiplex* 2. Double Columbine.
5. *vulgaris ftellata* - 3. Starry Columbine.
6. *vulgaris ariegata*   4. Striped Columbine.

N. B. Of each of thefe Varieties there are many different Colours, as Red, White, Blue, Striped, &c.

31. A R A B I S.

BASTARD TOWER MUSTARD.

L. G. Pl. 8 ,   Tetradynamia Siliquofa.   Cl. 15. Ord. 2.

1. alpina, ,   Alpine Baftard Tower Muftard.

32. A R E N A R I A.

ARENARIA,

L. G. Pl. 569.   Decandria Trigynia.   Cl. 10. Ord. 3.

1. grandiflora.   Large-flowering Arenaria,

33. A R E T I A.

ARETIA.

L. G. Pl. 195.   Pentandria Monogynia.   Cl. 5. Ord. 1.

1. alpina.   Alpine Aretia.

34. A R I S T O L O C H I A.

BIRTHWORT,——(Fr.)—Ariftoloche.

L. G. Pl. 1022.   Gynandria Hexandria,   Cl. 20. Ord. 5.

1. Clematitis.   Upright Birthwort.
2. longa.   Long-rooted Birthwort.
3. Piftolochia.   Birthwort.
4. rotunda.   Round Birthwort. .

35. ARNICA,

L. G. Pl. 958.   Syngenefia Polygamia Superflua.   Cl. 19. Ord. 2,

1. montana.   Mountain Arnica.
2. Scorpioides.   Scorpion-rooted Arnica,

36. ARTEMISIA.

MUGWORT,——(Fr.)—Armoife.

L. G. Pl. 945.   Syngenefia Polygamia Superflua.   Cl. 19. Ord. 1

1. vulgaris,   Mugwort.

ARTEMISIA-ABROTANUM,

SOUTHERNWOOD,——(Fr.)—Auronne.

1. campeftre.   Field Southernwood.
2. Santonicum,   Tartarian Southernwood.

ARTEMISIA-ABSYNTHIUM,

WORMWOOD,——(Fr.)—Abfinte.

1. cærulefcens.   Lavender-leaved Wormwood,
2. Dracunculus.   Tarragon.
3. integrifolia.   Entire-leaved Wormwood,
4. maritima.   Sea Wormwood.
5. pontica,   Roman Wormwood,

37. ARUM.

WAKE ROBIN, FRIAR's-COWL. DRAGONS.

L. G. Pl. 1028.   Gynandria Polygynia.   Cl. 20. Ord. 7.

1. Arifarum   - - 1. Broad-leaved Wake-Robin.
2. *Arifarum variegatum* 2. Striped Broad-leaved Wake-Robin,
3. Dracunculus.   Dragons.
4. italicum.   Italian Arum.
5. maculatum,   Spotted Wake-Robin.
6. triphyllum.   Three-leaved Arum,

38. ARUNDO.

REED,——(Fr.)—Roſeau,

L. G. Pl. 93.		Triandria Digynia.	Cl. 3. Ord. 2.
1. Donax - - -	1.	Evergreen Portugal Reed.	
2. *Donax variegata* -	2.	Striped Evergreen Portugal Reed.	
3. epigeios.		Reed.	
4. phragmitis.		Small Reed.	

39. ASARUM.

ASARABACCA,——(Fr.)—Cabaret,

L. G. Pl. 589.	Dodecandria Monogynia.	Cl. 11. Ord. 1.
1. canadenſe.	Canadian Aſarabacca.	
2. europæum.	European Aſarabacca,	
3. virginicum.	Virginian Aſarabacca,	

40. ASCLEPIAS.

SWALLOW-WORT,——(Fr.)—Dompte-venin.

L. G. Pl. 306.		Pentandria Digynia.	Cl. 5. Ord. 2.
1. amœna.		Oval-leaved Purple Dog's-bane.	
2. incarnata.		Fleſh-coloured Dog's-bane.	
3. nigra.		Black Swallow-wort.	
4. purpuraſcens.		Purple Dog's-bane.	
5. ſyriaca - - -	1.	Syrian Dog's-bane.	
6. *ſyriaca exaltata* -	2.	White Syrian Dog's-bane.	
7. tuberoſa,		Orange Apocynum.	
8. verticillata.		Toad-flax-leaved Swallow-wort.	
9. Vincetoxicum.		Swallow-wort.	

41. ASPARAGUS.

ASPARAGUS,——(Fr.)—Aſperge.

L. G. Pl. 424.	Hexandria Monogynia.	Cl. 6. Ord. 1.
1. altilis,	Aſparagus.	

42. ASPERULA.

WOODROOF.

L. G. Pl. 121.	Tetandria Monogynia.	Cl. 4. Ord. 1.
1. odorata.	Woodroof.	

43. ASPHODELUS.

ASPHODEL, or KING's-SPEAR,——(Fr.)—Asfodele.

L. G. Pl. 421.   Hexandria Monogynia.   Cl. 6. Ord. 1.

1. albus.   White Afphodel.
2. luteus.   Yellow Afphodel.
3. ramofus - - - 1. Branching Afphodel.
4. *ramofus minor* - 2. Small Branching Afphodel.

44. ASPLENIUM.

HART's TONGUE.

L. G. Pl. 1178.   Cryptogamia. Filix.   Cl. 24. Ord. 1.

1. Ceterach.   Spleen-wort.
2. Scolopendrium.   Hart's Tongue.
3. Trichomanes.   Maiden-hair.

45. ASTER.

ASTER, or STARWORT.

L. G. Pl. 954.   Syngenefia Polygamia Superflua, Cl. 19. Ord. 2.

* Integrifolii, pedunculis nudis.
Entire-leaved and Naked Footftalks.

1. alpinus.   Blue Mountain Starwort.
2. Amellus.   Sea Starwort.
3. divaricatus.   Branching Starwort.
4. Tripolium.   Sea Starwort.

** Integrifolii, pedunculis fquamofis.
Entire-leaved and Scaly Footftalks.

5. concolor.   Blue Starwort.
6. dumofus.   Bufhy White Starwort.
7. ericoides.   Heath-leaved Starwort.
8. linarifolius. Toad-flax-leaved Starwort.
9. linifolius.   Flax-leaved Starwort.
10. novanglicus. New-England Starwort.
11. rigidus.   Hard-leaved Starwort.
12. tenuifolius.   Slender-leaved Starwort.
13. undulatus.   Waved-leaved Starwort.

*** Serratifolii, pedunculis lævibus.
Serrated-leaved, and Smooth Footſtalks.

14. cordifolius,	Heart-ſhaped-leaved Starwort.
15. puniceus.	Purple-ſtalked Starwort.

**** Serratifolii, pedunculis ſquamoſis.
Serrated-leaved and Scaly Footſtalks.

16. grandiflorus.   Great-flowered Starwort.
17. lævis.   Smooth-ſtalked Starwort.
18. miſer.   Poor-flowered Starwort.
19. mutabilis.   Variable Starwort.
20. novibelgicus.   New-Holland Starwort.
21. tardiflorus - - 1. Late-flowering Starwort.
22. *tardiflorus minor* - 2. Leſſer Late-flowering Starwort.
23. Tradeſcantianus.   Tradeſcant's Starwort.

STARWORTS cultivated in the English Nurſeries, but not de-
ſcribed by Linnæus.

24. aculeatus.   Prickly-leaved Starwort.
25. alienatus.   Strange-flowered Starwort.
26. corymboſus.   Heart-ſhaped-leaved White Starwort.
27. purpureus.   Purple Starwort.
28. repens.   Creeping Broad-leaved Starwort.
29. ſalicifolius.   Willow-leaved Starwort.
30. umbellatus.   Umbellated Starwort.
31. virgatus.   Slender-branched Starwort.

46. ASTRAGALUS.

MILK-VETCH, or WILD LIQUORICE,——(Fr.)—Aſtragale.

L. G. Pl. 892.   Diadelphia Decandria.   Cl. 17. Ord. 3.

1. alopecuroides.   Fox-tail Milk-Vetch.
2. alpinus.   Alpine Milk-Vetch.
3. arenarius.   Sand Milk-Vetch.
4. Cicer.   Bladder-podded Milk-Vetch.
5. galegiformis.   Goat's-Rue-leaved Milk-Vetch.
6. glycyphyllus.   Wild Liquorice, or Liquorice M.V.
7. tragacanthoides.   Goat's-Thorn-leaved Milk-Vetch.

47. ASTRANTIA.

BLACK MASTERWORT.

L. G. Pl. 327.   Pentandria Digynia.   Cl. 5. Ord. 2.

1. major - - - 1. Great Black Masterwort.
2. *major candida* - 2. White-flowered Black Masterwort.
3. minor.   Lesser Black Masterwort.

48. ATHAMANTA.

SPIGNEL.

L. G. Pl. 338.   Pentandria Digynia.   Cl. 5. Ord. 2.

1. Meum.   Spignel.

49. ATROPA.

DEADLY NIGHTSHADE.

L. G. Pl. 249.   Pentandria Monogynia.   Cl. 5. Ord. 1.

1. Belladonna.   Deadly Nightshade.
2. Mandragora.   Mandrake.

50. BELLIS.

DAISY,——(Fr.)—Pàquerete.

L. G. Pl. 962.   Syngenesia Polygamia Superflua.   Cl. 19. Ord. 2.

1. perennis alba - 1. Double White Daisy.
2. *perennis incarnata* 2. Double Flesh-coloured Daisy.
3. *perennis rubra* - 3. Double Red Daisy.
4. *perennis variegata* 4. Double Red-and-white Daisy.
5. *perennis prolifera* 5. Proliferous Daisy.
6. *perennis cristata* - 6. Cock's-comb Daisy.

51. BETA.

BEET,——(Fr.)—Poirée.

L. G. Pl. 310.   Pentandria Digynia.   Cl. 5. Ord. 2.

1. vulgaris alba - - 1. White Beet.
2. *vulgaris rubra* - 2. Red Beet.
3. *vulgaris viridis* - 3. Green Beet.

52. BETONICA.

BETONY,——(Fr.)—Betoine.

L. G. Pl. 718.   Didynamia Gymnofpermia.   Cl. 14. Ord. 1.

1. alpina.   Alpine Betony.
2. danica.   Danifh Betony.
3. officinalis.   Betony.
4. orientalis.   Eaftern Betony.

53. BIDENS.

WATER-HEMP-AGRIMONY.

L. G. Pl. 932.   Syngenefia Polygamia Æqualis.   Cl. 19. Ord 1.

1. frondofa.   Canadian Bidens.

54. BLITUM.

STRAWBERRY SPINACH,——(Fr.)—Blete.

L. G. Pl. 14.   Monandria Digynia.   Cl. 1. Ord. 2,

1. capitatum,   Strawberry Spinach.
2. virgatum.

55. BORAGO.

BORAGE,——(Fr.)—Bourrache.

L. G. Pl. 188.   Pentandria Monogynia.   Cl. 5. Ord. 1.

1. orientalis.   Conftantinopolitan Borage.

56. BRASSICA.

CABBAGE,—(Fr.)—Choux.

L. G. Pl. 820.   Tetradynamia Siliquofa.   Cl. 15. Ord. 2.

1. oleracea - - - 1. Sea Cabbage.
2. *compreffa* - - - 2. Flat fided Cabbage.
3. *eboracenfis* - - - 3. Early Yorkfhire Cabbage.
4. *mufcovitica* - - - 4. Early Ruffian Cabbage.
5. *pyramidalis* - - - 5. Sugar-loaf Cabbage.
6. *pyramidalis præcox* 6. Early Sugar-loaf Cabbage.
7. *rubra* - - - - 7. Red Cabbage.
8. *fcotica* - - - - 8. Large White Scotch Cabbage.

BRASSICA SABAUDA.—SAVOY CABBAGE.

9. fabauda alba - - 1. White Savoy Cabbage.
10. *fabauda flava* - - 2. Yellow Savoy Cabbage.
11. *fabauda viridis* - 3. Green Savoy Cabbage.

BRASSICA SABELLICA.—BOORCALE, or KALE.

12. fabellica purpurea 1. Purple Boorcole.
13. *fabellica viridis* - 2. Green Boorcole.
14. *fabellica variegata* 3. Variegated Boorcole.

BRASSICA-BOTRYTIS.—CAULIFLOWER.

15. Botrytis præcox - 1. Early Cauliflower.
16. *Botrytis ferotina* - 2. Late Cauliflower.

BRASSICA-CAULORAPA.—CABBAGE-TURNEP.

17. Caulorapa.   Cabbage Turnep.

BRASSICA-NAPOBRASSICA.—TURNEP-ROOTED CABBAGE.

18. Napobraffica.   Turnep-rooted Cabbage.

BRASSICA-ITALICA.—BROCCOLI.

19. italica alba - - 1. White, or Cauliflower Broccoli.
20. *italica purpurea* - 2. Purple Broccoli.
21. *italica purp. præcox* 3. Early Purple Broccoli.

BRASSICA-RAPA.—TURNEP.

1. præcox - - - 1. Early Dutch Turnep.
2. *flavefcens* - - - 2. Yellow Turnep.
3. *viridis* - - - 3. Green-topped Turnep.
4. *candida* - - - 4. White-rooted Turnep.
5. *oblonga* - - - 5. Long-rooted Turnep.
6. *punicea* - - - 6. Purple-rooted Turnep.

BRASSICA-NAPUS.——NAVEW.

1. fylveftris - - 1. Wild Navew, or Rape-feed.
2. *fylveftris alba* - 2. White Navew, or French Turnep.

BRASSICA-ERUCA.—ROCKET.

1. Eruca.   Rocket.

57. BULBOCODIUM.

MOUNTAIN SAFFRON.

L. G. Pl. 407.   Hexandria Monogynia.   Cl. 6. Ord. 1.
1. alpinum.   Ruſh-leaved Bulbocodium.

58. BUPTHALMUM.

OX-EYE,——(Fr.)—Oeil de Boeuf.

L. G. Pl. 977.   Syngeneſia Polygamia Superflua.   Cl. 19. Ord. 2.
1. Helianthoides.   Ox-eye.

59. BUPLEURUM.

HARE'S-EAR.

L. G. Pl. 328.   Pentandria Digynia.   Cl. 5. Ord. 2.
1. longifolium.   Long-leaved Hare's Ear.

60. CACALIA.

FOREIGN COLTSFOOT.

L. G. Pl. 933.   Syngeneſia Polygamia Æqualis.   Cl. 19. Ord. 1.
1. alpina.   Alpine Coltsfoot.
2. atriplicifolia.   Orach-leaved Coltsfoot.
3. haſtata.   Spear-leaved Coltsfoot.
4. ſuaveolens.   Sweet-ſcented Coltsfoot.

61. CALENDULA.

MARYGOLD,——(Fr.)—Souci.

L. G. Pl. 990.   Syngeneſia Polygamia Neceſſaria.   Cl. 19. Ord. 4.
1. officinalis   - - 1. Marygold.
2. *officinalis citrina* - 2. Lemon-coloured Marygold.
3. pluvialis.   Cape Marygold.
4. hybrida.   Hybrid Marygold.

62. CALLA.

BASTARD ARUM.

L. G. Pl. 1030.   Gynandria Polyandria.   Cl. 20. Ord. 7.
1. paluſtris.   Marſh Baſtard Arum.

63. CALTHA.

MARSH MARYGOLD,

L. G. Pl. 703.   Polyandria Polygynia,   Cl. 13. Ord. 7.
1. paluſtris plena,   Double Marſh Marygold,

64. CAMPANULA.

BELL-FLOWER, or CAMPANULA,——(Fr.)—Campanule,

L. G. Pl. 218.   Pentandria Monogynia.   Cl. 5. Ord. 1.

* Foliis lævioribus anguſtioribus,
  With ſmooth narrow leaves.

1. americana.			American Bell-flower,
2. patula.			Field Bell-flower.
3. perſicifolia	-	1.	Blue Peach-leaved Bell-flower.
4. *perſicifolia alba*	-	2.	White Peach-leaved Bell-flower.
5. *perſicifolia plena*	-	3.	Double Blue Peach-leaved Bell-flo.
6. *perſicif. alba plena*		4.	Double White Peach-leaved Bell-flo.
7. pyramidalis.			Blue Pyramidal Bell-flower.
8. Rapunculus.			Rampion.
9. rotundifolia.			Round-leaved Bell-flower.

** Foliis ſcabris latioribus.
   With broad rough leaves.

10. glomerata	- -	1.	Leſſer Throatwort.
11. *glomerata alba*	-	2.	White Leſſer Throatwort.
12. latifolia	- - -	1.	Giant Throatwort.
13. *latifolia alba*	- -	2.	White Giant Throatwort.
14. medium	- - -	1.	Blue Canterbury Bell.
15. *medium album*	-	2.	White Canterbury Bell.
16. ſaxatilis.			Daiſy-leaved Throatwort.
17. thyrſoides.			Echium-leaved Bell-flower.
18. Trachelium	- -	1.	Great Throatwort.
19. *Trachelium album*		2.	Great White Throatwort.
20. *Trachelium plenum*		3.	Great Double Blue Throatwort.
21. *Trach. plenum album.*	4.		Great Double White Throatwort.

65. CANNABIS.

HEMP.

L. G. Pl. 1115,   Dioecia Pentandria.   Cl. 22. Ord. 5.
1. ſativa.   Hemp.
2. chinenſis.   Chineſe Hemp.

66. CAPSICUM.

CAPSICUM, INDIAN or GUINEA PEPPER,
(Fr.)—Poivre d'Inde.

L. G. Pl. 252.   Pentandria Monogynia.   Cl. 5. Ord. 1,

1. angulofum.   Angulated Scarlet Capficum. ☉
2. cerafiforme. - - 1. Red Cherry-fhaped Capficum. ☉
3. *cerafiforme luteum.* 2. Yellow Cherry-fhaped Capficum. ♂
4. cordiforme.   Heart-fhaped Capficum. ☉
5. olivæforme.   Olive-fhaped Capficum. ☉
6. propendens.   Long-podded Capficum. ☉
7. tetragonum.   Bell Pepper, or Pickling Capficum. ☉

N. B. No. 4. cordiforme, and No. 6. propendens, vary much in their
fhape. There are alfo both red and yellow of each fort.

67. CARDAMINE.

LADY's-SMOCK.

L. G. Pl. 812.   Tetradynamia Siliquofa.   Cl. 15. Ord. 2,

1. pratenfis - - - 1. Purple Lady's-fmock.
2. *pratenfis alba* - - 2. White Lady's-fmock.
3. *pratenfis plena* - 3. Double White Lady's-fmock.
4. *prat. plena purpurea* 4. Double Purple Lady's-fmock.
5. trifolia.   Three-leaved Lady's-fmock.

ANNUALS.

6. amara.   Bitter Creffes, or Lady's-fmock. ☉
7. hirfuta.   Hairy Lady's-fmock. ☉
8. impatiens.   Impatient Lady's-fmock. ☉
9. parviflora.   Small-flowered Lady's-fmock. ☉

68. CARDUUS.

THISTLE,——(Fr.)—Chardon.

L. G. Pl. 925.   Syngenefia Polygamia Æqualis.   Cl. 19. Ord 1.

1. acaulis.   Dwarf Carline Thiftle.
2. cafabonæ.   Fifh Thiftle. ♂
3. crifpus.   Thiftle upon Thiftle.
4. helenioides.   Melancholy Thiftle.
5. marianus - - - 1. Milk Thiftle.
6. *marianus maculatus* 2. Spotted Milk Thiftle.

F

69. CARTHAMUS.

BASTARD SAFFRON, or SAFFLOWER,
(Fr.)—Cartame, ou Saffran Batard.

L. G. Pl. 931.   Syngenefia Polygamia Æqualis.   Cl. 19. Ord. 1.
1. lanatus.   Diftaff Thiftle. ☉
2. tinctorius.   Baftard Saffron, or Safflower.

70. CASSIA.

CASSIA, or WILD SENA.

L. G. Pl. 514.   Decandria Monogynia.   Cl. 10. Ord. 1.
1. marilandica.   Maryland Sena.

71. CATANANCHE.

CANDY LION'S-FOOT.

L. G. Pl. 970.   Syngenefia Polygamia Æqualis.   Cl. 19. Ord. 1.
1. cærulea.   Blue Candy Lion's-foot.
2. lutea.   Yellow Candy Lion's-foot.

72. CELOSIA.

COCK'S-COMB AMARANTH.

L. G. Pl. 289.   Pentandria Monogynia.   Cl. 5. Ord. 1.

1. caftrenfis.   Branching-fpiked Cock's-comb. ☉
2. coccinea.   Scarlet Cock's-comb. ☉
3. criftata - - - 1. Cock's-comb Amaranth. ☉
4. *criftata humilis* - 2. Dwarf Cock's-comb Amaranth. ☉
5. *criftata lutea* - - 3. Yellow Cock's-comb Amaranth. ☉
6. *criftata variegata* - 4. Striped Cock's-comb Amaranth. ☉

73. CENTAUREA.

CENTAURY,——(Fr.)—Centaurée.

L. G. Pl. 984.   Syngenefia Polygamia Fruftranea.   Cl. 19. Ord. 3.
1. Centaurium.   Greater Centaury.
2. Cineraria.   Great Mountain Knapweed.
3. Crocodylium.   Great-headed Centaury.
4. glaftifolia.   Woad-leaved Centaury.

5. Jacea.   Knapweed.
6. montana.   Mountain Centaury.
7. pectinata.   Pectinated Centaury.
8. phrygia.   Ciliated Centaury.
9. Scabiosa.   Scabious-leaved Centaury.
10. sibirica.   Siberian Centaury.
11. splendens.   Shining-leaved Centaury.

ANNUALS.

12. benedicta.   Blessed Thistle. ☉
13. Cyanus   - - -   1.   Cornbottle. ☉
14. Cyanus albus   - -   2.   White Cornbottle. ☉
15. Cyanus ruber   - -   3.   Red Cornbottle. ☉
16. Cyanus variegatus   4.   Striped Cornbottle. ☉
17. melitensis.   Melitan Centaury. ☉
18. moschata   - - -   1.   Purple Sweet Sultan. ☉
19. moschata alba   -   2.   White Sweet Sultan. ☉
20. moschata Amberboi   3.   Yellow Sweet Sultan. ☉
21. moschata incarnata   4.   Flesh-coloured Sweet Sultan. ☉
22. nigra.   Black Knapweed. ☉
23. paniculata.   Purple panicled Knapweed. ☉

74. CERASTIUM.
MOUSE-EAR CHICKWEED.

L. G. Pl. 585.   Decandria Pentagynia.   Cl. 10. Ord. 4.

1. arvense.   Corn Mouse-ear Chickweed.
2. latifolium.   Broad-leaved Mouse-ear Chickweed.
3. repens.   Creeping Mouse-ear Chickweed.
4. tomentosum - - 1.   Woolly Mouse-ear Chickweed.
5. toment. angustifolium 2.   Narrow-leaved Mouse-ear Chickw.

75. CERINTHE.
HONEYWORT,——(Fr.)—Melinet.

L. G. Pl. 186.   Pentandria Monogynia.   Cl. 5. Ord. 1.

1. major.   Greater Honeywort. ☉
2. minor.   Lesser Honeywort. ☉

F 2

76. CHÆROPHYLLUM.

CHERVIL,——(Fr.)—Cerfeuil.

L. G. Pl. 358.   Pentandria Digynia.   Cl. 5. Ord. 2.

1. aromaticum.	Chervil.
2. aureum.	Yellow Wild Chervil.
3. bulbofum.	Hungarian Chervil.
4. hirfutum.	Myrrh.

77. CHEIRANTHUS.

STOCK JULY-FLOWER, and WALL-FLOWER,
(Fr.)—Giroflier, ou Violier.

L. G. Pl. 815.   Tetradynamia Siliquofa.   Cl. 15. Ord. 2.

1. annuus purpureus	1.	Purple Ten-weeks Stock.	⊙
2. *annuus albus* - -	2.	White Ten-weeks Stock.	⊙
3. *annuus leucojifolius*	3.	Wall-flower-leaved Ten-weeks S.	⊙
4. *an. leucojif. albus*	4.	White ditto.	⊙
5. *an. leucojif. coccineus*	5.	Scarlet ditto.	⊙
6. Cheiri - - -	1.	Wall-flower.	
7. *Cheiri plenus* - -	2.	Double Wall-flower.	
8. *Cheiri ferrugineus*	3.	Bloody Wall-flower.	
9. *Cheiri fer. plenus*	4.	Double Bloody Wall-flower.	
10. *Cheiri variegatus*	5.	Striped-leaved Bloody Wall-flower.	
11. *Cheiri albus* - -	6.	White Wall-flower.	
12. *Cheiri albus plenus*	7.	Double White Wall-flower.	
13. incanus albus -	1.	White Stock July-flower.	
14. *incanus coccineus* -	2.	Scarlet, or Brompton Stock.	
15. *incanus purpureus*	3.	Purple Stock July-flower.	
16. *incanus ruber* - -	4.	Pale-red, or Queen Stock.	
17. *incanus variegatus*	5.	Striped Stock July-flower.	

N. B. The wall-flowers and flocks are annual, biennial, or fhrubby, according to the foil and fituation where planted.

18. maritimus.	Dwarf Annual Stock.	⊙
19. tricufpidatus.	Three-pointed-leaved Stock.	

78. CHELIDONIUM.

CELANDINE,——(Fr.)—Chelidoine.

L. G. Pl. 647.　　Polyandria Monogynia.　　Cl. 13. Ord. 1.

1. majus　 -　-　- 　1. Celandine.
2. *majus plenum* -　- 　2. Double Celandine.
3. Glaucium.　　　.　　Horned Poppy. ♂

79. CHELONE.

CHELONE.

L. G. Pl. 748.　　Didynamia Angiofpermia.　　Cl. 14. Ord. 2.

1. glabra　 -　-　- 　1. White Chelone.
2. *glabra rofea* -　- 　2. Rofe-coloured Chelone.
3. hirfuta.　　　　Pale-blue Chelone.
4. Pentftemon.　　　Pentftemon Chelone.

80. CHRYSANTHEMUM.

CORN MARYGOLD.

L. G. Pl. 966.　　Syngenefia Polygamia Superflua.　　Cl. 19. Ord. 2.

1. atratum.　　　　Alpine Ox-eye Daify.
2. Balfamita.　　　Coftmary.
3. coronarium　-　- 　1. Chryfanthemum. ☉
4. *coronarium album*　2. White Chryfanthemum. ☉
5. Leucanthemum.　　Great Ox-eye Daify.
6. ferotinum.　　　.　　Creeping Ox-eye Daify.

81, CHRYSOCOMA.

GOLDYLOCKS.

L. G. Pl. 939.　　Syngenefia Polygamia Æqualis.　　Cl. 19. Ord. 1.

1. Linofyris.　　　German Goldylocks.

82. CHRYSOSPLENIUM.

GOLDEN SAXIFRAGE.

L. G. Pl. 558.　　Decandria Digynia.　　Cl. 10. Ord. 2.

1. alternifolium.　　Alternate-leaved Golden Saxifrage.
2. oppofitifolium,　　Oppofite-leaved Golden Saxifrage.

F 3

83. CICHORIUM.

SUCCORY,——(Fr.)—Chicorée,

L. G. Pl. 921.   Syngenesia Polygamia Æqualis.   Cl. 19. Ord. 1,

1. Endivia - - - 1. Endive. ⊙
2. *Endivia alba* - - 2. White Endive. ⊙
3. *Endivia latifolia* - 3. Broad-leaved Endive. ⊙

84. CIRCÆA.

ENCHANTER's NIGHTSHADE,——(Fr.)—Circée.

L. G. Pl. 24.   Diandria Monogynia.   Cl. 2. Ord. 1,

1. lutetiana.   Enchanter's Nightshade.
2. alpina.   Alpine Enchanter's Nightshade.

85. CLAYTONIA.

CLAYTONIA.

L. G. Pl. 287.   Pentandria Monogynia.   Cl. 5. Ord. 1.

1. virginica.   Virginian Claytonia.

86. CLEMATIS.

VIRGIN's BOWER,——(Fr.)—Clematite,

L. G. Pl. 696.   Polyandria Polygynia.   Cl. 13. Ord. 7,

1. integrifolia,   Entire-leaved Virgin's Bower.
2. recta,   Upright Virgin's Bower,

87. COCHLEARIA,

SCURVY-GRASS and HORSE-RADISH,

L. G. Pl. 803.   Tetradynamia Siliculosa.   Cl. 15. Ord. 1,

1. Armoracia,   Horse-Radish.

88. COLCHICUM.

COLCHICUM, or MEADOW SAFFRON——(Fr.)—Colchique,

L. G. Pl. 457.   Hexandria Trigynia.   Cl. 6. Ord. 3.

1. autumnale   - - 1. Colchicum.
2. *autumnale plenum* 2. Double Colchicum,
3. *autumnale variegat.* 3. Variegated Colchicum.

89. COLLINSONIA.
COLLINSONIA.

L. G. Pl. 40.   Diandria Monogynia.   Cl. 2. Ord. 1.
 1. canadenfis.   Canadian Collinfonia.

90. COMARUM.
MARSH CINQUEFOIL.

L. G. Pl. 638.   Icofandria Polygynia.   Cl. 12. Ord. 5.
 1. paluftre.   Marfh Cinquefoil.

91. CONVALLARIA.
LILY of the VALLEY,——(Fr.)—Muguet.

L. G. Pl. 425.   Hexandria Monogynia.   Cl. 6. Ord. 1.

1. majalis - - -	1.	Lily of the Valley.
2. majalis plena - -	2.	Double Lily of the Valley.
3. majalis rubra -	3.	Red Lily of the Valley.
4. majalis variegata	4.	Striped Lily of the Valley.

CONVALLARIA-POLYGONATUM.
SOLOMON's SEAL,——(Fr.)—Sceau de Solomon.

1. Polygonatum.	Solomon's Seal.
2. bifolia.	Two-leaved Solomon's Seal.
3. latifolia.	Broad-leaved Solomon's Seal.
4. multiflora.	Many-flowered Solomon's Seal.
5. racemofa.	Spiked-flowered Solomon's Seal.
6. trifolia.	Three-leaved Solomon's Seal.
7. verticillata.	Whirl-leaved Solomon's Seal.

92. CONVOLVULUS.
BINDWEED,——(Fr.)—Liferon.

L. G. Pl. 215.   Pentandria Monogynia.   Cl. 5. Ord. 1.

1. lineatus.	Dwarf Bindweed.
2. Soldanella.	Creeping Bindweed.
3. Scammonia.	Scammony.

F 4

ANNUALS,

4. coccineus,	Scarlet Convolvulus.	☉
5. hederaceus.	Great or Convolvulus Major.	☉
6. tricolor. - - 1.	Leſſer or Convolvulus Minor.	☉
7. *tricolor varieg.* - 2.	Striped Convolvulus Minor.	☉

93. COREOPSIS,
TICKSEED.

L. G. Pl. 981.   Syngeneſia Polygamia Superflua,   Cl. 19. Ord. 3.
1. alba.   White Tickſeed.
2. alternifolia.   Alternate-leaved Tickſeed.
3. lanceolata,   Long-leaved Tickſeed,
4. tripteris.   Three-leaved Tickſeed.
5. verticillata.   Whirl-leaved Tickſeed.

94. CORNUS.
DOGWOOD, or DOGBERRY,

L. G. Pl. 149.   Tetrandria Monogynia.   Cl. 4. Ord. 1,
1. canadenſis.   Canadian Dogberry.

95. CORTUSA.
BEAR's EAR SANICLE.

L. G. Pl. 198.   Pentandria Monogynia.   Cl. 5. Ord, 1,
1. Gmelini.   Siberian Bear's-Ear Sanicle,
2. Matthioli.   Alpine Bear's-Ear Sanicle.

96. CRAMBE.
SEA COLEWORT, or CABBAGE.

L. G. Pl. 825.   Tetradynamia Siliquoſa.   Cl. 15. Ord. 2,
1. maritima,   Sea Cabbage.
2. hiſpida.   Rough-leaved Sea Cabbage.

97. CRITHMUM.
SAMPHIRE,——(Fr.)—Bacille,

L. G. Pl. 340.   Pentandria Digynia.   Cl. 5. Ord. 2,
1. maritimum.   Samphire,

98. CROCUS.
Crocus and Saffron,——(Fr.)—Saffran.

L. G. Pl. 55. Triandria Monogynia. Cl. 3. Ord. 1.
1. officinalis. Saffron.
2. autumnalis albus 1. White Autumnal Crocus,
3. *autumnalis cæruleus* 2. Blue Autumnal Crocus.
4. *autumnalis purpureus* 3. Purple Autumnal Crocus.
5. vernus albus - - 1. White Crocus.
6. *vernus cæruleus* - 2. Blue Crocus.
7. *vernus luteus* - - 3. Yellow Crocus.
8. *vernus purpureus* 4. Purple Crocus.

N. B. In the different nurseries there are about twenty varieties of the spring, and four or five of the autumnal crocuses.

99. CUCUBALUS.
Berry-bearing Chickweed.

L. G. Pl. 566. Decandria Trigynia. Cl. 10. Ord. 3.
1. Behen. Behen.
2. catholicus - 1. Italian Lychnis.
3. *catholicus angustifol.* 2. Narrow-leaved Italian Lychnis.
4. Otites. Spanish Lychnis.
5. viscosus - - - 1. Night-flowering Dover Campion.
6. *viscosus albus* - 2. White Night-flowering Dover Cam.

100. CUCUMIS.
Cucumber,——(Fr.)—Concombre.

L. G. Pl. 1092. Monoecia Syngenesia. Cl. 21. Ord. 10.
1. sativus. Cucumber. ☉
2. anguinus. Snake Cucumber. ☉

CUCUMIS-ANGURIA.
Water-Melon.

1. Anguria. Water-Melon. ☉

CUCUMIS-MELO.
Melon,——(Fr.)—Melon.
1. melo vulgaris. Melon. ☉

N. B. For the cultivated varieties of the Cucumbers and Melons, see the Catalogue of the Kitchen-Garden Plants.

101. CUCURBITA.

GOURD,——(Fr.)—Calbaſſe.

L. G. Pl. 1091.   Monoecia Syngeneſia.   Cl. 21. Ord. 10.

1. aſpera.   Gourd.   ⊙

CUCURBITA-MELOPEPO.

SQUASH.

1. Melopepo.   Squaſh.   ⊙

CUCURBITA-PEPO.

PUMPION.

1. Pepo.   Pumpion.   ⊙

102. CYCLAMEN.

CYCLAMEN, or SOWBREAD,——(Fr.)—Pain de Pourceau.

L. G. Pl. 201.   Pentandria Monogynia.   Cl. 5. Ord. 1.

1. europæum   -   -   1. Autumnal Cyclamen.
2. *europæum album*   -   2. White Autumnal Cyclamen.
3. perſicum.   Perſian Cyclamen.
4. vernum   -   -   1. Spring Cyclamen.
5. *vernum album*   -   2. White Spring Cyclamen.

103. CYNARA.

ARTICHOKE,——(Fr.)—Artichauk.

L. G. Pl. 923.   Syngeneſia Polygamia Æqualis.   Cl. 19. Ord. 1.

1. Scolymus.   Artichoke.
2. Cardunculus.   Chardon.

104. CYNOGLOSSUM.

HOUND's TONGUE,——(Fr.)—Langue de Chien.

L. G. Pl. 183.   Pentandria Monogynia.   Cl. 5. Ord. 1.

1. officinale   -   -   1. Hound's Tongue.
2. *officinale virens*   -   2. Green-leaved Hound's Tongue.

CYNOGLOSSUM-OMPHALODES.

VENUS' NAVELWORT.

1. Omphalodes,   Venus' Navelwort.

105. CYPRIPEDIUM.

LADIES SLIPPER,——(Fr.)—Sabot.

L. G. Pl. 1015.   Gynandria Diandria.   Cl. 20. Ord. 1.

1. Calceolus purpur.   1. Purple Ladies Slipper.
2. *Calceolus luteus* -   2. Yellow Ladies Slipper.
3. canadenfe.   Canadian Ladies Slipper.

106. DATISCA.

BASTARD HEMP.

L. G. Pl. 1132.   Dioecia Dodecandria.   Cl. 22. Ord. 10.

1. Cannabina florif. -   1. Smooth Male Baftard Hemp. ☉
2. *Cannabina fruEtif.* -   2. Smooth Female Baftard Hemp. ☉
3. hir!uta florifera. -   1. Hairy Male Baftard Hemp. ☉
4. *hirfuta fruEtifera.* -   2. Hairy Female Baftard Hemp. ☉

107. DATURA.

THORNY APPLE, and STRAMONIUM.

L. G. Pl. 246.   Pentandria Monogynia.   Cl. 5. Ord. 1.

1. Stramonium. -   1. Thorny Apple. ☉
2. faftuofum. - -   1. Double White Stramonium. ☉
3. *faftuofum purp.* -   2. Double Purple Stramonium. ☉
4. Tatula.   Purple-ftalked Stramonium. ☉

108. DAUCUS.

CARROT,——(Fr.)—Carotte.

L. G. Pl. 333.   Pentandria Digynia.   Cl. 5. Ord. 2.

1. Carota.   Carrot. ♂

N. B. For the cultivated varieties, fee the Kitchen Garden Catalogue.

2. Gingidium.   White Carrot. -

109. DELPHINIUM.

LARKSPUR,——(Fr.)—Pié d'Alouette.

L. G. Pl. 681.   Polyandria Trigynia.   Cl. 13. Ord. 3.

1. americanum.   American Bee Larkſpur.
2. elatum.   Siberian Bee Larkſpur.
3. grandiflorum.   Great-flowering Bee Larkſpur.
4. Staphiſagria.   Staveſacre.

ANNUALS.

5. ambiguum.   Mauritanian Larkſpur. ☉
6. Ajacis. - - - 1.   Upright Larkſpur. ☉
7. *Ajacis plenum* - 2.   Double Upright Larkſpur.
8. Conſolida. - - 1.   Branching Larkſpur. ☉
9. *Conſolida variegata* 2.   Striped Branching Larkſpur.

N. B. The colours of the Annual Larkſpurs are white, blue, purple, roſe-coloured; and the ſtriped is blue and white.

110. DENTARIA.

TOOTHWORT,——(Fr.)—Dentaire.

L. G. Pl. 811.   Tetradynamia Siliquoſa.   Cl. 15. Ord. 2.

1. bulbifera.   Bulbiferous Toothwort.
2. enneaphyllus.   Three-leaved Toothwort.
3. pentaphyllus.   Five-leaved Toothwort.

111. DIANTHERA.

DIANTHERA.

L. G. Pl. 28.   Diandria Monogynia.   Cl. 2. Ord. 1.

1. americana.   Virginian Dianthera.

112. DIANTHUS.

CLOVE JULY-FLOWER, or CARNATION,——(Fr.)—Oeillet.

L. G. Pl. 565.   Decandria Digynia.   Cl. 10. Ord. 2.

1. alpinus.   Alpine Pink.
2. arenarius.   Stone Pink.
3. Armeria.   Deptford Pink. ☉
4. barbatus. - - 1.   Sweet William. ♂

5. *barbatus plenus*	-	2.	Double Sweet William.
6. *barbatus variegatus*		3.	Striped Sweet William.
7. Caryophyllus	-	1.	Clove July-flower, or Carnation.
8. *Caryophyllus plenus*		2.	Double Clove July-flower, or Carn.
9. chinenfis	- -	1.	Chinefe, or Indian Pink. ☉ ♂
10. *chinenfis plenus*	-	2.	Double Chinefe, or Indian Pink.
11. deltoides.			Pink.
12. glaucus.			Mountain Pink.
13. fuperbus.			Fringed Pink.

113. DICTAMNUS.

FRAXINELLA,——(Fr.)—Fraxinelle.

L. G. Pl. 522.   Decandria Monogynia.   Cl. 10. Ord. 1.

1. albus - - - 1. White Fraxinella.
2. *ruber* - - - - 2. Red Fraxinella.

114. DIGITALIS.

FOXGLOVE,——(Fr.)—Digitale.

L. G. Pl. 758.   Didynamia Angiofpermia.   Cl. 14. Ord. 2.

1. ferruginea.   Iron-coloured Foxglove.
2. lutea - - - - 1. Yellow Foxglove.
3. *lutea major* - - 2. Great Yellow Foxglove.
4. Thapfi.   Verbafcum-leaved Foxglove.
5. vulgaris - - - 1. Purple Foxglove.
6. *vulgaris alba* - - 2. White Foxglove.

115. DIONÆA.

VENUS's FLY-TRAP.

L. G. Pl.   Decandria Monogynia.   Cl. 10. Ord. 1.

1. mufcipula.   Venus's Fly-trap.

116. DIPSACUS.

TEASEL,——(Fr.)—Chardon à Bonnetier.

L. G. Pl. 114.   Tetrandria Monogynia.   Cl. 4. Ord. 1.

1. fullonum.   Teafel. ♂
2. laciniatus.   Jagged-leaved Teafel.

117. DODECATHEON.
AMERICAN COWSLIP.

L. G. Pl. 200. Pentandria Monogynia. Cl. 5. Ord. 1.
1. Meadia. American Cowslip.

118. DORONICUM.
LEOPARD's BANE,———(Fr.)—Doronic.

L. G. Pl. 959. Syngenesia Polygamia Superflua. Cl. 19. Ord. 2.
1. pardalianches. Great Leopard's Bane.
2. plantagineum. Plantain-leaved Leopard's Bane.

119. DRABA.
ALYSSON, or WHITLOW-GRASS.

L. G. Pl. 800. Tetradynamia Siliculosa. Cl. 15. Ord. 1.
1. alpina. Alpine Whitlow-grass.
2. pyrenaica. Pyrenean Trifid-leaved Whitlow-g.

120. DRACOCEPHALUM.
DRAGON's HEAD.

L. G. Pl. 729. Didynamia Gymnospermia. Cl. 14. Ord. 1.
1. austriacum. Austrian Dragon's Head.
2. Ruyschiana. Hyssop-leaved Dragon's Head.
3. sibiricum. Siberian Verticillated Dragon's Head.
4. virginianum. Virginian Purple Dragon's Head.

121. DRYAS.
AVENS.

L. G. Pl. 637. Icosandria Polygynia. Cl. 12. Ord. 5.
1. octopetala. Eight-petaled Avens.

122. ECHINOPS.
GLOBE-THISTLE.

L. G. Pl. 999. Syngenesia Polygamia Segregata. Cl. 19. Ord. 5.
1. Ritro. Lesser Globe-Thistle.
2. Sphærocephalus. Greater Globe-Thistle.

123. ECHIUM.

Viper's Bugloss,——(Fr.)—Viperine.

L. G. Pl. 191. Pentandria Monogynia. Cl. 5. Ord. 1.

1. vulgare - - - 1. Viper's Bugloſs.
2. *vulgare rubeſcens* - 2. Red Viper's Bugloſs.
3. italicum - - - 1. Italian Viper's Bugloſs.
4. *italicum album* - 2. White Italian Viper's Bugloſs.

124. EPILOBIUM.

Willow Herb, or French Willow.

L. G. Pl. 471. Octandria Monogynia. Cl. 8. Ord. L.

1. anguſtifolium - 1. French Willow.
2. *anguſtifolium album* 2. White French Willow.
3. latifolium. Broad-leaved French Willow.
4. hirſutum - - - 1. Hairy French Willow.
5. *hirſutum variegat.* 2. Striped-leaved Hairy French Willow.
6. ramoſum. Branching French Willow.

125. EPIMEDIUM.

Barren-wort.

L. G. Pl. 148. Tetrandria Monogynia. Cl. 4. Ord. 1.
1. alpinum. Alpine Barren-wort.

126. EQUISETUM.

Shave-grass.

L. G. Pl. 1169. Cryptogamia. Filix. Cl. 24. Ord. 1.
1. hyemale. Shave-graſs.

127. ERIGERON.

Fleabane.

L. G. Pl. 951. Syngeneſia Polygamia Superflua. Cl. 19. Ord. 2.
1. acre. Fleabane.

128. ERINUS.
ERINUS.

L. G. Pl. 771.   Didynamia Angiofpermia.   Cl. 14. Ord. 2.
1. alpinus.   Alpine Erinus.

129. ERVUM.
TARE,——(Fr.)—Ers.

L. G. Pl. 874.   Diadelphia Decandria.   Cl. 17. Ord. 3.
1. Lens.   Lentil. ☉
2. monænthus.   One-flowered Lentil. ☉
3. folonienfe.   Spring Tare. ☉

130. ERYNGIUM.
ERYNGO, or SEA HOLLY,——(Fr.)—Panicaut, Chardon Roland.

L. G. Pl. 324.   Pentandria Digynia.   Cl. 5. Ord. 2.
1. alpinum.   Alpine Sea Holly.
2. amethyftinum.   Amethyftine Sea Holly.
3. aquaticum.   Marfh Sea Holly.
4. campeftre.   Eryngo.
5. fœtidum.   Stinking Sea Holly.
6. maritimum.   Sea Holly.
7. planum.   Broad-leaved Sea Holly.

131. ERYSIMUM.
HEDGE MUSTARD,——(Fr.)—Velar ou Tortelle.

L. G. Pl. 814.   Tetradynamia Siliquofa.   Cl. 15. Ord. 2.
1. Barbarea - - - 1.   Winter Crefs.
2. *Barbarea plena* - 2.   Double Winter Crefs.

132. ERYTHRONIUM.
DOG's-TOOTH VIOLET.

L. G. Pl. 414.   Hexandria Monogynia.   Cl. 6. Ord. 1.
1. Dens canis - - 1.   Dog's-tooth Violet.
2. *Dens canis albus* 2.   White Dog's-tooth Violet.
3. anguftifolius.   Narrow-leaved Dog's-tooth Violet.

133. EUPATORIUM.

HEMP AGRIMONY,——(Fr.)—Eupatoire.

L. Gl. Pl. 935.   Syngenefia Polygamia Æqualis.   Cl. 19. Ord. 1.

1. altiffimum.	Tall Hemp Agrimony.
2. aromaticum.	Aromatic Hemp Agrimony.
3. cannabinum.	Hemp Agrimony.
4. maculatum.	Spotted-ftalked Hemp Agrimony.
5. perfoliatum.	Perfoliate-leaved Hemp Agrimony.
6. purpureum.	Purple Hemp Agrimony.
7. feffilifolium.	Seffile-leaved Hemp Agrimony.

134. EUPHORBIA.

SPURGE,——(Fr.)—Titimale.

L. G. Pl. 609.   Dodecandria Trigynia.   Cl. 11. Ord. 3.

1. amygdaloides	- 1.	Wood Spurge.
2. *amygdaloides varieg.*	2.	Striped Wood Spurge.
3. coralloides.		Coral-ftalked Spurge.
4. Efula	- - - 1.	Gromwel-leaved Spurge.
5. *Efula minor*	- - 2.	Leffer Gromwel-leaved Spurge.
6. myrfinites.		Dwarf Spurge.

ANNUALS.

7. heliofcopia.	Sun Spurge, or Waftwort. ⊙
8. Peplus.	Petty Spurge. ⊙
9. fegetalis.	Corn Spurge. ⊙

135. FERULA.

FENNEL-GIANT,——(Fr.)—Ferule.

L. G. Pl. 343.   Pentandria Digynia.   Cl. 5. Ord. 2.

1. canadenfis.	Canadian Fennel-Giant.
2. communis.	Fennel-Giant.
3. Galbanum.	Galbanum-bearing Fennel-Giant.
4. glauca.	Glaucous Fennel-Giant.
5. meoides.	Spignel-leaved Fennel-Giant.
6. tingitana.	Tangier Fennel-Giant.

G

.136. F R A G A R I A.

STRAWBERRY,——(Fr.)—Fraifier.

L. G. Pl. 633.   Icofandria Polygynia.   Cl. 12. Ord. 5.

1. *fylveftris* - - -	1.	Red Wood Strawberry.
2. *aureo-variegata* -	2.	Gold-ftriped-leaved Wood Strawb.
3. *alba* - - - -	3.	White Wood Strawberry.
4. *multiplex* - - -	4.	Double-flowering Wood Strawberry.
5. *eflagellis* - - -	5.	Red Bufh Strawberry.
6. *eflagellis alba* - -	6.	White Bufh Strawberry.
7. *monophylla* - -	7.	Verfailles, or One-leaved Strawberry.
8. *northumbricnfis* -	8.	Northumberland Wood Strawberry.
9. *imperialis* - -	9.	Royal Red Wood Strawberry.
10. *hortenfis* - - -	10.	Great Red Wood Strawberry.
11. *argenteo-variegata*	11.	Silver-ftriped Great Wood Strawb.
12. *alba* - - - -	12.	Great White Wood Strawberry.
13. *nigricans* - -	13.	Montreuil, or Dutch Wood Strawb.
14. *muricata* - -	14.	Plymouth Strawberry.
15. *fpinofa* - - -	15.	Prickly Strawberry.
16. *minor* - - -	16.	Leffer Red Wood Strawberry.
17. *minor alba* - -	17.	Leffer White Wood Strawberry.
18. *alpina* - - -	18.	Red Alpine Strawberry.
19. *alpina alba* - -	19.	White Alpine Strawberry.
20. *alpina phœnicea* -	20.	Scarlet Alpine Strawberry.
21. *alpina variegata*	21.	Striped-leaved Alpine Strawberry.
22. *alpina var. alba* -	22.	Striped-leaved White Alp. Strawb.
23. *alpina coccinea* -	23.	Scarlet-bloffomed Alpine Strawb.
24. *bargea* - - -	24.	Bargemon Strawberry.
25. *champagnienfis* -	25.	Champagne Strawberry.
26. *abertiva* - - -	26.	Blind Strawberry.
27. *granulofa* - -	27.	Minion Strawberry.
28. viridis - - -	1.	Green Wood Strawberry.
29. *viridis variegata* -	2.	Striped-leaved Green Strawberry.
30. *pratenfis* (Lin.) -	3.	Swedifh Green Field Strawberry.
31. *thuringiana* - -	4.	Thuringian Green Strawberry.
32. *fulphurea* - - -	5.	Yellow-bloffomed Strawberry.
33. *pendula* - - -	6.	Befançon Green Strawberry.
34. *procumbens* - -	7.	Ground Strawberry. .
35. mofchata - -	1.	Hautboy Strawberry.
36. *mofchata mafcula* -	2.	Male Hautboy Strawberry.
37. *mofchata rofea* -	3.	Rofe-coloured Hautboy.

38. *moschata globosa* - 4. Globe Hautboy Strawberry.
39. *moschata rubra* - 5. Red-blossomed Hautboy.
40. *mosc. albo' varieg* - 6. White-striped-leaved Hautboy.
41. *mosch. luteo variegata* 7. Yellow-striped-leaved Hautboy.
42. *mosch. hermaphrodita* 8. Royal Hautboy Strawberry.
43. *moschata hybrida* - 9. Green Bastard Hautboy Strawberry.
  ♀ *moschata.*   ♂ viridis.
44. *moschata viridis* - 10. Green Hautboy Strawberry.
45. *moschata bargea* 11. Bargemon Hautboy Strawberry.
  ♀ *moschata.*   ♂ viridis.
46. *moschata farinacea* 12. Virginian Mealy Hautboy.
  ♀ *moschata.*   ♂ virginiana.
47. *moschata ananassa* 13. Pine-apple Hautboy Strawberry.
  ♀ *moschata.*   ♂ ananassa.
48. *moschata crispa* - 14. Curled-leaved Hautboy.

49. chinensis - - 1 Chinese Strawberry.

50. virginiana - - 1. Virginian, or Scarlet Strawberry.
51. *virginiana variegata* 2. Striped-leaved Virginian Scarlet Str.
52. *virginiana argentata* 3. Silver-edged Virginian Scarlet Str.
53. *virginiana coccinea* 4. Scarlet-blossomed Virginian Strawb.
54. *virginiana campestris* 5. Wild Virginian Scarlet Strawberry.

55. chiloensis - - 1. Chili Strawberry.
56. *chiloensis mascula* - 2. Male Chili Strawberry.
57. *chiloensis hermaphrod.* 3. Royal Chili Strawberry.
  ♀ *chiloensis.*   ♂ ananassa.
58. *chiloensis alba* - - 4. White Chili Strawberry.
59. *chiloensis ananassa* - 5. Pine-apple Strawberry.
60. *chil. anan. variegata* 6. Yellow-striped Pine-apple Strawb.
61. *chiloensis bathonica* 7. Bath Chili Strawberry.
62. *chiloensis devonensis* 8. Devonshire Chili Strawberry.
63. *chiloensis belgica* - 9. Dutch Chili Strawberry.
64. *chiloensis peruviana* 10. Lima, or Peruvian Strawberry.
65. *chiloensis carolinensis* 11. Carolinian Strawberry.
60. *chil. carolin. alba* 12. White Carolinian Strawberry.

67. *ſterilis americana* 13. American Male Strawberry.
   ♀ ananaſſa.   ♂ moſchata maſcula.
68. capenſis maſcula   1. Male Cape Strawberry.

    Raiſed by Mr. Gordon, of Mile-End, from ſeeds ſent about 300
    miles from the Cape of Good Hope. One ſeed only grew,
    which proves to be a male.
  This mark ♂ ſignifies the male, and this ♀ the female plant.

    N. B. The Strawberries could not properly be deſcribed without
    inſerting the whole Catalogue of them, as mentioned in Vol. iii.
    of the Univerſal Botaniſt, p. 325. Particulars may there be ſeen
    from whence and how they were produced.

The following ſixteen Varieties are only what are generally cultivated in the Nurſeries.
No.
  1. Red Wood Strawberry.   38. Globe Hautboy.
  3. White Wood.   50. Virginian, or Scarlet.
13. Montreuil, or Dutch Wood. 55. Female Chili.
18. Alpine.   61. Bath Chili.
19. White Alpine.   62. Devonſhire Chili.
28. Green Wood.   63. Dutch Chili.
35. Female Hautboy.   65. Carolinian.
36. Male Hautboy.   66. White Carolinian.

137. FRANKENIA.
SEA HEATH.

L. G. Pl. 445.   Hexandria Monogynia.   Cl. 6. Ord. 1.
  1. hirſuta.   Hairy Sea Heath.
  2. lævis.   Smooth Sea Heath.

138. FRITILLARIA.
FRITILLARY,——(Fr.)—Fritillaire.

L. G. Pl. 411.   Hexandria Monogynia.   Cl. 6. Ord. 1.
  1. Meleagris.   Fritillary.

    For the varieties of theſe, ſee the Floriſts Catalogue.

  2. pyrenaica.   Pyrenean Fritillary.

FRITILLARIA—CORONA IMPERIALIS.

CROWN IMPERIAL,——(Fr.)—Courone Imperiale.

1. imperialis	- -	1.	Crown Imperial.
2. *duplex*	- - -	2.	Double Crown Imperial.
3. *latifolia*	- - -	3.	Broad-leaved Crown Imperial.
4. *lutea*	- - - -	4.	Yellow Crown Imperial.
5. *pallidè lutea*	- -	5.	Pale Yellow Crown Imperial.
6. *lutea striata*	- -	6.	Yellow-striped Crown Imperial.
7. *major*	- - - -	7.	Large-flowering Crown Imperial.
8. *plena lutea*	- -	8.	Double Yellow Crown Imperial.
9. *plena rubra*	- -	9.	Double Red Crown Imperial.
10. *rubens*	- - -	10.	Red Crown Imperial.
11. *triplex*	- - -	11.	Triple Crown Imperial.
12. *argenteo variegata*		12.	Silver-striped-leaved Crown Imperial.
13. *aureo variegata*	-	13.	Gold-striped-leaved Crown Imperial.

139. FUMARIA.

FUMATORY,——(Fr.)—Fumeterre.

L. G. Pl. 849.   Diadelphia Hexandria.   Cl. 17. Ord. 3.

1. bulbosa	- - -	1.	Bulbous-rooted Fumatory.
2. *bulbosa cava*	- -	2.	Hollow-rooted Fumatory.
3. capnoides.			Yellow Fumatory.
4. sempervirens.			Ever-green Fumatory,

140. GALANTHUS.

SNOWDROP,——(Fr.)—Perce-niege.

L. G. Pl. 401.   Hexandria Monogynia.   Cl. 6. Ord. 1.

1. nivalis	- - -	1.	Snowdrop.
2. *nivalis plenus*	-	2.	Double Snowdrop.

141. GALEGA.

GOAT'S RUE.

L. G. Pl. 890.   Diadelphia Decandria.   Cl. 17. Ord. 3.

1. officinalis	- -	1. Goat's Rue.
2. *officinalis alba*	-	2. White Goat's Rue.
3. *officinalis variegata*		3. Striped Goat's Rue.

G 3

142. GALEOPSIS.

HEDGE-NETTLE.

L. G. Pl. 717. Didynamia Gymnofpermia. Cl. 14. Ord. 1.
1. Galeobdolon - 1. Hedge-Nettle.
2. *Galeob. variegatum* 2. Striped-leaved Hedge-Nettle.

143. GALIUM.

LADIES BEDSTRAW.

L. G. Pl. 125. Tetrandria Monogyn'a. Cl. 4. Ord. 1.

1. boreale. Northern Ladies Bedftraw.
2. verum. Ladies Bedftraw.

144. GAURA.

LOOSESTRIFE.

L. G. Pl. 470. Octandria Monogynia. Cl. 8. Ord. 1.
1. biennis. Virginian Loofeftrife. ♂

145. GENTIANA.

GENTIAN, or FELLWORT,——(Fr.)—Gentiana.

L. G. Pl. 322. Pentandria Digynia. Cl. 5. Ord. 2.

1. acaulis. Gentianella.
2. afclepiades. Swallow-wort-leaved Gentian.
3. Cruciata. Crofswort Gentian.
4. imperialis. Imperial Gentian.
5. lutea. Yellow Gentian.
6. Pneumonanthe. Marfh Gentian.
7. purpurea. Purple Gentian.
8. Saponaria. Soapwort-leaved Gentian.
9. verna. Small Blue Gentian.

146. GERANIUM.

CRANE'S-BILL,——(Fr.)—Bec de Grüe.

L. G. Pl. 832. Monadelphia Decandria. Cl. 16. Ord. 2.
  * *Staminibus quinque fertilibus.*
  With five fertile Stamina.

1. maritimum. Sea Crane's-bill.
2. romanum. Roman Crane's-bill.

** *Staminibus decem fertilibus.*
With ten fertile Stamina.

3. maculatum.   Spotted-leaved Crane's-bill.
4. macrorhizum.   Long-rooted Crane's-bill.
5. nodofum.   Knotty Crane's-bill.
6. paluftre.   Marfh Crane's-bill.
7. phæum.   Black-flowered Crane's-bill.
8. pratenfe.   Meadow Crane's-bill.
9. robertianum.   Herb Robert.
10. ftriatum.   Striped-flowered Crane's-bill.
11. fylvaticum.   Wood Crane's-bill.

*** *Uniflora—Uniflorøus.*

12. fanguineum - - 1. Bloody Crane's-bill.
13. *fang. lancaftrienfe* 2. Lancafhiıe Crane's-bill.

147. GEUM.

AVENS, or HERB BENNET,——(Fr.)—Benoite.

L. G. Pl. 636.   Icofandria Polygynia.   Cl. 12. Ord 5.

1. montanum.   Mountain Avens.
2. pyrenaicum.   Pyrenean Avens.
3. rivale.   Marfh Avens.
4. urbanum.   Avens, or Herb Bennet.
5. virginianum.   Virginian Avens.

148. GLADIOLUS.

CORNFLAG,——(Fr.)—Glaieul.

L. G. Pl. 57.   Triandria Monogynia.   Cl. 3. Ord. 1.

1. communis - - 1. Cornflag.
2. *communis variegatus* 2. Striped-flowered Cornflag.

149. GLOBULARIA.

GLOBULARIA, or BLUE DAISY.

L. G. Pl. 112.   Tetrandria Monogynia.   Cl. 4. Ord. 1.

1. vulgaris.   Blue Daify.

G 4

150. GLYCYRRHIZA.

LIQUORICE,——(Fr.)—Regliffe.

L. G. Pl. 88?.   Diadelphia Decandria.   Cl. 17. Ord. 3.
1. echinata.   Prickly Liquorice.
2. glabra.   Liquorice.

151. GNAPHALIUM.

CUDWEED, EVERLASTING,——(Fr.)—Immortel.

L. G. Pl. 946.   Syngenefia Polygamia Superflua.   Cl. 19. Ord. 2.

1. dioicum mafculum 1. Male Mountain Cudweed.
2. *dioicum fœmineum* 2. Female Mountain Cudweed.
3. fœtidum - - - 1. Stinking Everlafting.
4. *fœtidum aureum* - 2. Golding Stinking Everlafting.
5. margaritaceum.   White Everlafting.
6. plantaginifolium.   Plantain-leaved Everlafting.
7. fylvaticum.   Wood Everlafting.

152. GOMPHRENA.

GLOBE AMARANTH, or EVERLASTING FLOWER,
(Fr.)—Immortelle.

L. G. Pl. 314.   Pentandria Digynia.   Cl. 5. Ord. 2.
1. globofa - - - 1. Purple Globe Amaranth.
2. *globofa argentea* - 2. White Globe Amaranth.
3. *globofa ftriata* - 3. Striped Globe Amaranth.

153. GRATIOLA.

HEDGE HYSSOP.

L. G. Pl. 29.   Diandria Monogynia.   Cl. 2. Ord. 1.
1. officinalis.   Hedge Hyffop.

154. GUNDELIA.

GUNDELIA.

L. G. Pl. 1000.   Syngenefia Polygamia Segregata.   Cl. 19. Ord. 5.
1. Tournefortia.   Oriental Gundelia.

155. HEDYSARUM.

FRENCH HONEYSUCKLE, SAINTFOIN,
(Fr.)—Saintfoin.

L. G. Pl. 887.   Diadelphia Decandria.   Cl. 17. Ord. 3.

1. canadense.		Canadian Saintfoin.
2. Caput galli	- - 1.	French Honeysuckle.
3. *Caput galli album*	2.	White French Honeysuckle.
4. Onobrychis.		Saintfoin, or Cock's-head.
5. paniculatum.		Virginian Saintfoin.
6. violaceum.		Violet Saintfoin.

156. HELENIUM.

BASTARD SUNFLOWER.

L. G. Pl. 961.   Syngenesia Polygamia Superflua.   Cl. 19. Ord. 2.

1. autumnale.   Bastard Sunflower.

157. HELIANTHUS.

SUNFLOWER,——(Fr.)—Soleil.

L. G. Pl. 979.   Syngenesia Polygamia Frustranea.   Cl. 19. Ord. 3.

1. altissimus.		Tallest Virginian Sunflower.
2. decapetalus.		Ten-petaled Canadian Sunflower.
3. divariegatus.		Opposite-leaved Sunflower.
4. giganteus.		Giant Sunflower.
5. multiflorus	- - 1.	Perennial Sunflower.
6. *multiflorus plenus*	- 2.	Double Perennial Sunflower.
7. strumosus.		Spindle-rooted Sunflower.
8. tuberosus.		Jerusalem Artichoke.

ANNUALS.

9. annuus	- - - 1.	Peruvian Annual Sunflower. ☉
10. *annuus plenus*	- 2.	Double Peruvian Annual Sunflower.
11. *annuus pumilus*	- 3.	Dwarf Sunflower.
12. *annuus pum. plenus*	4.	Double Dwarf Sunflower.

158. HELONIAS.

HELONIAS.

L. G. Pl. 458.   Hexandria Trigynia.   Cl. 6. Ord. 3.

1. asphodeloides.	Asphodel-leaved Helonias.
2. bullata.	Bullated-flowered Helonias.

159. HELLEBORUS.

BLACK HELLEBORE,——(Fr.)—Ellebore Noir.

L. G. Pl. 702. Polyandria Polygynia. Cl. 13. Ord. 7.

1. fœtidus.	Stinking Bear's-foot.
2. hyemalis.	Winter Aconite.
3. latifolius.	Broad-leaved Black Hellebore.
4. niger.	Black Hellebore, or Christmas Rose.
5. trifolius.	Three-leaved Black Hellebore.
6. viridis.	Green-flowered Black Hellebore.

160. HEMEROCALLIS.

DAY-LILY, or LILY-ASPHODEL,——(Fr.)—Lis-Asfodele.

L. G. Pl. 433. Hexandria Monogynia. Cl. 6. Ord. 1.

1. flava.	Yellow Day-Lily.
2. fulva.	Saint Bruno's Lily.

161. HESPERIS.

DAME's VIOLET, or ROCKET,——(Fr.)—Julienne.

L. G. Pl. 817. Tetradynamia Siliquofa. Cl. 15. Ord. 2.

1. matronalis - -	1.	Rocket. ♂
2. matronalis plena -	2.	Double Rocket.
3. matronalis rubra -	3.	Red Rocket.
4. matr. rubra plena	4.	Double Red Rocket.
5. triftis.		Night-fmelling Dame's Violet.

162. HEUCHERA.

AMERICAN HEUCHERA, or SANICLE.

L. G. Pl. 320. Pentandria Digynia. Cl. 5. Ord. 2.

1. americana.	American Heuchera, or Sanicle.

163. HIBISCUS.

MALLOW.

L. G. Pl. 846. Monadelphia Polyandria. Cl. 16. Ord. 5.

1. paluftris.	Marfh Althea.

HERBACEOUS PLANTS. 91

164. HIERACIUM.
HAWKWEED.

L. G. Pl. 913.   Syngenefia Polygamia Æqualis.   Cl. 19. Ord. 1.

1. aurantiacum. — Orange-flowered Hawkweed.
2. Pilofella. — Creeping Moufe-ear.
3. fabaudum — - 1. Oval-leaved Hawkweed.
4. *fabaudum variegatum* 2. Striped Oval-leaved Hawkweed.
5. umbellatum. — Umbellated Hawkweed.

165. HIPPOCREPIS.
HORSE-SHOE VETCH,——(Fr.)—Fer de Cheval.

L. G. Pl. 885.   Diadelphia Decandria.   Cl. 17. Ord. 3.

1. comofa. — Horfe-fhoe Vetch.

166. HORDEUM.
BARLEY,——(Fr.)—Orge.

L. G. Pl. 98.   Triandria Digynia.   Cl. 3. Ord. 2.

1. diftichon. — Sprat, or Battledore Barley. ☉
2. hexaftichon. — Six-rowed, or Winter Barley. ☉
3. murinum. — Wall Barley-grafs. ☉
4. vulgare. — Spring Barley. ☉

167. HORMINUM.
CLARY.

L. G. Pl. 730.   Didynamia Gymnofpermia.   Cl. 14. Ord. 1.

1. pyrenaicum. — Pyrenean Clary.
2. virginicum. — Virginian Clary.

168. HUMULUS.
HOP,——(Fr.)—Houblon.

L. G. Pl. 1116.   Dioecia Pentandria.   Cl. 22. Ord. 5.

1. Lupulus fœminea 1. Female Hop.
2. *Lupulus mafcula* - 2. Male Hop.

169. HYACINTHUS.

Hyacinthus,——(Fr.)—Jacinte.

L. G. Pl. 427.   Hexandria Monogynia.   Cl. 6. Ord. 1.

1. *botryoides* - -	1.	Grape Hyacinth.
2. *botryoides albus* -	2.	White Grape Hyacinth.
3. comofus.		Comofe, or Greater Grape Hyacinth.
4. monftrofus.		Blue-feathered Hyacinth.
5. Mufcari.		Mufk Hyacinth.
6. nonfcriptus -	1.	Harebells, or Englifh Hyacinth.
7. *nonfcriptus albus*	2.	White Harebells.
8. orientalis albus -	1.	White Oriental Hyacinth.
9. *orientalis cœruleus*	2.	Blue Oriental Hyacinth.
10. *orientalis flavus* -	3.	Yellow Oriental Hyacinth.
11. *orientalis rofeus* -	4.	Rofe-coloured Oriental Hyacinth.

For feveral hundred cultivated varieties, fee the Florifts Catalogues.

170. HYDRASTIS.

Hydrastis, or Yellow Root.

L. G. Pl. 704.   Polyandria Polygynia.   Cl. 13. Qrd. 7.

1. canadenfis.   Yellow Root.

171. HYDROPHYLLUM.

Water-leaf.

L. G. Pl. 204.   Pentandria Monogÿnia.   Cl. 5. Ord. 1.

1. canadenfe.   Canadian Water-leaf.
2. virginianum.   Virginian Water-leaf.

172. HYPERICUM.

St. Johnswort,——(Fr.)—Millepertuis.

L. G. Pl. 902.   Polyadelphia Polyandria.   Cl. 18. Ord. 3.

1. Afcyron.   Great-flowered St. Johnswort.
2. elodes.   Marfh St. Peterswort.
3. humifufum.   Trailing St. Peterswort.
4. montanum.   Mountain St. Johnswort.

5. perforatum.   Perforated St. Johnswort.
6. pulchrum.   Upright St. Johnswort.
7. quadrangulum.   Square-ftalked St. Johnswort.
8. tomentofum.   Downy St. Johnswort.
9. virginicum.   Virginian St. Johnswort.

173. HYPOXIS.

Hypoxis.

L. G. Pl. 417.   Hexandria Monogynia.   Cl. 6. Ord. 1.

1. erecta.   Upright Hypoxis.

174. HYSSOPUS.

Hyssop,——(Fr.)—Hifope.

L. G. Pl. 709.   Didynamia Gymnofpermia.   Cl. 14. Ord. 1.

1. Lophanthus.   Catmint-leaved Hyffop.
2. officinalis.   Hyffop.
3. nepetoides.   Square-ftalked Hyffop.

175. IBERIS.

Candytuft, or Sciatica Cress,——(Fr.)—Iberiette.

L. G. Pl. 804.   Tetradynamia Siliculofa.   Cl. 15. Ord. 1.

1. umbellata alba - 1. White Candytuft. ⊙
2. *umbellata purpurea* 2. Purple Candytuft.
3. *umbellata rubra* - 3. Red Candytuft.
4. odorata.   4. Sweet-fcented Candytuft. ⊙
5. femperflorens.   Everflowering Candytuft.

176. IMPATIENS.

Balsam,——(Fr.)—Balfamine.

L. G. Pl. 1008.   Syngenefia Monogamia.   Cl. 19. Ord. 4.

1. Balfamina - - 1. Balfam. ⊙
2. *Balfamina plena* - 2. Double Balfam.
3. noli me tangere - 1. Touch me not. ⊙
4. *noli me tangere maj.* 2. Greater Touch me not.

177. IMPERATORIA.

MASTERWORT,——(Fr.)—Imperatoire.

L. G. Pl. 359.   Pentandria Digynia.   Cl. 5. Ord. 2.
1. Oftruthium.   Mafterwort, or Baftard Pellitory.

178. INULA.

ELECAMPANE.

L. G. Pl. 956.   Syngenefia Polygamia Superflua.   Cl. 19. Ord. 2.

1. crithmoides.	Golden Sampire.
2. Helenium.	Elecampane.
3. hirta.	Hairy-leaved Fleabane.
4. Oculus Chrifti.	Woolly Fleabane.
5. falicina.	Willow-leaved Fleabane.
6. fquarrofa.	Montpelier Fleabane.

179. IRIS.

FLOWER-DE-LUCE,——(Fr.)—Flambe.

* *Barbatæ : nectariis petalorum reflexorum.*
  Bearaed, the Nectaria formed by Petals reflexed.

1. biflora.			Two-flowered Portugal Iris.
2. florentina	-	- 1.	White Florentine Iris.
3. *florentina lutea*	-	2.	Yellow Florentine Iris.
4. germanica.			German Iris.
5. pumila.			Dwarf Purple Iris.
6. fambucina.			Elder-fcented Iris.
7. fqualens.			Brown-coloured Iris.
8. fufiana.			Chalcedonian Iris.
9. variegata.			Variegated Iris.

** *Imberbes: petalis deflexis lævibus.*
   Without Beards : fmooth deflexed Petals.

10. fœtidiffima	-	- 1.	Stinking Gladwin.
11 *fœtidif. varieg. folia*	2.		Striped-leaved Stinking Gladwin.
12. graminea.			Grafs-leaved Iris.
13. martinicenfis.			Martinican Yellow and Black Iris.
14. ochroleuca.			Oriental Iris.
15. perfica.			Perfian Iris.

16. Pfeudacorus - - 1. Yellow Water Flower-de-luce.
17. *Pfeudacorus pallida* 2. Pale Yellow Water Flower-de-luce.
18. fibirica. Siberian Iris.
19. Sifyrinchium. Crocus-rooted Iris.
20. fpuria. Baftard Iris.
21. tuberofa. Snake's-head Iris.
22. verna. Blue Spring Iris.
23. verficolor. Various-coloured Iris.
24. virginica. Virginian Iris.
25. Xiphium. Bulbous-rooted Iris.

For whofe varieties, fee the Florifts Catalogues.

180. ISATIS.

WOAD,——(Fr.)—Paftel.

L. G. Pl. 824. Tetradynamia Siliquofa. Cl. 15. Ord. 2.

1. tinctoria. Woad. ♂

181. IXIA.

IXIA.

L. G. Pl. 56. Triandria Monogynia. Cl. 3. Ord. 1.

1. Bulbocodium. Crocus-leaved Ixia.
2. chinenfis. Chinefe Ixia.

182. LACTUCA.

LETTUCE,——(Fr.)—Laituë.

L. G. Pl. 909. Syngenefia Polygamia Æqualis. Cl. 19. Ord. 1.

1. fativa. Lettuce. ☉

For whofe cultivated varieties, fee the Kitchen-Garden Catalogue.

2. Scariola. Italian Lettuce, or Scariola.

183. LAMIUM.

DEAD NETTLE, or ARCHANGEL.

L. G. Pl. 716. Didynamia Gymnofpermia. Cl. 14. Ord. 1.

1. album. White Archangel.
2. garganicum. Red Archangel.
3. helveticum. Switzerland Archangel.
4. Orvala. Purple Archangel.

184. LASERPITIUM.

LASERWORT.

| L. G. Pl. 344. | Pentandria Digynia. | Cl. 5. Ord. 2. |

1. latifolium.   Broad-leaved Laferwort.
2. Siler.   Mountain Laferwort.
3. trilobum.   Three-leaved Laferwort.

185. LATHYRUS..

CHICKLING VETCH,——(Fr.)—Geffe.

| L. G. Pl. 872. | Diadelphia Decandria. | Cl. 18. Ord. 3. |

1. Cicera.   Chick Pea.
2. latifolius.   Broad-leaved Everlafting Pea.
3. fylveftris.   Narrow-leaved Everlafting Pea.

186. LAVATERA.

LAVATERA.

| L. G. Pl. 842. | Monodelphia Polyandria. | Cl. 16. Ord. 5. |

1. arborea.   Sea Tree Mallow.   ♂
2. cretica - - -   1. White Lavatera.   ☉
3. *cretica rubra* - -   2. Red Lavatera.   ☉
4. olbia.   Provence Lavatera.   ☉
5. thuringiaca.   Thuringian Lavatera.   ☉
6. trimeftris - -   1. Spanifh Lavatera.   ☉
7. *trimeftris rubra* -   2. Red Spanifh Lavatera.   ☉

187. LEONTODON.

DANDELION,——(Fr.)—Dent de Lion.

| L. G. Pl. 912. | Syngenefia Polygamia Æqualis. | Cl. 19. Ord. 1. |

1. aureum.   Golden Dandelion.
2. autumnale.   Autumnal Dandelion.
3. Taraxacum.   Dandelion.

188. LEONURUS.

LION's-TAIL, or MOTHERWORT.

| L. G. Pl. 722. | Didynamia Gymnofpermia. | Cl. 14. Ord. 1. |

1. Cardiaca.   Motherwort.
2. tataricus.   Tartarian Motherwort.

189. LEPIDIUM.

DITTANDER, or PEPPERWORT,——(Fr.)—Paſſerage:

L. G. Pl. 801.　　Tetradynamia Siliculoſa.　　Cl. 15. Ord. 1.

  1. latifolium.　　　　Dittander, or Pepperwort.

190. LEUCOJUM.

GREATER SNOWDROP.

L. G. Pl. 402.　　Hexandria Monogynia.　　Cl. 6. Ord. 1.

  1. vernum.　　　　　Greater Spring Snowdrop.
  2. æſtivum.　　　　　Greater Summer Snowdrop.

191. LIGUSTICUM.

LOVAGE.

L. G. Pl. 346.　　Pentandria Digynia.　　Cl. 5. Ord. 2.

  1. Leviſticum.　　　　Lovage.
  2. ſcoticum.　　　　　Scotiſh Sea Parſley.
  3. peloponneſiacum.　　Peloponneſian Lovage.
  4. peregrinum.　　　　Foreign Lovage.

192. LILIUM.

LILY,——(Fr.)—Lis.

L. G. Pl. 410.　　Hexandria Monogynia.　　Cl. 6. Ord. 1.

  1. aurantiacum.　　　　Orange Lily.

  2. bulbiferum　-　-　1.　Bulbiferous Orange Lily.
  3. bulbiferum anguſtif. 2.　Narrow-leaved Bulbiferous Lily.
  4. bulbiferum plenum　3.　Double Bulbiferous Lily.
  5. bulbiferum variegat. 4.　Striped-leaved Bulbiferous Lily.

  6. canadenſe.　　　　Canadian Martagon.

  7. candidum　-　-　1.　White Lily.
  8. candidum ſtriatum　2.　Striped-leaved White Lily.
  9. candidum maculatum 3.　Spotted, or Bloatched-leaved Wh. L.
  10. candidum plenum　-　4.　Double White Lily.
  11. candidum purpureum 5.　Purple-ſtriped-flowered White Lily.

H

12. chalcedonicum.   Chalcedonian Scarlet Martagon.

13. Martagon - - 1. Martagon Lily.
14. *Martagon album* - 2. White Martagon Lily.
15. *Martagon imperiale* 3. Imperial Martagon Lily.

16. philadelphicum.   Philadelphian Lily.
17. pomponium.   Pompony Martagon.
18. fuperbum.   Superb Canadian Martagon.

193. L I N U M.

FLAX,——(Fr.)—Lin.

L. G. Pl. 389.   Pentandria Pentagynia.   Cl. 5. Ord. 5.

1. perenne.   Perennial Flax.

194. L I T H O S P E R M U M.

GROMWELL,——(Fr.)—Gremil.

L. G. Pl. 181.   Pentandria Monogynia.   Cl. 5. Ord. 1.
1. officinale - - - 1. Gromwell.
2. *officinale purpureum* 2. Purple-flowered Gromwell.

195. L O B E L I A.

CARDINAL FLOWER.

L. G. Pl. 1006.   Syngenefia Monogamia.   Cl. 19. Ord. 6.

1. Cardinalis.   Scarlet Cardinal Flower.
2. fiphilitica - - 1. Blue Cardinal Flower.
3. *fiphilitica alba* - 2. White Cardinal Flower.

196. L O T U S.

BIRD's-FOOT TREFOIL.

L. G. Pl. 897.   Diadelphia Decandria.   Cl. 17. Ord. 3.
1. maritimus.   Sea Bird's-foot Trefoil.

197. LUNARIA.

MOONWORT, SATTEN-FLOWER, or HONESTY.

L. G. Pl. 809.   Tetradynamia Siliculofa.   Cl. 15. Ord. 1.

1. rediviva - - - 1. White Moonwort.
2. *rediviva purpurea* 2. Purple Moonwort.

198. LUPINUS.

LUPINE,——(Fr.)—Lupin.

L. G. Pl. 865.   Diadelphia Decandria.   Cl. 17. Ord. 3.

1. albus.   White Lupine.
2. anguftifolius.   Narrow-leaved Blue Lupine.
3. hirfutus - - - 1.   Hairy Large Blue Lupine.
4. *hirfutus rofeus* - 2. Hairy Rofe-coloured Large Lupine.
5. luteus.   Yellow Lupine.
6. perennis.   Perennial Lupine.
7. varius.   Montpelier Blue Lupine.

199. LYCHNIS.

CAMPION, LYCHNIS, &c.

L. G. Pl. 584.   Decandria Pentagynia.   Cl. 10. Ord. 4.

1. chalcedonica   - 1. Scarlet Lychnis.
2. *chalcedonica plena* 2. Double Scarlet Lychnis.

3. dioica   - - - 1. Wh. Campion, or Batchelor's Button.
4. *dioica plena* - - 2. Double White Batchelor's Button.
5. *dioica rubra* - - 3. Red Batchelor's Button.
6. *dioica rubra plena* 4. Double Red Batchelor's Button.

7. Flos cuculi - - - 1. Meadow Pink, Cuckow Flower,
                          Wild Williams, Ragged Robin.

8. *Flos cuculi plenus* - 2. Double Meadow Pink.
9. *Flos cuculi albus* - 3. White Meadow Pink.

10. Vifcaria - - - 1. Catchfly.
11. *Vifcaria plena* - 2. Double Catchfly.

H 2

200. LYCOPUS.
WATER HOREHOUND.

L. G. Pl. 33.   Diandria Monogynia.   Cl. 2. Ord. 1.

1. europæus.   Water Horehound.
2. virginicus.   Virginian Water Horehound.

201. LYSIMACHIA.
LOOSESTRIFE,——(Fr.)—Corneille.

L. G. Pl. 205.   Pentandria Monogynia.   Cl. 5. Ord. 1.

1. ciliata.   American Loosestrife.
2. hispanica.   Spanish Loosestrife.
3. nemorum.   Wood Moneywort.
4. Nummularia.   Moneywort.
5. tenella.   Purple Loosestrife.
6. vulgaris.   Loosestrife.
7. salicifolia.   Willow-leaved Loosestrife.

202. LYTHRUM.
WILLOW HERB.

L. G. Pl. 604.   Dodecandria Monbgynia.   Cl. 11. Ord. 1.

1. Salicaria.   Willow Herb.

203. MALVA.
MALLOW,——(Fr.)—Mauve.

L. G. Pl. 840.   Monadelphia Polyandria.   Cl. 16. Ord. 5.

1. Alcea.   Vervain Mallow. ♂
2. americana.   Dwarf American Mallow. ☉
3. capensis.   Cape Mallow. ☉
4. cretica.   Cretan Mallow. ☉
5. crispa.   Curled-leaved Mallow. ☉
6. Limosella.   Blue Mallow. ☉
7. moschata.   Jagged-leaved Vervain Mallow. ♂
8. parviflora.   Small-flowered Mallow. ☉
9. siriaca.   Syrian Mallow. ☉
10. sylvestris.   Mallow.
11. verticillata.   Verticillated Mallow. ☉

204. MARRUBIUM.

HOREHOUND,——(Fr.)—Marrube.

L. G. Pl. 721.   Didynamia Gymnofpermia.   Cl. 14. Ord. 1.

1. acetabulofum.   Baftard Dittany.
2. candidiffimum.   White Horehound.
3. vulgare.   Horehound.

205. MATRICARIA.

FEVERFEW,——(Fr.)—Matricaire.

L. G. Pl. 967.   Syngenefia Polygamia Superflua.   Cl. 19. Ord. 2.

1. Parthenium - - 1. Feverfew.
2. *Parthenium plenum* 2. Double Feverfew.

206. MEDICAGO.

MEDICK.

L. G. Pl. 899.   Diadelphia Decandria.   Cl. 17. Ord. 3.

1. falcata.   Yellow Medick.
2. polymorpha.   Polymorphous Trefoil, or Snails
                       and Hedge-Hogs. ⊙
3. fativa.   Lucern.

207. MELISSA.

BALM,——(Fr.)—Meliffe.

L. G. Pl. 728.   Didynamia Gymnofpermia.   Cl. 14. Ord. 1.

1. Calamintha.   Calamint.
2. grandiflora.   Great-flowered Balm.

3. Nepeta - - - 1. Catmint-leaved Balm.
4. *Nepeta montana* - 2. Mountain Catmint-leaved Balm.

5. officinalis - - 1. Balm.
6. *officinalis variegata* 2. Variegated-leaved Balm.

7. romana.   Roman Balm.

H 3

208. MELITTIS,

BASTARD BALM.

L. G. Pl. 731.   Didynamia Gymnospermia·   Cl. 14. Ord. 1.
1. melissophyllum.   Bastard Balm.

209. MENTHA.

MINT,——(Fr.)—Menthe.

L. G. Pl. 713.   Didynamia Gymnospermia.   Cl. 14. Ord. 1,

* Spicatæ.—With spiked Flowers.

1. longifolia (L. sylvestris)   Long-leaved Horse-Mint,
2. rotundifolia,   Round-leaved Horse-Mint,
3. rubra,   Red Mint.
4. spicata (L. viridis) 1.   Spear-Mint.
5. spic. argenteo var. 2.   Silver-striped Spear-Mint.
6. spicata aureo var. 3.   Gold-striped Spear-Mint.

** Capitatæ.—The Flowers growing in Heads.

7. aquatica,   Water-Mint.
8. crispa,   Curled-leaved Mint,
9. piperita.   Pepper-Mint.

*** Verticillatæ.—The Flowers growing in Whorls.

10. arvensis.   Corn-Mint.
11. Cervina.   Montpelier Mint.

12. Pulegium   -   1.   Penny Royal,
13. Pulegium erectum   2.   Upright Penny Royal.
14. Pulegium latifolium   3.   Broad-leaved Penny Royal.

210. MILIUM.

MILLET.

L. G. Pl. 79.   Triandria Digynia.   Cl. 3. Ord. 2,
1. lendigerum.   Millet, ☉

211. MIMULUS.

BASTARD FOXGLOVE.

L. G. Pl. 783,   Didynamia Angiospermia,   Cl. 14. Ord. 2,
1. ringens,   Bastard Foxglove,

212. MIRABILIS.

MARVEL OF PERU;———(Fr.)—Belle de Nuit.

L. G. Pl. 242.   Pentandria Monogynia.   Cl. 5. Ord. 1.

1. Jalapa alba - - 1. White Marvel of Peru. ⊙ ♃.
2. *Jalapa flava* - - 2. Yellow Marvel of Peru.
3. *Jalapa purpurea* - 3. Purple Marvel of Peru.
4. *Jalapa rubra* - 4. Red Marvel of Peru.

There are also many with striped Flowers and different Colours on the same Plant.

213. MOMORDICA.

BALSAM APPLE,———(Fr.)—Pomme de Merveille.

L. G. Pl. 1090.   Monoecia Syngenesia.   Cl. 21. Ord. 10.

1. Elaterium.   Spurting Cucumber. ⊙

214. MONARDA.
LIONSTAIL.

L. G. Pl. 37.   Diandria Monogynia.   Cl. 2. Ord. 1.

1. clinopodia - - 1. Lionstail.
2. *clinopodia alba* - 2. White Lionstail.
3. didyma.   Ofwego Tea, or Scarlet Lionstail.
4. fiftulofa.   Purple Lionstail.
5. punctata.   Yellow-fpotted Lionstail.

215. MYAGRUM.
GOLD OF PLEASURE.

L. G. Pl. 796.   Tetradynamia Siliculofa.   Cl. 15. Ord. 1.

1. fativum - - - 1. Gold of Pleafure.
2. *fativum minus* - 2. Smaller Gold of Pleafure.

216. NAPÆA.
NAPÆA.

L. G. Pl. 838.   Monadelphia Polyandria.   Cl. 16. Ord. 5.

1. dioica.   Virginian Dioicous Napæa.
2. hermaphrodita.   Hermaphrodite Napæa.

H 4

217. NARCISSUS.

NARCISSUS, or DAFFODIL,——(Fr.)—Narcisse.

L. G. Pl. 403.   Hexandria Monogynia.   Cl. 6. Ord. 1.

1. bicolor - - -	1.	Two-coloured Narciffus, Daffodil.
2. *bicolor plenus* - -	2.	Double Daffodil.
3. Bulbocodium.		Hoop-petticoat Narciffus.
4. Jonquilla - - -.	1.	Jonquil.
5. *Jonquilla plena* - -	2.	Double Jonquil.
6. minor.		Leffer Winter Narciffus.
7. moschatus.		Mufk Narciffus.
8. odorus.		Sweet-fcented Narciffus.
9. poeticus - - -	1.	Poetic or Pale Daffodil, or Primrofe.
10. *poeticus purpureus*	2.	Peerlefs Purple-cupped Narciffus.
11. *poeticus albus* -	3.	White Narciffus.
12. *poeticus multiplex*	4.	Semi-double Narciffus.
13. *poeticus plenus* -	5.	Double Narciffus.
14. Pfeudo Narciffus	1.	Wild Englifh Daffodil.
15. *Pf. Nar. multiplex*	2.	Semi-double Daffodil.
16. *Pf. Na. plenus* -	3.	Double Daffodil.
17. *Pf.N.tradescantianus*	4.	Tradefcant's Double Daffodil.
18. *Pfeudo Nar. albus*	5.	Yellow and White Daffodil.
19. Tazetta.		Polyanthus Narciffus.

For above 130 cultivated Varieties, fee the Florift's Catalogue. Bot. Vol. 2.

218. NEPETA.

CATMINT,——(Fr.)—Herbe aux Chats.

L. G. Pl. 710.   Didynamia Gymnofpermia.   Cl. 14. Ord. 1.

1. Cataria - - -	1.	Catmint.
2. *Cataria minor* -	2.	Leffer Catmint.
3. hirfuta.		Hairy Catmint.
4. italica.		Italian Catmint.
5. Nepetella.		Small Red Catmint.
6. nuda.		White Catmint.
7. Scordotis.		Long-leaved Purple Catmint.
8. tuberofa.		Tuberous-rooted Catmint.
9. violacea.		Violet-coloured Catmint.

219. NICOTIANA.

TOBACCO,——(Fr.)—Nicotiane ou Tabac.

L. G. Pl. 248.   Pentandria Monogynia.   Cl. 5. Ord. 1.

1. glutinofa.   Clammy-leaved Tobacco. ☉
2. paniculata.   Brafilian Tobacco. ☉
3. ruftica.   English Tobacco. ☉
4. Tabacum   — — 1. Virginian Tobacco. ☉
5. *Tabacum anguftifol.* 2. Narrow-leaved Virginian Tobacco.

220. NIGELLA.

FENNEL-FLOWER, or DEVIL IN A BUSH.

L. G. Pl. 685.   Polyandria Pentagynia.   Cl. 13. Ord. 5.

1. damafcena.   Nigella. ☉
2. hifpanica.   Spanish Nigella. ☉
3. lutea.   Yellow Nigella. ☉
4. orientalis.   Oriental Nigella. ☉
5. fativa.   Cretan Nigella.

221. NOLANA.

NOLANA.

L. G. Pl. 193.   Pentandria Monogynia.   Cl. 5. Ord. 1.

1. proftrata.   Nolana.

222. NYMPHÆA.

WATER LILY,——(Fr.)—Nenufar.

L. G. Pl. 653.   Polyandria Monogynia.   Cl. 13. Ord. 1.

1. alba.   White Water Lily.
2. lutea.   Yellow Water Lily.
3. Nelumbo virginica. Virginian Water Lily.

223. OCIMUM.

BASIL,——(Fr.)—Bafilie.

L. G. Pl. 732.   Didynamia Gymnofpermia.   Cl. 14. Ord. 1.

1. Bafilicum.   Bafil. ☉
2. minimum.   Bush Bafil. ☉

224. ONOCLEA.

Onoclea.

L. G. Pl. 1170,   Cryptogamia Filix.   Cl. 24. Ord. 1.
1. fenfibilis.   Virginian Onoclea.

225. OENOTHERA.

Tree Primrose.

L. G. Pl. 469.   Octandria Monogynia.   Cl. 8. Ord. 1.
1. biennis.   Biennial Tree Primrofe.
2. fruticofa.   Shrubby Tree Primrofe.
3. pumila.   Dwarf Tree Primrofe.

226. ONOSMA.

Onosma.

L. G. Pl. 187.   Pentandria Monogynia.   Cl. 5. Ord. 1.
1. echioides.   Auftrian Onofma.
2. orientalis.   Oriental Onofma.

227. OPHRYS.

Twyblade.

L. G. Pl. 1011.   Gynandria Diandria.   Cl. 20. Ord. 1.

* *Bulbis ramofis.*—*With Bulbs branching.*

1. Nidus Avis.   Bird's-neft Ophrys.
2. ovata.   Twyblade.
3. fpiralis.   Ladies Traces.

** *Bulbis rotundis.*—*With Round Bulbs.*

4. anthropophora.   Man Orchis.
5. apifera fphegodes.   Green-winged Orchis.
6. infectifera   -   1. Great Fly Orchis.
7. *infectifera adrachnites* 2. Humble Bee Orchis.
8. Monorchis.   Mufk Orchis.

228. ORCHIS,

ORCHIS.

L. G. Pl. 1009. Gynandria Diandria. Cl. 20. Ord. 1.

* *Bulbis indivisis.—With Bulbs undivided.*

1. bifolia.   Butterfly Orchis.
2. mascula.   Spotted-leaved Male Orchis.
3. militaris.   Man Orchis.
4. Morio.   Female Orchis.
5. pyramidalis.   Pyramidal Orchis.

** *Bulbis palmatis.—With palmated Bulbs.*

6. latifolia.   Broad-leaved Orchis.
7. maculata.   Spotted-leaved Orchis.

*** *Bulbis fasciculatis.—With fasciculated Bulbs.*

8. abortiva.   Bird's-nest Orchis.

229. ORIGANUM.

MARJORAM.

L. G. Pl. 726. Didynamia Gymnospermia. Cl. 14. Ord. 1.

1. vulgare   -   -   -   1. Marjoram.
2. *vulgare luteum*   ~   2. Yellow-leaved Marjoram.

230. ORNITHOGALUM.

STAR OF BETHLEHEM.

L. G. Pl. 418. Hexandria Monogynia. Cl. 6. Ord. 1.

1. luteum.   Yellow Star of Bethlehem.
2. pyramidale.   Large-spiked White Star of Bethleh.
3. pyrenaicum.   Pyrenean Star of Bethlehem.
4. umbellatum,   Umbellated Star of Bethlehem.

231. OROBUS.

BITTER VETCH.

L. G. Pl. 871. Diadelphia Decandria. Cl. 17. Ord. 3.

1. lathyroides,   Bastard Chickling Vetch.
2. luteus,   Yellow Vetch.

3. niger.   Black Vetch.
4. sylvaticus.   Wood Vetch.
5. tuberosus.   Tuberous-rooted Vetch.
6. vernus.   Spring Vetch. ☉

232. OSMUNDA.

OSMUNDA.

L. G. Pl. 1172.   Cryptogamia Filix.   Cl. 24. Ord. 1.

1. crifpa.   Stone Fern.
2. Lunaria.   Moonwort.
3. regalis.   Flowering Fern.
4. fpicata.   Rough Spleenwort.
5. Struthiopteris.   Ruffian Fern.
6. virginica.   Virginian Fern.

233. OTHONNA.

RAGWORT.

L. G. Pl. 993.   Syngenefia Polygamia Neceffaria.   Cl. 19. Ord. 4.

1. cheirifolia.   African Ragwort.

234. OXALIS.

WOOD SORREL.

L. G. Pl. 582.   Decandria Pentagynia.   Cl. 10. Ord. 4.

1. Acetofella - - 1. Wood Sorrel.
2. *Acetofella cærulea*   2. Blue Wood Sorrel.
3. ftricta.   Upright Virginian Wood Sorrel.

235. PÆONIA.

PIONY,——(Fr.)——

L. G. Pl. 678.   Polyandria Digynia.   Cl. 13. Ord. 2.

1. mafcula - - - 1. Single Piony.
2. *alba plena* - - 2. Double White Piony.
3. *rofea plena* - - - 3. Double Rofe-coloured Piony.
4. *hemerina plena* - - 4. Double Crimfon Piony.
5. lufitanica.   Portugal Larkfpur-leaved Piony.

236. PANAX.

GINSENG.

L. Gli Pl. 1166.	Polygamia Diœcia.	Cl. 23. Ord. 2
1. quinquefolium.	Ginfeng.	

237. PANCRATIUM.

PANCRATIUM.

L. G. Pl. 404.	Hexandria Monogynia.	Cl. 6. Ord. 1
1. maritimum.	Sea Daffodil.	

238. PAPAVER.

POPPY,——(Fr.)—

L. G. Pl. 648.	Polyandria Monogynia.	Cl. 13. Ord. 1
1. cambricum.	Yellow Welch Poppy.	
2. orientale.	Oriental Poppy.	
3. Rhœas - - - 1.	Dwarf Corn Poppy.	
4. *Rhœas plenum* - 2.	Double Dwarf Corn Poppy. ☉	

There are various colours of this fort, as Scarlet, Purple, White, Variegated, &c.

5. fomniferum - - 1.	Somniferous Poppy. ☉	
6. *fomniferum album* 2.	White Somniferous Poppy.	
7. *fomniferum plenum* 3.	Double Poppy.	

The Carnation, Feathered, &c. are varieties of this.

239. PARIETARIA.

PELLITORY.

L. G. Pl. 1152.	Polygamia Monoecia.	Cl. 23. Ord. 1
1. officinalis.	Pellitory.	

240. PARIS.

TRUE LOVE, or ONE BERRY.

L. G. Pl. 500.	Octandria Tetragynia.	Cl. 8. Ord. 4
1. quadrifolia.	True Love, or One Berry.	

241. PARNASSIA.
GRASS OF PARNASSUS.

L. G. Pl. 384.   Decandria Monogynia.   Cl. 10. Ord. 1.
1. paluftris.   Grafs of Parnaffus.

242. PARTHENIUM.
BASTARD FEVERFEW.

L. G. Pl. 1058.   Monoecia Pentandria.   Cl. 21. Ord. 5.
1. Hyfterophorus.   Baftard Feverfew.
2. integrifolium.   Entire-leaved Baftard Feverfew.

243. PASTINACA.
PARSNEP,——(Fr.)—Panais.

L. G. Pl. 362.   Pentandria Digynia.   Cl. 5. Ord. 2.
1. fativa.   Parfnep. ♂
2. Opopanax.   Gum Parfnep.

244. PELTARIA.
PELTARIA.

L. G. Pl. 806.   Tetradynamia Siliculofa.   Cl. 15. Ord. 1.
1. alliacea.   Auftrian Peltaria.

245. PEUCEDANUM.
HOG'S FENNEL.

L. G. Pl. 339.   Pentandria Digynia.   Cl. 5. Ord. 2.
1. officinale.   Hog's Fennel.
2. minus.   Small Hog's Fennel.

246. PHALARIS.
CANARY GRASS.

L. G. Pl. 74.   Triandria Digynia.   Cl. 3. Ord. 2.
1. canarienfis.   Canary Grafs. ☉

247. PHASEOLUS.

KIDNEY or FRENCH BEAN,———(Fr.)—

L. G. Pl. 866.   Diadelphia Decandria.   Cl. 17. Ord. 3

1. nanus.   Dwarf Kidney Bean.

For the varieties of thefe, fee the Kitchen Garden Catalogue.

2. vulgaris - - - 1.   Scarlet-flowering Kidney Bean.
3. *vulgaris alba* - 2.   White-flowering Kidney Bean.

248. PHLOMIS.

JERUSALEM SAGE, or PHLOMIS.

L. G. Pl. 723.   Didynamia Gymnofpermia.   Cl. 14. Ord. 1

1. herba venti.   Narbone Phlomis.
2. tuberofa.   Tuberofe-rooted Phlomis.

249. PHLOX.

LYCHNIDEA, or BASTARD LYCHNIS.

L. G. Pl. 214.   Pentandria Monogynia.   Cl. 5. Ord. 1.

1. alba.   White Lychnidea.
2. carolina.   Rough-ftalked Carolina Lychnidea.
3. divaricata.   Pale-blue Dwarf Lychnidea.
4. glaberrima.   Smooth Lychnidea.
5. maculata - - 1.   Spotted-ftalked Lychnidea.
6. *maculata alba* - 2.   Spotted-ftalked White Lychnidea.
7. ovata.   Ovate-leaved Lychnidea.
8. paniculata.   Paniculated Lychnidea.

250. PHYSALIS.

WINTER CHERRY, or ALKEKENGI.

L. G. Pl. 250.   Pentandria Monogynia.   Cl. 5. Ord. 1

1. Alkekengi.   Winter Cherry.

HERBACEOUS PLANTS

251. PHYTEUMA.
RAMPION.

L. G. Pl. 220. Pentandria Monogynia. Cl. 5. Ord. 1.
1. orbicularis. Round-headed Rampion.
2. pauciflora. Leafy-spiked Rampion.

252. PHYTOLACCA.
AMERICAN NIGHTSHADE.

L. G. Pl. 588. Decandria Decagynia. Cl. 10. Ord. 5.
1. decandra. American Nightshade.

253. PIMPINELLA.
BURNET SAXIFRAGE.

L. G. Pl. 366. Pentandria Digynia. Cl. 5. Ord. 2.
1. Anisum Anise. ⊙
2. major Great Burnet Saxifrage.

254. PINGUICULA.
BUTTER-WORT.

L. G. Pl. 30. Diandria Monogynia. Cl. 2. Ord. 1.
1. vulgaris. Butter-wort.

255. PISUM.
PEA——(Fr.)—Pois.

L. G. Pl. 870. Diadelphia Decandria. Cl. 17. Ord. 3.
1. americanum. Cape Horn, or Lord Anson's Pea.
2. Ochrus. Italian winged Pea. ⊙
3. sativum. Garden Pea. ⊙
For whose cultivated varieties see the Kitchen-Garden Catalogue.
4. umbellatum. Rose, or Crown Pea. ⊙

256. PLANTAGO.

PLANTAIN.

L. G. Pl. 142.   Tetrandria Monogynia.   Cl. 4. Ord. 1.

1. alpina.   Alpine Plantain.
2. afiatica.   Siberian Plantain.
3. Coronopus.   Buck's-horn Plantain.
4. maritima.   Sea Plantain.
5. Pfillium.   Branching Plantain.

257. PLUMBAGO.

LEADWORT.

L. G. Pl. 213.   Pentandria Monogynia.   Cl. 5. Ord. 1.

1. europæa.   Leadwort.

258. PODOPHYLLUM.

DUCK'S-FOOT.

L. G. Pl. 646.   Polyandria Monogynia.   Cl. 13. Ord. 1.

1. peltatum.   Duck's-foot.

259. POLEMONIUM.

GREEK VALERIAN.

L. G. Pl. 217.   Pentandria Monogynia.   Cl. 5. Ord. 1.

1. cœruleum - - 1. Blue Greek Valerian.
2. cær. variegatifolium 2. Striped-leaved Blue Greek Valerian.
3. album - - - - 3. White Greek Valerian.
4. reptans.   Creeping-rooted Greek Valerian.

260. POLIANTHES.

TUBEROSE.—(Fr.)

L. G. Pl. 426.   Hexandria Monogynia.   Cl. 6. Ord. 1.

1. tuberofa - - - - - 1. Tuberose.
2. tuberofa plena - - - 2. Double Tuberose.
3. tuberofa variegata - 3. Gold-striped-leaved Tuberose.

I

261. POLYGONUM.

KNOTGRASS.

L. G. Pl. 495.   Pentandria Trigynia.   Cl. 5. Ord. 3.

1. Biftorta.	Biftort.
2. Fagopyrum.	Buckwheat. ⊙
3. Perficaria.	Perficaria. ⊙
4. virginianum.	Virginian Knot-grafs.
5. viviparum.	Narrow-leaved Knot-grafs.

262. POLYMNIA.

POLYMNIA.

L. G. Pl. 987.   Syngenefia Polygamia Neceffaria.   Cl. 19. Ord. 4.

1. canadenfis.	Canadian oppofite-leaved Polymnia.
2. Uvedalia.	Virginian alternate-leaved Polymnia.

263. POLYPODIUM.

POLYPODY.

L. G. Pl. 1179.   Cryptogamia Filix.   Cl. 24. Ord. 1.

1. aculeatum.	Prickly Polypody.
2. cambricum.	Welfh Polypody.
3. Dryopteris.	Branching Polypody.
4. Filix mas - - - 1.	Male Fern.
5. *Filix fœmina* - - - 2.	Female Fern.
6. fragile.	Brittle Polypody.
7. fragrans.	Sweet Polypody.
8. Lonchitis.	Great Spleenwort.
9. rhæticum.	Stone Polypody.
10. vulgare.	Polypody.

264. PORTULACA.

PURSLANE.

L. G. Pl. 603.   Dodecandria Monogynia.   Cl. 11. Ord. 1.

1. oleracea aurea - - 1.	Golden Purflane. ⊙
2. *oleracea viridis* - - 2.	Green Purflane. ⊙

265. POTENTILLA.

CINQUEFOIL.

L. G. Pl. 634.   Icofandria Polygynia.   Cl. 12. Ord. 5.

1. argentea.   Silver-leaved Cinquefoil.
2. aurea.   Golden-leaved Cinquefoil.
3. canadenfis.   Canadian Cinquefoil.
4. fragarioides.   Strawberry-leaved Cinquefoil.
5. hirta.   Hairy Cinquefoil.
6. monspelienfis.   Montpelier Cinquefoil.
7. recta.   Upright Cinquefoil.
8. rupeftris,   Rock Cinquefoil.

266. POTERIUM.

BURNET.

L. G. Pl. 1069.   Monoecia Polyandria.   Cl. 21. Ord. 8.

1. hybridum.   Sweet Agrimony-leaved Burnet.
2. Sanguisorba.   Garden Burnet.

267. PRIMULA.

PRIMROSE,——(Fr.)—Prime vere.

L. G. Pl. 197.   .   Pentandria Monogynia.   Cl. 5. Ord. 1.

1. veris - - - - 1.   Primrofe.
2. *veris lutea plena* - - 2.   Double Yellow Primrofe.
3. *veris purpurea plena* 3.   Double Purple Primrofe.
4. *veris rubra plena* - 4.   Double Red Primrofe.
5. *veris alba* - - - 5.   White, or Paper Primrofe.
6. elatior - . - - - 1.   Cowflip.
7. *elatior plena* - - 2.   Double Cowflip.
8. farinofa.   Bird's-Eye Primrofe.

PRIMULA—AURICULA.

AURICULA, or BEAR's EAR,——(Fr.) Oreille d'ours.

1. Auricula.   Auricula.

For many cultivated varieties, fee the Florifts Catalogues.

PRIMULA—POLYANTHUS.

POLYANTHUS.

1. Polyanthus.   Polyanthus.

For many cultivated varieties, fee the Florifts Catalogues.

268. PRUNELLA.

SELF-HEAL.

L. G. Pl 735.   Didynamia Gymnofpermia.   Cl. 14. Ord. 1.
1. laciniata.   Jagged-leaved Self-heal.
2. vulgaris - - - - 1. Self-heal.
3. *vulgaris grandiflora* 2. Great-flowered Self-heal.

269. PTERIS.

BRAKES.

L. G. Pl. 1174.   Cryptogamia Filix.   Cl. 24. Ord. 1.
1. aquilina.   Brakes.
2. atropurpurea.   Virginian Brakes.

270. PULMONARIA.

LUNGWORT——(Fr.)—Pulmonaire.

L. G. Pl. 184.   Pentandria Monogynia.   Cl. 5. Ord. 1.

1. anguftifolia.   Narrow-leaved Lungwort.
2. officinalis - - - 1. Lungwort.
3. *officinalis alba* - - 2. White-flowered Lungwort.
4. virginica.   Virginian Lungwort.

271. RANUNCULUS.

CROWFOOT, or RANUNCULUS——(Fr.)—Ranoncule.

L. G. Pl. 699.   Polyandria Polygynia.   Cl. 13. Ord. 7.

1. aconitifolius - - 1. White Mountain Ranunculus, or
                         'Fair Maid of France.'
2. *aconitifolius plenus* 2. Double white Mountain Ranunculus
3. acris. - -   Double yellow Crowfoot.

4. alpeſtris.	Little Alpine Crowfoot.
5. amplexicaulis.	Plantain-leaved Crowfoot.
6. aſiaticus.	Perſian Ranunculus.

For about a thouſand cultivated varieties, ſee the Floriſts Catalogues.

7. auricomus plenus.	Double Wood Crowfoot.
8. Ficaria plena.	Double Pilewort.
9. Flammula.	Leſſer Spearwort.
10. gramineus.	Graſs-leaved Crowfoot.
11. illyricus.	Illyrian Crowfoot.
12. Thora.	Alpine Crowfoot.
13. tuberoſus.	Tuberous-rooted Crowfoot.

272. RAPHANUS.

RADISH——(Fr.)

L. G. Pl. 822.   Tetradynamia Siliquoſa.   Cl. 15. Ord. 2.

1. ſativus - - -	1. Radiſh. ⊙
2. ſativus brevifolius -	2. Short-topped Radiſh. ⊙
3. ſativus longifolius -	3. Long-topped Radiſh. ⊙
4. ſativus roſeus - -	4. Pale red or Salmon Radiſh. ⊙
5. niger.	Black Spaniſh Radiſh. ⊙
6. orbiculatus.	Turnep-rooted or white Spaniſh Radiſh. ⊙

273. RESEDA.

BASTARD ROCKET.

L. G. Pl. 608.   Dodecandria Trigynia.   Cl. 11. Ord. 3.

| 1. odorata. | Sweet Reſeda, or Mignonette. ⊙ |
| 2. Seſamoides. | Weld. |

274. RHEUM.

RHUBARB—— (Fr.)—Rhubarbe.

L. G. Pl. 506.   Enneandria Trigynia.   Cl. 9. Ord. 2.

1. compactum.	Plain-leaved Rhubarb.
2. palmatum.	True Palmated-leaved Rhubarb.
3. rhaponticum.	Rhapontic Rhubarb.
4. undulatum.	Waved-leaved Rhubarb.

I 3

275. RHEXIA.

RHEXIA.

L. G. Pl. 468. Octandria Monogynia. Cl. 8. Ord. 1.

1. mariana. Maryland Rhexia.
2. virginica, Virginian Rhexia.

276. RHODIOLA.

ROSE-ROOT.

L. G. Pl. 1124. Dioecia Octandria. Cl. 22. Ord. 7.

1. rosea. Rose-root.

277. RUBIA.

L. G. Pl. 127. Tetrandia Monogynia. Cl. 4. Ord. 1.

1. peregrina. Four-leaved Canadian Madder.
2. Tinctorum, Madder.

278. RUBUS.

RASPBERRY——(Fr.)—Ronce.

L. G. Pl. 632. Icosandria Polygynia. Cl. 12. Ord. 5.

1. arcticus. Cloud Berry.
2. Chamæmorus, Dwarf, or Bastard Mulberry.

279. RUDBECKIA.

AMERICAN SUNFLOWER.

L. G. Pl. 980. Syngenesia Polygamia Frustranea. Cl. 19. Ord. 3.

1. atropurpurea. Dark purple American Sunflower.
2. hirta. Hairy American Sunflower.
3. laciniata. Jagged-leaved American Sunflower.
4. purpurea. Purple American Sunflower.

280. RUMEX.

Dock.

L. G. Pl. 451.	Hexandria Trigynia.	Cl. 6. Ord. 3.
1. Acetosa.	Sorrel.	
3. britannicus.	Water Dock.	
4. Patientia.	Garden Patience.	
5. sanguineus.	Bloody Dock.	
6. tuberosus.	French Sorrel.	

281. SALVIA.

SAGE.

L. G. Pl. 39.	Octandria Monogynia.	Cl. 8. Ord. 1.
1. indica.	Indian Sage.	
2. sylvestris.	Wood Sage.	

SALVIA—SCLAREA,

CLARY.

1. Sclarea.	Clary.
2. glutinosa.	Gummy-leaved Clary,
3. tomentosa.	Broad-leaved Clary.

282. SAMBUCUS.

ELDER——(Fr.)—Saureau.

L. G. Pl. 372.	Pentandria Trigynia.	Cl. 5. Ord. 3.
1. Ebulus.	Dwarf Elder.	

283. SAMOLUS.

ROUND-LEAVED WATER PIMPERNEL.

L. G. Pl. 222.	Pentandria Monogynia.	Cl. 5. Ord. 1.
1. Valerandi.	Round-headed Water Pimpernel.	

284. SANGUINARIA.

PUCCOON.

L. G. Pl. 645.	Polyandria Monogynia.	Cl. 13. Ord. 1.
1. canadensis.	Canadian Puccoon.	

I 4

285. SANGUISORBA.

BURNET.

L. G. Pl. 146.   Tetrandia Monogynia.   Cl. 4. Ord. 1.

1. canadenfis.   Canadian Burnet.
2. officinalis.   Burnet.

286. SANICULA.

SANICLE, or SELF-HEAL.

L. G. Pl. 326.   Pentandria Digynia.   Cl. 5. Ord. 2.

1. europæa.   Sanicle, or Self-heal.

287. SAPONARIA.

SOAP-WORT,

L. G. Pl. 564.   Decandria Digynia.   Cl. 10. Ord. 2.

1. officinalis   -   -   - 1. Soapwort.
2. *officinalis plena* - - - 2. Double Soapwort.
3. *officinalis hybrida* - 3. Hollow-leaved Soap-wort.

288. SARRACENIA.

SIDE-SADDLE FLOWER.

L. G. Pl. 653.   Polyandria Monogynia.   Cl. 13. Ord 1.

1. flava.   Yellow Side-Saddle Flower.
2. purpurea.   Purple Side-Saddle Flower.

289. SATUREJA.

SAVORY.—(Fr.)

L. G. Pl. 707.   Didynamia Gymnospermia.   Cl. 14. Ord. 1.

1. capitata.   Headed Savory.
2. hortenfis.   Summer Savory.   ☉
3. montana.   Winter Savory.
4. virginiana.   Virginian Savory.

290. SAURURUS.

LIZARD'S-TAIL.

L. G. Pl. 464.   Heptandria Trigynia.   Cl. 7. Ord. 3.

1. cernuus.   Lizard's-Tail.

291. SAXIFRAGA.

SAXIFRAGE.

L. G. Pl. 559.   Decandria Digynia.   Cl. 10. Ord. 2.

1. autumnalis - - 1.   Autumnal Saxifrage.
2. *autumnalis plena* - - 2.   Double Autumnal Saxifrage.
3. Cotyledon.   Narrow-leaved Saxifrage.
4. craffifolia.   Thick-leaved Saxifrage.
5. cuneifolia.   Wedge-leaved Saxifrage.
6. Geum.   London Pride.
7. granulata - - 1.   White Saxifrage.
8. *granulata plena* - - 2.   Double White Saxifrage.
9. Hynoides.   Hypnum-leaved Saxifrage.
10. mutata.   Lesser Saxifrage.
11. nivalis.   Snowy Saxifrage.
12. oppofitifolia.   Opposite-leaved Saxifrage.
13. penfylvanica.   Penfylvanian Saxifrage.
14. punctata.   Dotted Saxifrage.
15. pyramidata.   Pyramidal Saxifrage.
16. rivularis.   Palmate-leaved Saxifrage.
17. rotundifolia.   Round-leaved Saxifrage.
18. umbrofa.   Hairy-footftalked Saxifrage.

292. SCABIOSA.

SCABIOUS.

L. G. Pl. 115.   Tetrandria Monogynia.   Cl. 4. Ord. 1.

1. alpina.   Alpine Scabious.
2. altiffima.   Tall Scabious.
3. arvenfis.   Field Scabious.
4. atropurpurea.   Sweet Scabious.
5. graminifolia.   Grafs-leaved Scabious.
6. gramontia.   Cut-leaved Scabious.
7. leuvantha.   Snowy Scabious.
8. fuccifa.   Devil's Bit.

293. SCANDIX.

L. G. Pl. 357.   Pentandria Digynia.   Cl. 5. Ord. 2.
1. odorata.   Sweet Fern, or Myrrh.

294. SCILLA.

SQUILL.

L. G. Pl. 419.   Hexandria Monogynia.   Cl. 6. Ord. 1.
1. amœna.   Byzantine Squill, or Starry Hyacinth
2. autumnalis.   Autumnal Squill.
3. bifolia alba - - 1.   White Starry Hyacinth.
4. *bifolia cœrulea* - - 2.   Blue Starry Hyacinth.
5. italica.   Italian blue-fpiked Squill.
6. peruviana alba - - 1.   White Peruvian Hyacinth.
7. *peruviana cœrulea* - 2.   Blue Peruvian Hyacinth.

295. SCORZONERA.

VIPER's-GRASS, or SCORZONERA.

L. G. Pl. 906.   Syngenefia Polygamia Æqualis.   Cl. 19. Ord. 1.
1. hifpanica.   Scorzonera. ♂

296. SCROPHULARIA.

FIGWORT.——(Fr.)—Scrofulaire.

L. G. Pl. 756.   Didynamia Angiofpermia.   Cl. 14. Ord. 2.
1. aquatica - - 1.   Water Figwort, or Water Betony.
2. *aquatica variegata* - 2.   Striped-leaved Water Figwort.
3. frutefcens.   Vervain-leaved Figwort.
4. lucida.   Shining-leaved Figwort.
5. marilandica.   Maryland Figwort.
6. nodofa.   Knobbed-rooted Figwort.
7. peregrina.   Nettle-leaved Figwort.
8. fambucifolia.   Elder-leaved Figwort.
9. Scorodonia.   Balm-leaved Figwort.

297. SCUTELLARIA.

SKULLCAP.

L. G. Pl. 734.   Didynamia Gymnofpermia.   Cl. 14. Ord. 1.

1. alpina.   Alpine Skullcap.
2. altiffima.   Nettle-leaved Skullcap.

3. cretica.   Cretan Skullcap.
4. galericulata.   Skullcap, or Helmet-flower.
5. minor.   Leffer Skullcap.
6. peregrina,   Florentine Skullcap.

298. SECALE.
RYE.

L. G. Pl. 97.   Triandria Digynia.   Cl. 3. Ord. 2.
1,   Rye.

299. SEDUM.
HOUSELEEK, or STONECROP.

L. G. Pl. 579.   Decandria Pentagynia.   Cl. 10. Ord. 4,

1. acre   -   -   -   1. Stonecrop, or Wall Pepper.
2. *acre grandiflorum* - 2. Large-flowered Stonecrop.
3. Aizoon.   Yellow-flowered Houfeleek.
4. album.   White Houfeleek.
5. Anacampferos,   Evergreen leffer Houfeleek.
6. hybridum,   Germander-leaved Houfeleek.
7. reflexum,   Reflexed-leaved Houfeleek, or Prick
                              Madam.
8. rupeftre.   Rock Houfeleek.
9. fe angulare,   Six-angled Houfeleek.
10. Telephium.   Orpine.

300. SEMPERVIVUM.
HOUSELEEK.

L. G. Pl. 612.   Dodecandria Polygynia.   Cl. 11. Ord. 1.

1. arachnoideum.   Cobweb Houfeleek.
2. globiferum.   Round-headed Houfeleek,
3. Tectorum,   Houfeleek.

301. SENECIO.
GROUNDSEL.

L. G. Pl. 953.   Syngenefia Polygamia Superflua.   Cl. 19. Ord. 2.
1. Doria.   Sea Lavender-leaved Groundfel.
2. Doronicum.   Alpine Groundfel,

3. luridus.   Purple-leaved Groundfel.
4. faracenicus.   Saracens All-heal.

302.   SERAPIAS.

BASTARD HELLEBORE.

L. G. Pl. 1012.   Gynandria Digynis.   Cl. 20. Ord. 1.

1. Helleborine.   Baftard Hellebore.
2. latifolia.   Broad-leaved Baftard Hellebore.
3. longifolia.   White-flowered Baftard Hellebore,

303.   SERRATULA.

SAW-WORT.

L. G. Pl. 924.   Syngenefia Polygamia Æqualis.   Cl. 19. Ord. 1.

1. præalta.   Virginian Peached-leaved Saw-wort.
2. fcariofa.   Broad-leaved Saw-wort.
3. fpicata.   Spiked-flowered Saw-wort.
4. fquarrofa.   Rough-headed Saw-wort.
5. tinctoria.   Saw-wort.

304.   SIBBALDIA.

SIBBALDIA.

L. G. Pl. 393.   Pentandria Pentagynia.   Cl. 5. Ord. 5.

1. procumbens.   Trailing Sibbaldia.

305.   SIBTHORPIA.

BASTARD MONEY-WORT.

L. G. Pl. 775.   Didynamia Angiofpermia.   Cl. 14. Ord. 2,

1. europæa.   Baftard Money-wort.

306.   SIDERITIS.

IRON-WORT.

L. G. Pl. 712.   Didynamia Gymnofpermia.   Cl. 14. Ord. 1.

1. hyffopifolia.   Hyffop-leaved Ironwort.

307. SILENE.

VISCOUS CAMPION.

L. G. Pl. 567.   Decandria Trigynia.   Cl. 10. Ord. 3.

1. amœna.   Sea Viscous Campion.
2. Armeria alba   -   -   1.   White Lobel's Catchfly. ☉
3. *Armeria purpurea* • 2. Purple Lobel's Catchfly. ☉
4. *Armeria rubra*   -   3.   Red Lobel's Catchfly. ☉
5. nutans.   Nodding Viscous Campion.
6. quinquagvulnera.   Dwarf Lychnis. ☉

308. SILPHIUM.

BASTARD MARYGOLD, or CHRYSANTHEMUM.

L. G. Pl. 986.   Syngenesia Polygamia Necessaria.   Cl. 19. Ord. 4.

1. conatum.   Conated Bastard Marygold.
2. laciniatum.   Jagged-leaved Bastard Marygold.
3. latifolium.   Broad-leaved Bastard Marygold.
4. perfoliatum.   Perfoliate-leaved Bastard Marygold.
5. trifoliatum.   Three-leaved Bastard Marygold.

309. SINAPIS.

MUSTARD—(Fr.)—Moutarde.

L. G. Pl. 821.   Tetradynamia Siliquosa.   Cl. 15. Ord. 2.

1. alba.   White Mustard.
2. nigra.   Black Mustard.
3. arvensis.   -   -   -   1.   Durham Mustard.
4. *arvensis laciniata* - 2. Jagged-leaved Durham Mustard.

310. SISYMBRIUM.

WATER CRESS.

L. G. Pl. 813.   Tetradynamia Siliquosa.   Cl. 15. Ord. 2.
1. Nasturtium aquaticum. Water Cress.

311. SISYRINCHIUM.

L. G. Pl. 1017.   Gynandria Triandria.   Cl. 20. Ord. 2.
1. angustifolia.   Narrow-leaved Sisyrinchium.
2. Bermudiana.   Bermudian Sisyrinchium.

312. SIUM.
SKIRRET.

L. G. Pl. 348.   Pentandria Digynia.   Cl. 5. Ord. 2.
1. Sifarum.   Skirret. ♂

313. SMYRNIUM.
ALEXANDER, or ALISANDER.

L. G. Pl. 363.   Pentandria Digynia.   Cl. 5. Ord. 2.
1. Olufatrum.   Alexander.

314. SOLANUM.
NIGHTSHADE.

L. G. Pl. 251.   Pentandria Monogynia.   Cl. 5. Ord. 1.
1. efculentum.   Potatoe.

For the cultivated varieties, fee the Kitchen-Garden Catalogue.

315. SOLIDAGO.
GOLDEN-ROD.

L. G. Pl. 955.   Syngenefia Polygamia Superflua.   Cl. 19. Ord. 2.
1. alba.   White Golden-rod.
2. altiffima.   Tall Golden-rod.
3. cœfia.   Smooth-ftalked Golden-rod.
4. cambrica.   Welfh Golden-rod.
5. canadenfis.   Canadian Golden-rod.
6. flexicaulis.   Flexible-ftalked Golden-rod.
7. lateriflora.   Sideflowering Golden-rod.
8. latifolia.   Broad-leaved Golden-rod.
9. mexicana.   Mexican Golden-rod.
10. minor.   Small Golden-rod.
11. minuta.   Very fmall Golden-rod.
12. noveboracenfis.   New-York Golden-rod.
13. odorata.   Sweet-fcented Golden-rod.
14. rigida.   Rigid-ftalked Golden-rod.
15. rugofa.   Wrinkled-leaved Golden-rod.
16. fempervirens - - - 1. Evergreen Golden-rod.
17. femperv. latifolia - - 2. Broad-leaved Evergreen Golden-rod.
18. Virga aurea.   Golden-rod.

316. SOPHORA.
SOPHORA.

L. G. Pl. 508.　　　Decandria Monogynia.　　　Cl. 10. Ord. 1.

1. alopecuroides.　　　Levantine Sophora.
2. purpurea.　　　Purple Sophora.
3. tinctoria - - - 1.　Dyers Sophora.
4. *tinctoria alba* - - 2.　White flowered Dyer's Sophora.

317. SPIGELIA.
WORM-SEED, or WORM-GRASS.

L. G. Pl. 209.　　　Pentandria Monogynia.　　　Cl. 5. Ord. 1.

1. marilandica.　　　Maryland Worm-seed.

318. SPINACIA.
SPINACH.

L. Gl. PL 1112.　　　Dioecia Pentandria.　　　Cl. 22. Ord. 5.

1. glabra.　　　Smooth-seeded Spinach.　⊙
2. oleracea.　　　Prickly-seeded Spinach.　⊙

319. SPIRÆA.
SPIRÆA.

L. G. Pl. 630.　　　Icosandria Pentagynia.　　　Cl. 12. Ord. 4.

1. Aruncus.　　　Goat's-beard Spiræa.
2. Filipendula - - 1.　Dropwort.
3. *Filipendula plena* - 2.　Double Dropwort.
4. lobata.　　　Purple Spiræa.
5. rubra.　　　Red-flowered Spiræa.
6. trifoliata.　　　Three-leaved Spiræa.
7. Ulmaria - - - 1.　Meadow-sweet.
8. *Ulmaria plena* - - 2.　Double Meadow-sweet.
9. *Ulmaria variegatifolia* 3.　Striped-leaved Meadow-sweet.

320. STACHYS.
BASE HOREHOUND.

L. G. Pl. 719.　　　Didynamia Gymnospermia.　　　Cl. 14. Ord. 1.

1. cretica.　　　Cretan Base Horehound.
2. germanica.　　　German Base Horehound.
3. palustris.　　　Marsh Base Horehound.

321. STATICE.

THRIFT, or SEA PINK.

L. G. Pl. 388.   Pentandria Pentagynia.   Cl. 5. Ord. 5.

1. Armeria - - - 1. Thrift.
2. *Armeria alba* - - 2. White Thrift.
3. *Armeria latifolia* - 3. Broad-leaved Thrift.
4. Limonium.   Sea Lavender.
5. montana.   Mountain Thrift.
6. fpeciofa.   Plantain-leaved Sea Lavender.
7. tatarica.   Tartarian Sea Lavender.

322. STIPA.

FEATHER-GRASS.

L. G. Pl. 90.   Triandria Digynia.   Cl. 3. Ord. 2.

1. juncea.   Rufh-leaved Feather-grafs.
2. pennata.   Feather-grafs.

323. SWERTIA.

MARSH GENTIAN.

L. G. Pl. 321.   Pentandria Digynia.   Cl. 5. Ord. 2.

1. perennis.   Marfh Gentian.

324. SYMPHYTUM.

COMFREY.

L. G. Pl. 185.   Pentandria Monogynia.   Cl. 5. Ord. 1.

1. officinale.   Comfrey.
2. tuberofum.   Tuberous-rooted Comfrey.

325. TABERNÆMONTANA.

TABERNÆMONTANA.

L. G. Pl. 301.   Pentandria Monogynia.   Cl. 5. Ord. 1.

1. Amfonia.   Virginian Amfonia.

326. TAGETES.

AFRICAN and FRENCH MARYGOLD.

L. G. Pl. 964.   Syngenefia Polygamia Superflua.   Cl. 19. Ord. 2.

1. erecta aurantiaca - 1. Orange-coloured African Maryg. ⊙
2. erecta lutea   - - 2. Yellow African Marygold.
3. erecta fulphurea - 3. Brimstone-coloured African Maryg.
4. erecta odorata   - - 4. Sweet-fcented African Marygold.
   Of thefe there are fingle, double, and fiftulous Flowers.
5. patula -   -   - 1. French Marygold. ⊙
6. patula odorata - - 2. Sweet-fcented French Marygold.
7. patula ftriata - - 3. Striped French Marygold.

327. TANACETUM.

TANSEY.

L. G. Pl. 944.   Syngenefia Polygamia Superflua.   Cl. 19. Ord. 2

1. vulgare   - - - - 1. Tanfey.
2. vulgare crifpum - - 2. Curled-leaved Tanfey.
3. vulgare variegatifol. 3. Striped-leaved Tanfey.
4. Balfamita.   Coftmary.

328. TELEPHIUM.

ORPINE.

L. G. Pl. 377.   Pentandria Trigynia.   Cl. 5. Ord. 3.
1. Imperati.   Orpine, or Live-long.

329. TETRAGONOTHECA.

BASTARD-SUNFLOWER.

L. G. Pl. 976.   Syngenefia Polygamia Superflua.   Cl. 19. Ord. 2.
1. Helianthoides.   Baftard Sunflower.

330. TEUCRIUM.

GERMANDER.

L. G. Pl. 706.   Didynamia Gymnofpermia.   Cl. 14. Ord. 1.
1. canadenfe.   Canadian Germander.
2. Chamædrys.   Creeping Germander.
3. lucidum.   Shining-leaved Germander.

K

4. montanum.	Mountain Germander.
5. pyrenaicum.	Pyrenean Germander.
6, Scordium.	Water Germander.
7. Scorodonia.	Wood Sage.
8. virginicum,	Virginian Germander.

331. THALICTRUM.
MEADOW RUE.

L. G. Pl. 697.　　Polyandria Polygynia.　　Cl. 13. Ord. 7.

1. alpinum.	Alpine Feathered Columbine.
2. angustifolium.	Narrow-leaved Feathered Columbine
3. aquilegifolium.	Feathered Columbine.
4. Cornuti.	Canadian Meadow Rue.
5. flavum.	Great Meadow Rue.
6. fœtidum.	Stinking Meadow Rue.
7. minus.	Dwarf Meadow Rue.
8. tuberosum.	Tuberous-rooted Meadow Rue.

332. TIARELLA.
SANICLE.

L. G. Pl. 560.　　Decandria Digynia.　　Cl. 10. Ord. 2.

| 1. cordifolia. | Heartshaped-leaved Sanicle. |

333. TORMENTILLA.
TORMENTIL.

L. G. Pl. 635.　　Icosandria Polygynia.　　Cl. 12. Ord. 5.

| 1. erecta. | Upright Tormentil. |
| 2. reptans. | Creeping Tormentil. |

334. TRACHELIUM.
THROATWORT.

L. G. Pl. 221.　　Pentandria Monogynia.　　Cl. 5. Ord. 1.

| 1. cœruleum, | Blue Mountain Throatwort. |

335. TRADESCANTIA.

SPIDERWORT.

L. G. Pl. 398. Hexandria Monogynia. Cl. 6. Ord. 1.

1. virginiana - - - 1. Virginian Spiderwort.
2. virginiana alba - - 2. White Virginian Spiderwort.

336. TRAGOPOGON.

GOATS-BEARD.

I. G. Pl. 905. Syngenesia Polygamia Æqualis. Cl. 19. Ord. 1.

1. Dalechampii. Cretan Goats-beard.
2. pratense. Goats-beard.

337. TRICHOMANES.

MAIDENHAIR.

L. G. Pl. 1181. Crytogamia Filix. Cl. 24. Ord. 1.

1. tunbrigiense. Tunbridge Maidenhair.

338. TRIENTALIS.

CHICKWEED WINTER GREEN.

L. G. Pl. 461. Heptandria Monogynia. Cl. 7. Ord. 1.

1. europæa. Chickweed Winter Green.

339. TRIFOLIUM.

TREFOIL.

L. G. Pl. 896. Diadelphia Decandria. Cl. 17. Ord. 5.

1. agrarium. Hop Clover, or Yellow Meadow Trefoil.
2. alpestre. Long-spiked Trefoil.
3. alpinum. Alpine Trefoil.
4. filiforme. Least Yellow Hop Trefoil, None-such or Black seed.
5. fragiferum. Strawberry Trefoil.
6. Lupinaster. Bastard Lupin.
7. ochroleucrum. Trefoil.

K 2

8. pratenfe.	·	··	Red or Dutch Clover.
9. repens.			,. White Dutch Clover, or Honey-fuckle-grafs.
10. rubens.			Red-fpecked Trefoil.

340. TRILLIUM.

HERB PARIS, or TRUE LOVE.

L. G. Pl. 456.   Hexandria Trigynia.   Cl. 6. Ord. 3.

1. erectum.   Upright Herb True Love.

341. TRIOSTEUM.

FALSE IPECACUANA.

L. G. Pl. 234.   Pentandria Monogynia.   Cl. 5. Ord. 1.

1. perfoliatum.   Falfe Ipecacuana, or Dr. Tinkar's Weed.

342. TRITICUM.

WHEAT.

L. G. Pl. 99.   Triandria Trigynia.   Cl. 3. Ord. 3.

1. æftivum.	•	Summer or Spring Wheat.
2. hybernum.	,	Winter Wheat.
3. polonicum.		Poland Wheat.
4. quadratum album	- 1.	White Cone Wheat.
5. *quadratum rubrum*	- 2.	Red Cone Wheat.
6. fibiricum.		Siberian Wheat or Barley.
7. turgidum.		Gray Pollard, or Duckbill **Wheat.**

Befides the above Species there are the following Varieties,

Red Wheat without Awns.   Red-eared bearded Wheat.
Many-eared Wheat.

343. TROLLIUS.

GLOBE RANUNCULUS.

L. G. Pl. 700.   Polyandria Polygynia.   Cl. 13. Ord. 7.

1. europæus.   Globe Ranunculus, or Locker Gowlans.

344. TULIPA.
TULIP——(Fr.)——Tulipe.

L. G. Pl. 415.　　Hexandria Monogynia.　　Cl. 6. Ord. 1.
1. gefneriana.　　　　Tulip.

For feveral hundred cultivated varieties of which, fee the Florifts Catalogue.

2. fylveftris - - - 1. Wild Yellow Tulip.
3. *fylveftris minor* - - 2. Leffer Wild Yellow Tulip.

345. TURRITIS.
TOWER MUSTARD.

L. G. Pl. 819.　　Tetradynamia Siliquofa.　　Cl. 15. Ord. 2.
1. glabra.　　　　Great Tower Muftard.
2. hirfuta.　　　　Hairy Tower Muftard.

346. TUSSILAGO.
COLTSFOOT.

L. G. Pl. 952.　Syngenefia Polygamia Superflua.　Cl. 19. Ord. 2.
1. alba.　　　　White Coltsfoot.
2. alpina.　　　　Alpine Coltsfoot.
3. Farfara.　　　Coltsfoot.
4. hybrida.　　　Long-ftalked Coltsfoot.
5. Petafites.　　Butter Burr.

347. VALANTIA.
CROSS-WORT.

L. G. Pl. 1151.　　Polygamia Monoecia.　　Cl. 23. Ord. 1.
1. Cruciata.　　　　Crofs-wort.

348. VALERIANA.
VALERIAN.

L. G. Pl. 44.　　Triandria Monogynia.　　Cl. 3. Ord. 1.
1. dioica.　　　　Marfh Valerian.
2. montana.　　　Mountain Valerian.

K 3

3. officinalis.   Wild Valerian.
4. Phu.   Garden Valerian.
5. pyrenaica.   Pyrenean Valerian.
6. rubra - - - - 1.   Red Valerian.
7. *alba* - - - - - 2. White Valerian.
8. Tripteris.   Small Alpine Valerian.

349. VERATRUM.

WHITE HELLEBORE.

L. G. Pl. 1144.   Polygamia Monoecia.   Cl. 23. Ord. 1.

1. album.   White Hellebore.
2. nigrum,   Black Hellebore.

350. VERBASCUM.

MULLEIN.

L. G. Pl. 245.   Pentandria Monogynia.   Cl. 5. Ord. 1.

1. Blattaria.   Yellow Moth Mullein.
2. Lychnitis,   White Mullein.   ♂
3. Myconi.   Bear's Ear Mullein.
4. nigrum.   Sage-leaved Black Mullein.
5. phœniceum.   Purple Moth Mullein.
6. phlomoides.   Alpine Mullein.
7. Thapfus,   Mullein, or High-taper.

351. VERBENA,

VERVAIN.

L. G. Pl. 32,   Diandria Monogynia.   Cl. 2. Ord. 1.

1. bonariense.   Tall Buenos Ayres Vervain.
2. haftata.   Spear-leaved Vervain.
3. officinalis,   Vervain,

352. VERONICA.

SPEEDWELL.

L. G. Pl. 25.   Diandria Monogynia.   Cl. 2. Ord. 1.

1. acinifolia.   Needle-leaved Speedwell.
2. auftriaca,   Auftrian Speedwell,

3. cœrulea.	Blue Speedwell.
4. hybrida.	Welſh Speedwell.
5. incana.	Hoary-leaved Speedwell.
6. longifolia.	Long-leaved Speedwell.
7. maritima - - - 1.	Sea Speedwell.
8. *maritima alba* - - 2.	White Sea Speedwell.
9. *maritima incarnata* - 3.	Fleſh-coloured Sea Speedwell.
10. montana.	Mountain Speedwell.
11. officinalis.	Speedwell.
12. ſibirica.	Siberian Speedwell.
13. ſpicata.	Spiked-flowered Speedwell.
14. ſpuria.	Narrow-leaved Speedwell.
15. Teucrium.	Germander-leaved Speedwell.
16. virginica - - - 1.	Virginian Speedwell.
17. *virginica incarnata* - 2.	Fleſh-coloured Virginian Speedwell.

353. VICIA.
VETCH, or TARE.

L. G. Pl. 873.   Diadelphia Decandria.   Cl. 17. Ord. 3.

1. narbonenſis.	Narbone Vetch.
2. *ſativa alba* - - 1.	White Vetch.
3. *ſat:va nigra* - - 2.	Black Vetch.
4. ſylvatica.	Wood Vetch.

354. VIOLA.
VIOLET——(Fr.)—Violier.

L. G. Pl. 1007.   Syngeneſia Monogamia.   Cl. 19. Ord. 6.

1. biflora.	Two-flowered Violet.
2. canadenſis.	Canadian Violet.
3. hirta.	Hairy Violet.
4. lutea.	Yellow Violet.
5. mirabilis.	Mutable Violet.
6. montana.	Mountain Violet.
7. odorata - - - 1.	Violet.
8. *odorata plena* - - 2.	Double Violet.
9. *odorata plena alba* - - 3.	Double White Violet.
10. palmata.	Palmated Violet.
11. paluſtris.	Marſh Violet.

K 4

12. pedata.   Pedated Violet.
13. tricolor.   Hearts-eafe, or Panfie. ⊙
           Of this there are many feminal varieties.

355. URTICA,
NETTLE.

L. G. Pl. 1054.   Monoecia Tetrandria,   Cl. 21. Ord. 4.
1. canadenfis.   Canadian Nettle.
2. cannabina.   Tartarian Nettle.
3. nivea.   Snowy Nettle.

356. UVULARIA.
UVULARIA.

L. G. Pl. 412.   Hexandria Monogynia.   Cl. 6. Ord. 1.
1. amplexifolia.   Amplexicaul Uvularia,
2. perfoliata.   Perfoliate Uvularia.

357. XERANTHEMUM.
ETERNAL-FLOWER.

L. G. Pl. 947.   Syngenefia Polygamia Superflua.   Cl. 19. Ord. 2.
1. annuum album - - 1.   White Eternal-flower.
2. *annuum album plenum* 2. Double White Eternal-flower.
3. *annuum rubrum* - - 2.   Red Eternal-flower.
4. *annuum rubrum plen.* 4. Double Red Eternal-flower.

358. ZEA.
INDIAN CORN, or MAIZE.

L. G. Pl. 1042.   Monoecia Triandria.   Cl. 21. Ord. 3.
1. alba.   Slender-fpiked Indian Corn.
2. americana.   Long-fpiked Indian Corn.
3. vulgaris.   Short-fpiked Indian Corn.

359. ZINNIA.
ZINNIA.

L. G. Pl. 974.   Syngenefia Polygamia Superflua.   Cl. 19. Ord. 2.
1. pauciflora lutea - - 1. Yellow Zinnia. ⊙
2. *pauciflora rubra* - 2. Red Zinnia. ⊙

CHAP. III.

GREENHOUSE PLANTS.

1. ACHILLEA.

MILFOIL, YARROW, and SNEEZEWORT.
(Fr.)—Mille-feuille.

Lin. Gen. Pl. 971. Syngenefia Polygamia Superflua. Claffis 19. Ord. 2.

1. ægyptiaca.   Ægyptian Milfoil.
2. Clavennæ.   Silver-leaved Milfoil.

2. ADIANTHUM.
MAIDEN-HAIR.

L. G. Pl. 1180.   Crytogamia Filix.   Cl. 24. Ord. 1.
1. capillus Veneris.   Maiden-hair,

3. AGAVE.
AMERICAN ALOE, or AGAVE.

L. G. Pl. 431.   Hexandria Monogynia.   Cl. 6. Ord. 1.

1. americana - - - 1.   American Agave.
2. *americ. argenteo-var.* 2.   Silver-ftriped American Agave.
3. *americ. aureo-varieg.* 3.   Gold-ftriped American Agave.
4. virginiana.   Virginian Agave.

360. ZYGOPHYLLUM.
BEAN CAPER.

L. G. Pl. 530.   Decandria Monogynia.   Cl. 10. Ord. 1.
1. Fabago.   Bean Caper.

4. ALBUCA.

BASTARD STAR OF BETHLEHEM.

L. G. Pl. 416.   Hexandria Monogynia.   Cl. 6. Ord. 1,

1. major.   Baftard Star of Bethlehem.
2. minor.   Leffer Baftard Star of Bethlehem.

4. ALETRIS.

ALETRIS.

L. G. Pl. 428.   Hexandria Monogynia.   Cl. 6. Ord. 1

1. farinofa.   Mealy-leaved Virginian Aletris.
2. Uvaria.   Uvaria Aletris.

6. ALOE.

ALOE.

L. G. Pl. 430.   Hexandria Monogynia.   Cl. 6. Ord. 1,

1. arachnoidea.   Cobweb Aloe.
2. arborefcens.   Sword Aloe.
3. barbadenfis.   Barbadoes Aloe.
4. brevifolia.   Short-leaved Aloe.
5. carinata.   Keel-fhaped Aloe.
6. caroliniana.   Carolinian Aloe.
7. difticha.   Soap Aloe.
8. ferox.   Great Prickly Aloe.
9. herbacea.   Leaft Cobweb Aloe.
10. humilis.   Hedgehog Aloe.
11. linguiformis.   Tongue-fhaped Aloe.
12. margaritifera   - - 1.   Pearl Aloe.
13. *margaritifera minor*   2.   Small Pearl Aloe.
14. mitriformis.   Mitre-fhaped Aloe.
15. perfoliata. ,   Perfoliate-leaved Aloe.
16. plicatilis.   Fan Aloe.
17. retufa.   Cufhion Aloe.
18. fpiralis.   Upright round-leaved Aloe.
19. variegata.   Partridge-breaft Aloe.
20. vera.   Succotrine Aloe.
21. verrucofa.   Pearl-tongue Aloe.
22. vifcofa.   Upright triangular vifcous Aloe.

7. ALSTRŒMERIA.

ALSTRŒMERIA.

L. G. Pl. 432.	Hexandria Monogynia.	Cl. 6. Ord. 1
1. Ligta.	Striped Alftrœmeria.	
2. pelegias.	Spotted Alftrœmeria.	

8. AMARYLLIS.

AMARYLLIS, or LILY-DAFFODIL——(Fr.)—Lis Narciſſe.

L. G. Pl. 400.	Hexandria Monogynia.	Cl. 2. Ord. 1.
1. farnienſis.	Guernſey, or Japoneſe Lily.	

9. AMBROSIA.

AMBROSIA.

L. G. Pl. 1054.	Monoecia Pentandria.	Cl. 21. Ord. 5.
1. arboreſcens.	Shrubby Mexican Ambroſia.	

10. ANAGALLIS.

PIMPERNEL.

L. G. Pl. 206.	Pentandria Monogynia.	Cl. 6. Ord. 1.
1. Monelli.	♂ Blue Pimpernel.	

11. ANAGYRIS.

STINKING BEAN TREFOIL.

L. G. Pl. 509.	Decandria Monogynia.	Cl. 10. Ord. 1.
1. fœtida.	Stinking Bean Trefoil.	

12. ANTHEMIS.

CAMOMILE.

L. G. Pl. 970.	Syngeneſia Polygamia Superflua.	Cl. 19. Ord. 2.
1. maritima.	Sea Camomile.	

13. ANTHERICUM.

SPIDERWORT.

L. G. Pl. 422.　　Hexandria Monogynia.　　Cl. 6. Ord. 1.
1. aloides.　　　　Aloe-leaved Spiderwort.
2. Afphodeloides　　Afphodel-leaved Spiderwort.
3. frutefcens.　　　Shrubby Spiderwort.

14. ANTHOLYZA.

ANTHOLYZA.

L. G. Pl. 58.　　Triandia Monogynia.　　Cl. 3. Ord. 1.
1. Cunonia.　　　Perfian Antholyza.
2. Meriana.　　　Cape Antholyza.

15. ANTHOSPERMUM.

AMBER-TREE.

L. G. Pl. 1164.　　Polygamia Dioecia.　　Cl. 23. Ord. 2.
1. æthiopicum.　　　Æthiopian Amber-tree.

16. ANTHYLLIS.

SILVER BUSH, or JUPITER's BEARD.

L. G. Pl. 864.　　Diadelphia Decandria.　　Cl. 17. Ord. 4.
1. Barba Jovis.　　Jupiter's Beard.
2. Cytifoides.　　Spanifh Silver Bufh.
3. heterophylla.　　Various-leaved Silver Bufh.

17. ANTIRRHINUM.

SNAP-DRAGON.

L. G. Pl. 750.　　Didynamia Angiofpermia.　　Cl. 14. Ord 2
1. trifte - - - - - 1. Black-flowered Snap-dragon.
2. trifte variegatum - 2. Striped-leaved Snap-dragon.

18. APOCYNUM.

DOG's-BANE.

L. G. Pl. 305.　　Pentandria Digynia.　　Cl. 5. Ord. 2.
1. reticulatum.　　　Indian Dog's-bane.

19. ARCTOTIS.

ARCTOTIS.

L. G. Pl. 991.　　Syngenesia Polygamia Necessaria.　　Cl. 19. Ord. 4.
1. acaulis.　　　　　Stalkless Arctotis.
2. angustifolia.　　Narrow-leaved Arctotis.
3. aspera.　　　　　Rough-leaved Arctotis.
4. aurantia.　　　　Orange-coloured Arctotis.
5. plantaginea.　　Plantain-leaved Arctotis.
6. superba.　　　　Superb Arctotis.

20. ARISTOLOCHIA.

BIRTHWORT——(Fr.)—Aristoloche.

L. G. Pl. 1022.　　Gynandria Hexandria.　　Cl. 20. Ord. 5.

1. maxima.　　　　Great-flowered Birthwort.
2. Pistolochia.　　Notched-leaved Birthwort.
3. sempervirens.　Evergreen Birthwort.
4. Serpentaria.　　Virginian Snake-root.

21. ARTEMISIA.

MUGWORT.——(Fr.)—Armoise.

L. G. Pl. 945.　　Syngenesia Polygamia Superflua.　　Cl. 19. Ord. 2.

1. arborescens.　　Tree Wormwood.
2. campestris.　　　Wild Wormwood.
3. coerulescens.　　Lavender-leaved Wormwood.
4. nilotica.　　　　Ægyptian Wormwood.

22. ASCLEPIAS.

SWALLOW-WORT.

L. G. Pl. 306.　　Pentandra Digynia.　　Cl. 5. Ord. 2.
1. fruticosa.　　　Shrubby Swallow-wort.

23. ASCYRUM.

SAINT PETER's-WORT.

L. G. Pl. 903.　　Polyadelphia Polyandria.　　Cl. 11. Ord. 3.
1. Crux Andreæ.　　Maryland Saint Peter's-wort.

24. ASPARAGUS.

ASPARAGUS——(Fr.)—Afperge.

L. G. Pl. 424.   Hexandria Monogynia.   Cl. 6. Ord. 1

1. acutifolius.   Needle-leaved Afparagus.
2. albus.   White Deciduous Afparagus.
3. declinatus.   Briftly-leaved Afparagus.
4. retrofractus.   Larch-leaved Afparagus.
5. farmentofus.   Triple-fpined Afparagus.

25. ASPALATHUS.

ASPALATHUS, or AFRICAN BROOM.

L. G. Pl 860.   Diadelphia Decandria.   Cl. 17. Ord. 3.

1. chenopoda.   Hairy-flowered Afpalathus.
2. cretica.   Cretan Afpalathus.

26. ASPHODELUS.

ASPHODEL, or KING'S-PEAR.

L. G. Pl. 421.   Hexandria Monogynia.   Cl. 6. Ord. 1.

1. fiftulofus.   Leffer King's-pear.

27. ASTER.

STARWORT.

L. G. Pl. 954.   Syngenefia Polygamia Superflua.   Cl. 19. Ord. 2.
1. fruticofus.   Shrubby Starwort.

28. ATRAPHAXIS.

ATRAPHAXIS.

L. G. Pl. 449.   Polygamia Monoecia.   Cl. 23. Ord. 1.

1. undulata.   Waved-leaved Atraphaxis.

29. BACCHARIS.

PLOUGHMAN'S SPIKENARD.

L. G. Pl. 949.   Syngenesia Polygamia Superflua.   Cl. 19. Ord. 2.
1. ivæfolia.   Peruvian Ploughman's Spikenard.
2. neriifolia.   Oleander-leaved Ploughman's Sp.

30. BIGNONIA.

TRUMPET-FLOWER.

L. G. Pl. 759.   Didynamia Angiofpermia.   Cl. 14. Ord. 1.
1. Unguis cati.   Evergreen Trumpet-flower.

31. BONTIA.

BARBADOES WILD OLIVE.

L. G. Pl. 791.   Didynamia Angiofpermis.   Cl. 14. Ord. 2.
1. daphnoides.   Barbadoes Wild Olive.

32. BOSEA.

GOLDEN-ROD-TREE.

L. G. Pl. 315.   Pentandria Digynia.   Cl. 5. Ord. 2.
1. yervamora.   Golden-rod-tree.

33. BUBON.

MACEDONIAN PARSLEY.

L. G. Pl. 350.   Pentandria Digynia.   Cl. 5. Ord. 2.
1. Galbanum.   Gum Galbanum.
2. macedonicum.   Macedonian Parsley.

34. BUPHTHALMUM.

OX-EYE——(Fr.)—Oeil de Boeuf.

L. G. Pl. 977.   Syngenesia Polygamia Superflua.   Cl. 19. Ord. 2.
1. arborefcens.   Tree Ox-eye.
2. frutefcens.   Shrubby Ox-eye.
3. maritimus.   Sea Ox-eye.

35. BUPLEURUM.

HARE'S-EAR.

L. G. Pl. 328.   Pentandria Digynia.   Cl. 5. Ord. 2.

1. difforme.   Rush-leaved Hare's-ear.

36. CACALIA.

CACALIA, or FOREIGN COLTSFOOT.

L. G. Pl. 933.   Syngenesia Polygamia Æqualis.   Cl. 19. Ord. 1.

1. Anteuphorbium.
2. Ficoides.   Ficoides-leaved Cacalia.
3. Kleinia.   Cabbage-tree.
4. papillaris.   Thorny Cacalia.

37. CACTUS.

MELON THISTLE.

L. G. Pl. 613.   Icosandria Monogynia.   Cl. 12. Ord. 1.

1. mammillaris.   Red-spined Lesser Melon Thistle.
2. Melocactus.   Great Melon Thistle.
3. mitis.   Small Melon Thistle.

CACTUS-CEREUS.

TORCH-THISTLE——(Fr.)—Cierge-epineux.

1. flagelliformis.   Lesser Creeping Cereus.
2. grandiflorus.   Great Creeping Cereus.
3. heptagonus.   Seven-angled Torch-thistle.
4. hexagonus.   Six-angled Torch-thistle.
5. lanuginosus.   Woolly Torch-thistle.
6. pentagonus.   Five-angled Torch-thistle.
7. peruvianus.   Peruvian Torch-thistle.
8. repandus.   Obtuse-angled Torch-thistle.
9. Royeni.   Ten-angled Torch-thistle.
10. tetragonus.   Four-angled Torch-thistle.
11. triangularis.   Triangular Torch-thistle.

CACTUS-OPUNTIA.

INDIAN FIG——(Fr.)—Raquette.

1. cochinillifer.	Cochineal-bearing Indian Fig.
2. curaſſavicus.	Curaſſavian Indian Fig.
3. Ficus Indicus.	Many-jointed Indian Fig.
4. moniliformis.	Round-jointed Indian Fig.
5. Opuntia.	Indian Fig.
6. Pereſkia.	American Gooſeberry.
7. phyllanthus.	Spleenwort-leaved Indian Fig.
8. ſpinoſiſſimus.	Pricklieſt Indian Fig.
9. Tuna.	Branching-jointed Indian Fig.

N. B. A dry ſtove is the proper place for all the varieties of Cactus, except Cactus-Opuntia, No. 5

38. CALENDULA.

SHRUBBY AFRICAN MARYGOLD.

L. G. Pl. 990.   Syngeneſia Polygamia Neceſſaria.   Cl. 19. Ord. 4.

1. fruticoſa.	Shrubby African Marygold.
2. graminifolia.	Graſs-leaved African Marygold.

39. CALLA.

WAKE-ROBIN, or ARUM.

L. G. Pl. 1030.   Gynandria Polyandria.   Cl. 20. Ord. 4.

1. æthiopica.	Æthiopian Arum.

40. CALLICARPA.

CALLICARPA.

L. G. Pl. 135.   Tetrandria Monogynia.   Cl. 4. Ord. 1.

1. americana.	American Callicarpia.

41. CAMELLIA.

CAMELLIA.

L. G. Pl. 848.   Monadelphia Polyandria.   Cl. 16. Ord. 3.

1. japonica - - -	1.	Japoneſe Camellia.
2. *japonica plena* - -	2.	Double Japoneſe Camellia.

L

42. CAMPANULA.

BELL-FLOWER, or CAMPANULA——(Fr.)—Campanule.

L. G. Pl. 218.   Pentandria Monogynia.   Cl. 5. Ord. 1.

1. americana   * - - 1. American Campanula.
2. *americana alba* * - - 2. White American Campanula.
3. canarienfis.   Canary Campanula.

43. CAPPARIS.

CAPER-TREE——(Fr.)—Caprier.

L. G. Pl. 643.   Polyandria Monogynia.   Cl. 13. Ord. 1.

1. fpinofa.   Caper-tree.

44. CASSINE.

SOUTH-SEA TEA-TREE.

L. G. Pl. 371.   Pentandria Trigynia.   Cl. 5. Ord. 3.

1. Maurocenia   - - 1. Hottentot Cherry.
2. *Maurocenia minor* - 2. Smaller Hottentot Cherry.
3. Paragua.   *   Yapon, or South-Sea Tea-tree.
4. Phyllyrea.   Cape Phyllyrea.

45. CEANOTHUS.

CEANOTHUS.

L. G. Pl. 267.   Pentandria Monogynia.   Cl. 5. Ord. 1.

1. africanus.   African Ceanothus.

46. CELASTRUS.

STAFF-TREE.

L. G. Pl. 270.   Pentandria Monogynia.   Cl. 5. Ord. 1.

1. buxifolius.   Box-leaved Staff-tree.
2. Pyracanthus.   Pyracantha-leaved Staff-tree.

47. CENTAUREA.

CENTAURY——(Fr.)—Centaurée.

L. G. Pl. 984.   Syngenefia Polygamia Fruftranea.   Cl. 19. Ord. 3.

1. fruticofa.   Shrubby Centaury.
2. ragufina.   Ragufian Centaury.
3. fempervirens.   Evergreen Centaury.

48. CERATONIA.

CAROB-TREE, or SAINT JOHN's BREAD—(Fr.)—Carouge.

L. G. Pl. 1167.   Polygamia Trioecia.   Cl. 23. Ord. 1.
1. Siliqua.   Carob-tree.

49. CHENOPODIUM.

WILD ORACH.

L. G. Pl. 309.   Pentandria Digynia.   Cl. 5. Ord. 2.

1. anthelminticum.   Water Horehound-leaved Orach.
2. capenfe.   Cape Wild Orach.
3. multifidum.   Shrubby Orach.

50. CHIRONIA.

CHIRONIA, or SHRUBBY AFRICAN CENTAURY.

L. G. Pl. 255.   Pentandria Monogynia.   Cl. 5. Ord. 1

1. baccifera.   Berry-bearing Chironia.
2. frutefcens.   Capfular Chironia.

51. CHRYSANTHEMUM.

SHRUBBY CORN MARYGOLD.

L. G. Pl. 966.   Syngenefia Polygamia Superflua.   Cl. 19. Ord. 2.

1. flofculofum.   Cape Shrubby Corn Marygold.
2. frutefcens.   Canary Shrubby Corn Marygold.

52. CHRYSOCOMA.

GOLDEN LOCKS.

L. G. Pl. 939.　　Syngenesia Polygamia Æqualis.　　Cl. 19. Ord. 1.

1. cernua.　　　　　　Lesser Shrubby Golden Locks.
2. ciliata.　　　　　　Ciliated Shrubby Golden Locks.
3. Coma aurea.　　　　Greater Shrubby Golden Locks.

53. CINERARIA.

RAGWORT——(Fr.)—Jacobeé.

L. G. Pl. 957.　　Syngenesia Polygamia Superflua.　　Cl. 19. Ord. 2.

1. Amelloides.　　　　Opposite-leaved Cape Ragwort.
2. geifolia.　　　　　Avens-leaved Cape Ragwort.
3. othonnites.　　　　Alternate-leaved Cape Ragwort.

54. CISTUS.

CISTUS, or ROCK ROSE——(Fr.)—Ciste.

L. G. Pl. 673.　　Polyandria Monogynia.　　Cl. 13. Ord. 1.

1. albidus. 　*　　　　White-leaved Cistus.
2. creticus 　*　　　　Cretan Cistus.
3. crispus., 　*　　　　Curled-leaved Cistus.
4. halimifolius. 　*　　Sea-Purslane-leaved Cistus.
5. incanus. 　*　　　　Hoary-leaved Cistus.
6. pilosus. 　*　　　　Hairy-leaved Cistus.
7. populifolius. 　*　　Poplar-leaved Cistus.

Except in very severe Winters, these will live in the open ground.

55. CITRUS.

CITRON-TREE——(Fr.)—Citronier.

L. G. Pl. 901.　　Polyadelphia Icosandria.　　Cl. 18. Ord. 2.

1. Medica.　　　　　Citron-tree.

CITRUS-AURANTIUM.

ORANGE-TREE——(Fr.)—Oranger.

1. acris.　　　　　　　Seville Orange-tree.
2. chinensis - - - 1.　Chinese-Orange-tree.
3. chi. argenteo-varieg.- 2.　Silver-striped Chinese Orange-tree.

4. *chi. aureo-varieg.* - 3. Gold-ftriped Chinefe Orange-tree.
5. corniculata - - 1. Horned Orange-tree.
6. *corniculata aureo-var.* 2. Gold-ftriped Horned Orange-tree.
7. crifpa. Curled-leaved Orange-tree.
8. crifpa variegata. Gold-ftriped curled Orange-tree.
9. decumana. Shaddock Orange-tree.
10. hermaphrodita. Hermaphrodite Orange-tree.
11. humilis. Dwarf, or Nutmeg Orange-tree.
12. myrtifolia. Myrtle-leaved Orange-tree.
13. plena. Double flowering Orange-tree.
14. falicifolia - - 1. Willow-leaved, or Turkey Orange.
15. *falicifolia variegata* 2. Striped Willow-leaved Orange.
16. trifoliata. Three-leaved Orange-tree.

CITRUS—LIMON.
LEMON-TREE——(Fr.)—Limonier.

1. vulgaris - - - 1. Lemon-tree.
2. *vulgaris argenteo-var.* 2. Silver-ftriped Lemon-tree.
3. *vulgaris aureo-var.* 3. Gold-ftriped Lemon-tree.
4. dulcis. Sweet Lemon-tree.
5. imperialis. Imperial Lemon-tree.
6. plena. Double-flowered Lemon-tree.
7. Pomum Adami. Adam's-Apple Lemon-tree.
8. prolifera. Proliferous Lemon-tree.
9. pyriformis. Pear-fhaped Lemon-tree.

CITRUS—LIMA.
LIME-TREE——(Fr.)—Limonet.

1. americana. Lime-tree.
2. plena. Double-flowered Lime-tree.

56. CLIFFORTIA.
CLIFFORTIA.

L. G. Pl. 1133. Dioecia Polyandria. Cl. 22. Ord. 10.
1. ilicifolia. Ilex-leaved Cliffortia.

57. CLUTIA.
CLUTIA.

L. G. Pl. 1140. Dioecia Gynandria. Cl. 22. Ord. 13.
1. alaternoides. Narrow-leaved Clutia.
2. pulchella. Purflane-leaved Clutia.

L 3

58. COLUTEA.

BLADDER SENA——(Fr.)—Baguenaudier.

L. G. Pl. 880.   Diadelphia Decandria.   Cl. 17. Ord. 3.
1. frutefcens,   Scarlet Bladder Sena.

59. COMMELINA.

COMMELINA.

L. G. Pl. 61,   Triandria Monogynia.   Cl. 3. Ord. 1,
1. africana,   African Commelina.
2. criftata.   Crefted Commelina.
3. tuberofa.   Tuberous-rooted Commelina.

60. CONVOLVULUS.

BINDWEED——(Fr.)—Liferon.

L. G. Pl. 215.   Pentandria Monogynia.   Cl. 5. Ord. 1.
1. canarienfic.   Evergreen Canary Convolvulus.
2. Cantabrica.   Flax-leaved Convolvulus,
3. Cneorum.   Silver-leaved Convolvulus.

61. CONYZA,

FLEA-BANE——(Fr.)—Conife.

L. G. Pl. 950.   Syngenefia Polygamia Superflua,   Cl. 19. Ord. 2.
1. candida.   White-leaved Cretan Flea-bane.

62. CORONILLA.

CORONILLA, or JOINTED-PODDED COLUTEA.

L. G. Pl. 883.   Diadelphia Decandria.   Cl. 17. Ord. 4.
1. argentea,   Silver eleven-leaved Coronilla.
2. coronata.   Nine-leaved Coronilla.
3. glauca.   Seven-leaved Coronilla.
4. juncea.   Rufh-leaved Coronilla.
5. valentina,   Leffer Nine-leaved Coronilla.

63. COTYLEDON.

NAVELWORT.

L. G. Pl. 578.   Decandria Pentagynia.   Cl. 10. Ord. 4.
1. arborefcens.   Tree Navelwort.
2. hemifphærica,   Semiglobular-leaved Navelwort.

3. laciniata. Jagged-leaved Navelwort.
4. orbiculata. Round-leaved Navelwort.
5. ferrata. Sawed-leaved Navelwort.
6. fpuria. Long-leaved Navelwort.

64 CRASSULA.
ORPINE.

L. G. Pl. 392. Pentandria Pentagynia. Cl. 5. Ord. 5.
1. coccinea. Scarlet Orpine.
2. cultrata. Orpine-leaved Craffula.
3. perfoliata. Perfoliate-leaved Orpine.
4. Portulacaria. Purflane-leaved Orpine.
5. tetragona. Four-fquared-leaved Orpine.

65. CRINUM.
CRINUM, or LILY ASPHODEL.

L. G. Pl. 405. Hexandria Monogynia. Cl. 6. Ord. 1.
1. africanum. Blue African Crinum.

66. CROTALARIA.
CROTALARIA.

L. G. Pl. 862. Diadelphia Decandria. Cl. 17. Ord. 3.
1. laburnifolia. Laburnum-leaved Crotalaria.

67. CROTON.
BASTARD RICINUS.

L.G. Pl. 1083. Monoecia Monadelphia. Cl. 21. Ord. 9.
1. febiferum. Chinefe Tallow-tree.

68. CYCLAMEN.
SOW-BREAD, or CYCLAMEN——(Fr.)—Pain de Pourceau.
L. G. Pl. 201. Pentandria Monogynia. Cl. 5. Ord. 1.
1. perficum album * - 1. White Perfian Cyclamen.
2. *perficum carneum* * - 2. Flefh-coloured Perfian Cyclamen.

69. DIGITALIS.
FOXGLOVE.
L. G. Pl. 758. Didynamia Angiofpermia. Cl. 14. Ord. 2.
1. canarienfis. Shrubby Canary Foxglove.

L 4

70. DIOSMA.
DIOSMA, or AFRICAN SPIRÆA.

L. G. Pl. 272.   Pentandria Monogynia.   Cl. 5. Ord. 1.
  1. ciliata.   Ciliated-leaved Diosma.
  2. ericoides.   Heath-leaved Diosma.
  3. hirsuta.   Hairy-leaved Diosma.
  4. odorata.   Sweet-scented Diosma.
  5. oppositifolia.   Opposite-leaved Diosma.
  6. rubra.   Red-flowered Diosma.

71. DRACOCEPHALON.
DRAGON'S-HEAD.

L. G. Pl. 729.   Didynamia Gymnospermia.   Cl. 14. Ord. 1.
  1. canariense.   Canary Balm of Gilead.

72. EBENUS.
EBONY-TREE.

L. G. Pl. 895.   Diadelphia Decandria.   Cl. 17. Ord. 3.
  1. cretica.   Cretan Ebony-tree.

73. ELEPHANTOPUS.
ELEPHANT'S-FOOT.

L. G. Pl. 997.   Syngenesia Polygamia Segregata.   Cl. 19. Ord. 5.
  1. scaber.   Rough-leaved Elephant's foot.

74. EMPETRUM.
EMPETRUM, or CROW-BERRY.

L. G. Pl. 1100.   Dioecia Tetrandria.   Cl. 22. Ord. 4.
  1. album.   White Portugal Crow-berry.

75. ERICA.
HEATH——(Fr.)—Bruyere.

L. G. Pl. 484.   Octandria Monogynia.   Cl. 8. Ord. 1.
  1. mediterranea.   Mediterranean Heath.
  2. multiflora.   *   Many-flowered Heath.
  3. triflora.   *   Three-flowered African Heath.

76. ERIOCEPHALUS.
ERIOCEPHALUS.
L. G. Pl. 994.   Syngenesia Polygamia Necessaria.   Cl. 19. Ord. 4.
1. africanus.   African Eriocephalus.
2. pectinifolius.   Pectinated Eriocephalus.
3. racemosus.   Silvery narrow-leaved Eriocephalus.

77. ERYTHRINA.
CORAL-TREE.
L. G. Pl. 855.   Diadelphia Decandria.   Cl. 17. Ord. 3.
1. herbacea.   Carolinian Herbaceous Coral.

78. EUPHORBIA.
SPURGE——(Fr.)—Euphorbia——(Fr.)—Titimale.
L. G. Pl. 609.   Dodecandria Trigynia.   Cl. 11. Ord. 3.
1. amygdaloides - - 1.   Wood Spurge.
2. *amygd. variegatifolia* 2.   Striped-leaved Wood Spurge.
3. Caput Medusæ.   Medusa's-head Spurge.
4. Characias.   Red Spurge.
5. corallioides.   Red-stalked Spurge.
6. dendroides.   Cretan Spurge.
7. Tithymaloides.   Myrtle-leaved Spurge.
8. viminalis.   Naked African Spurge.

79. FERRARIA.
FERRARIA.
L. G. Pl. 1018.   Gynandria Triandria.   Cl. 20. Ord. 2.
1. undulata.   Waved-leaved Ferraria.

80. FERULA.
FENNEL-GIANT.
L. G. Pl. 343.   Pentandria Digynia.   Cl. 5. Ord. 2.
1. Ferulago.   Galbanum-bearing Fennel-giant.

81. GALENIA.
GALENIA.
L. G. Pl. 492.   Octandria Trigynia.   Cl. 8. Ord. 3.
1. africana.   Rosemary-leaved African Galenia.

82. GARDENIA.

GARDENIA, or CAPE JASMIN.

L. G. Pl. 296. Pentandria Monogynia. Cl. 5. Ord. 1,

1. florida - - - - 1. Cape Jasmin.
2. *florida plena* - - 2. Double-flowered Cape Jasmin.

83. GENISTA.

BROOM——(Fr.)—Genêt.

L. G. Pl. 859. Diadelphia Decandria. Cl. 17. Ord. 34,

1. canarienfis. Canary Broom.
2. candicans. * Montpelier Broom.

84. GERANIUM.

CRANE'S-BILL——(Fr.)—Bec de Grüe.

L. G. Pl. 832. Monadelphia Decandria. Cl. 16. Ord. 2,

1. acetofum.		Sorrel-leaved Crane's-bill Geranium
2. alchemilloides	⁊ ⅟	Ladies-Mantle-leaved Geranium.
3. Althæoides - - - ⅟		Marſh-mallow-leaved Geranium.
4. betulinum.		Birch-leaved Geranium.
5. capitatum.	•	Rofe-fcented Geranium.
6. carnofum.		Alcea-leaved Geranium.
7. coriandrifolium.		Coriander-leaved Geranium.
8. cucullatum - - 1.		Marſh-mallow-leaved Geranium.
9. *cucul. angulatum* - 2.		Angular Marſh-mallow-leaved Ge.
10. ferulaceum.		Fennel-leaved Geranium.
11. fulgidum.		Vervain-mallow-leaved Geranium.
12. gibbofum.		Columbine-leaved gouty-ſtalkedGe.
13. groſſularioides ⁊ ⅟		Goofeberry-leaved Geranium.
14. hirtum.		
15. inquinans.		Shining Mallow-leaved Geranium.
16. lobatum - - - ⅟		Vine-leaved Geranium.
17. maritimum.		Sea Geranium.
18. odoratiſſimum ⁊ ⅟		Mallow-leaved fweet-fcented Ger.
19. papillionaceum.		Pointed mallow-leaved ButterflyGe,
20. peltatum.		Ivy-leaved Geranium.
21. pinnatum - 7 - ⅟		Milk-Vetch-leaved Geranium.
22. prolificum - - - ⅟		Myrrh-leaved Night-fmelling Ger,
23. fcabrum.		Rough-leaved Geranium.
24. triſte - - - - ⅟		Night-fmelling Geranium.

multifidum ——
lanceolatum ——
+ *triquetrum* ——
+ *Terebinthinum* ——

+ 25. vitifolium - - 1. Vine-leaved Balm-fcented Geran.
26. *vitifolium argentatum* 2. Silver-edged Vine-leaved Geranium.
27. zonale - - - 1. Horfefhoe-leaved Geranium.
28. *zon. coccineum* - - 2. Scarlet-flowered Horfefhoe Geran.
29. *zon. argentatum* - - 3. Silver-edged Horfefhoe Geranium.
30. *zon. argenteo-var.* - 4. Silver-ftriped Geranium.
31. *zon. aureo-var.* - - 5. Scarlet Gold-ftriped Geranium.
32. *zon. var. grandifol.* - 6. Large Scarlet Gold-ftriped Geran,

85. GLADIOLUS.

Cornflag——(Fr.)—Glaieul.

L. G. Pl. 57.   Triandria Monogynia.   Cl. 3. Ord. 1.

1. anguftus.   Narrow-leaved Cornflag.
2. fpicatus.   Spiked-flowered Cornflag.
3. triftis.   Square-ftalked Cornflag.

86. GNAPHALIUM.

Cudweed, or Eternal-flower.

L. G. Pl. 946.   Syngenefia Polygamia Superflua.   Cl. 19. Ord. 2.

1. arboreum,   Tree Eternal-flower.
2. cymofum.   Long-leaved Eternal-flower.
3. niveum.   Snowy Eternal-flower.
4. odoratiffimum.   Sweet-fmelling Eternal-flower.
5. orientale.   Eaftern Eternal-flower.
6. patulum.   Spreading Eternal-flower.
7. Stoechas,   Eternal-flower.

87. GNIDIA.

Gnidia.

L. G. Pl. 487.   Octandria Monogynia,   Cl. 8. Ord. 1.
1. pinifolia.   White-flowering Gnidia.

88. GOMPHRENA.

Globe Amaranth, or Everlasting-flower.

L. G. Pl. 314.   Pentandria Digynia.   Cl. 5. Ord. 2.

1. globofa purpurea * 1. Purple Globe Amaranth.
2. *globofa argentea* * - 2. White Globe Amaranth.
3. *globofa ftriata* * - 3. Striped Globe Amaranth.

89. GORDONIA.

1. Lafianthus.   Loblolly Bay.

90. GORTERIA.
GORTERIA.

L. G. Pl. 982.   Syngenefia Polygamia Fruftranea.   Cl. 19. Ord. 3.
1. ciliaris.   Ciliated Gorteria.
2. ringens.   Narrow-leaved Gorteria.

91. GREWIA.
GREWIA.

L. G. Pl. 1026.   Gynandria Polyandria.   Cl. 20. Ord. 7.
1. occidentalis.   Elm-leaved Grewia.

92. HÆMANTHUS.
BLOODFLOWER, or AFRICAN TULIP.

L. G. Pl. 400.   Hexandria Monogynia.   Cl. 6. Ord. 1.
1. ciliaris.   Ciliated-leaved Hæmanthus.
2. coccineus.   Scarlet Hæmanthus.
3. puniceus.   Spotted-ftalked Hæmanthus.

93. HALLERIA.
AFRICAN FLY HONEYSUCKLE.

L. G. Pl. 761.   Didynamia Angiofpermia.   Cl. 14. Ord. 2.
1. lucida.   Shining-leaved African Fly Honeyf

94. HELIOTROPIUM.
TURNSOLE.

L. G. Pl. 179.   Pentandria Monogynia.   Cl. 5. Ord. 1.
1. fruticofum.   Shrubby Turnfole.
2. peruvianum.   Peruvian Sweet-fcented Turnfole.

95. HERMANNIA.
HERMANNIA.
L. G. Pl. 828. Monadelphia Pentandria. Cl. 16. Ord. 1.
1. alnifolia. Alder-leaved Hermannia.
2. althæifolia. Althæa-leaved Hermannia.
3. grossularifolia. Gooseberry-leaved Hermannia.
4. lavendulifolia. Lavender-leaved Hermannia.

96. HYOSCYAMUS.
HENBANE.
L. G. Pl. 247. Pentandria Monogynia. Cl. 5. Ord. 1.
1. aureus. Golden Cretan Henbane.

97. HYPERICUM.
SAINT JOHN'S-WORT.
L. G. Pl. 902. Polyadelphia Polyandria. Cl. 18. Ord. 3.
1. balearicum. Minorca warted St. John's-wort.
2. monogynum. Chinese St. John's-wort.

98. JASMINUM.
JASMIN——(Fr.)—Jafmin.
L. G. Pl. 17. Diandria Monogynia. Cl. 2. Ord. 1.
1. azoricum. Azorian Jafmin.
2. grandiflorum. Catalonian Jafmin.
3. odoratissimum. Yellow Indian Jafmin.

99. JUNIPERUS.
JUNIPER-TREE——(Fr.)—Genevrier.
L. G. Pl. 1134. Dioecia Monadelphia. Cl. 22. Ord. 12.
1. bermudiana. Bermudian Cedar-tree.

100. JUSTICIA.
MALABAR NUT-TREE.
L. G. Pl. 27. Diandria Monogynia. Cl. 2. Ord. 1.
1. Adhatoda. Malabar Nut-tree.

101. IBERIS.
TREE CANDY-TUFT.

L. G. Pl. 804.　Tetradynamia Siliculofa.　Cl. 15. Ord. 1.
1. femperflorens.　Everflowering Tree Candy-tuft.
2. fempervirens - - - 1.　Evergreen Tree Candy-tuft.
3. *fempervirens varieg.* 2.　Striped Evergreen Tree Candy-tuft.

102. ILLECEBRUM.
KNOT-GRASS.

L. G. Pl. 290.　Pentandria Monogynia.　Cl. 5. Ord. 1.
1. Paronychia.　Pyrenean Knot-grafs.

103. ILLICIUM.
ILLICIUM.

L. G. Pl. 611.　Dodecandria Dodecagynia.　Cl. 11. Ord. 6.
1. anifatum.　Chinefe Illicium.

104. IXIA.
IXIA.

L. G. Pl. 56.　Triandria Monogynia.　Cl. 3. Ord. 1.
1. africana.　Woolly-flowered Ixia.
2. bulbifera.　Bulbiferous yellowifh-white Ixia.
3. chinenfis.　Chinefe fpotted yellow Ixia.
4. crocata.　White blue-ftriped Ixia.
5. flexuofa.　White bending-ftalked Ixia.
6. polyftachia.　White many-fpiked Ixia.
7. fcillaris.　Blue-fpiked Ixia.

105. KIGGELARIA.
KIGGELARIA.

L. G. Pl. 1128.　Dioecia Decandria.　Cl. 22. Ord. 9.
1. africana.　African Kiggelaria.

106. LANTANA.
AMERICAN VIBURNUM.

L. G. Pl. 765.　Didynamia Angiofpermia.　Cl. 14. Ord. 2.
1. africana　Ilex-leaved Jeffamine.
2. falvifolia.　Sage-leaved American Viburnum.

107. LAVANDULA.
LAVENDER——(Fr.)—Lavande.

L. G. Pl. 711.　　Didynamia Gymnofpermia.　　Cl. 14. Ord. 1.
1. dentata.　　　　Sawed-leaved Lavender.
2. multifida.　　　Jagged-leaved Canary Lavender.

108. LAVATERA.
LAVATERA.

L. G. Pl. 842.　　Monadelphia Polyandria.　　Cl. 16. Ord. 3.
1. olbia.　　　　　Small-flowered Lavatera.

109. LAURUS.
BAY-TREE——(Fr.)—Laurier.

L. G. Pl. 503.　　Enneandria Monogynia.　　Cl. 19. Ord. 1.
1. æftivalis.　　　Deciduous Bay-tree.
2. Borbonia. *　　Carolinian Blue-berried Bay-tree.
3. Camphora.　　　Camphire-tree.
4. indica.　　　　Portugal, or Royal Bay-tree.

110. LIMODORUM.
LIMODORUM.

L. G. Pl. 1013.　　Gynandria Diandria.　　Cl. 20. Ord. 1.
1. tuberofum.　　Tuberous-rooted American Limod.

111. LINUM.
FLAX.

L. G. Pl. 389.　　Pentandria Pentagynia.　　Cl. 5. Ord. 5.
1. maritimum.　　Montpelier Yellow-flowered Flax.

112. LOBELIA.
CARDINAL-FLOWER.

L. G. Pl. 1006.　　Syngenefia Monogamia.　　Cl. 19. Ord. 6.
1. Cardinalis. *　　Cardinal-flower.
2. fiphilitica. *　　Blue Virginian Cardinal-flow.

113. LOTUS.

BIRD'S-FOOT TREFOIL——(Fr.)—Lotier.

L. G. Pl. 897.   Diadelphia Decandria.   Cl. 17. Ord. 3.

1. creticus.   Cretan Silver-leaved Lotus.
2. Dorycnium.   Montpelier White Lotus.
3. hirfutus. *   Tall Hairy Bird's-foot Trefoil.
4. jacobæus.   Purple and yellow Lotus.
5. maritimus. *   Sea Bird's-foot Trefoil.
6. rectus. *   Upright Bird's-foot Trefoil.

114. LYCIUM.

BOXTHORN.

L. G. Pl. 262.   Pentandria Monogynia.   Cl. 5. Ord. 1.

1. afrum.   African Boxthorn.
2. capfulare.   Mexican Boxthorn.

115. MEDEOLA.

CLIMBING AFRICAN ASPARAGUS.

L. G. Pl. 455.   Hexandria Trigynia.   Cl. 6. Ord. 3.

1. anguftifolia.   Narrow Myrtle-leaved Afparagus.
2. afpargoides.   Myrtle-leaved Afparagus.

116. MEDICAGO.

MOON-TREFOIL.

L. G. Pl. 899.   Diadelphia Decandria.   Cl. 17. Ord. 3.

1. arborea.   Shrubby Moon-trefoil.

117. MELIA.

BEAD-TREE.

L. G. Pl. 537.   Decandria Monogynia.   Cl. 10. Ord. 1.

1. Azedarac   Bipinnated Bead-tree.
   Azediracta.   Pinnated Bead-tree.

118. MELIANTHUS.
HONEY-FLOWER.

L. G. Pl. 795.   Didynamia Angiofpermia.   Cl. 14. Ord. 2.
1. major.   *   Honey-flower.
2. minor.   Small Stinking Honey-flower.

119. MENTHA.
MINT——(Fr.)—Menthe.

L. G. Pl. 713.   Didynamia Gymnofpermia.   Cl. 14. Ord. 1.
1. canarienfis.   Shrubby Canary Mint.

120. MESEMBRYANTHEMUM.
FIG-MARYGOLD, or FICOIDES.

L. G. Pl. 628.   Icofandria Pentagynia.   Cl. 12. Ord. 4.

   * *Albis Corollis.*   *With white Corollas.*

1. calamiforme.   Quill-leaved Ficoides.
2. copticum. ☉   Coptic Ficoides.
3. cryftallinum. ☉   Diamond Ficoides.
4. geniculiflorum.   Jointed-ftalked Ficoides.
5. noctiflorum - * 1.   Purple and white Night-flow. Fic.
6. *noctifl. ftramineum* - 2.   Straw-colour and white Nightfl. Fic.
7. nodiflorum. ☉   Ægyptian Kali, or Ficoides.
8. fplendens.   Shining-leaved Ficoides.
9. umbellatum.   Umbellated Ficoides.
10. Tripolium.   Tripolium-leaved Ficoides.

   ** *Rubicundis Corollis.*   *With reddifh Corollas.*

1. acinaciforme.   Scymeter-leaved Ficoides.
2. barbatum - - - 1.   Bearded Ficoides.
3. *barbatum majus* - 2.   Greater Bearded Ficoides.
4. *barbatum minus* - 3.   Leffer Bearded Ficoides.
5. bellidiflorum.   Daify-flowered Ficoides.
6. craffifolium.   Thick-leaved Creeping Ficoides.
7. deltoide - - - 1.   Delta-leaved Ficoides.
8. *deltoide majus* - - 2.   Great Delta-leaved Ficoides.
9. *deltoide minus* - - 3.   Leffer Delta-leaved Ficoides.
10. emarginatum.   Notched-flowered Ficoides.
11. falcatum.   Crooked-leaved Ficoides.
12. filamentofum.   Six-angled-ftalked Ficoides.
13. forficatum.   Forked Ficoides.

M

14. glomeratum.   Glomerated Ficoides:
15. hifpidum - - - 1.   Briftly-ftalked Ficoides.
16. *hifpidum purpurafcens* 2.   Pale purple Briftly-ftalked Ficoides,
17. *hifpidum ftriatum* - 3.   Striped Briftly-ftalked Ficoides.
18. loreum.   Leathery-ftalked Ficoides.
19. fcabrum.   Rough-leaved Ficoides.
20. fpinofum.   Thorny Ficoides.
21. ftipulaceum.   Upright Ficoides.
22. tenuifolium.   Slender-leaved Ficoides.
23. tuberofum.   Tuberous-rooted Ficoides.
24. villofum.   Hairy-ftalked Ficoides.
25. uncinatum - - 1.   Buck's-horn Ficoides.
26. *uncinatum majus* - 2.   Great Buck's-horn Ficoides.
     *** *Luteis Corollis.*   *With yellow Corollas.*

1. albidum.   White-leaved Ficoides.
2. bicolore.   Yellow and purple Ficoides.
3. corniculatum - - 1.   Horned-leaved Ficoides.
4. *corniculatum breve* - 2.   Short-horned-leaved Ficoides.
5. difforme.   Deformed-leaved Ficoides.
6. dolabriforme.   Hatchet-leaved Ficoides.
7. edule.   Eatable-fruited Ficoides.
8. expanfum.   Expanded-leaved Ficoides.
9. felinum.   Cat's-chap Ficoides.
10. glaucum.   Glaucous-leaved Ficoides.
11. linguiforme - - 1.   Tongue-leaved Ficoides.
12. *linguiforme anguftum* 2.   Narrow Tongue-leaved Ficoides,
13. *linguiforme latum* - - 3.   Broad Tongue-leaved Ficoides.
14. *linguiforme longum* - 4.   Long Tongue-leaved Ficoides.
15. micans.   Glittering Ficoides.
16. pomeridianum. ☉   Afternoon-flowering Ficoides,
17. pugioniforme.   Dagger-leaved Ficoides.
18. ringens - - - 1.   Ringent-flowered Ficoides.
19. *ringens caninum* - - 2.   Dog's-chap Ficoides.
20. roftratum.   Heron's-billed Ficoides.
21. ferratum.   Serrated-leaved Ficoides.
22. tortuofum.   Twifted-leaved Ficoides.
23. verruculatum.   Warted-leaved Ficoides.

The following are defcribed by Miller, &c.

1. aureum.   Gold-coloured-flowered Ficoides.
2. auftriale.   Auftrian Ficoides.
3. decumbens.   Trailing Ficoides.
4. fubulatum.   Awl-fhaped-leaved Ficoides.

THE
MESEMBRYANTHEMA
Have also been arranged by LINNÆUS in the following Manner.

ANNUA——ANNUAL:
Copticum, cryſtallinum, nodiflorum,——pomeridianum.

ACAULIA——WITHOUT STALKS:
Calamiforme—bellidiflorum—albidum, difforme, dolabriforme,
linguiforme, ringens, roſtratum.

LAXA, CAULE PENDULO—SUPPLE, WITH A PENDULOUS STALK:
Tripolium—acinaciforme, craſſifolium, loreum, filamentoſum,
forficatum, tenuifolium——corniculatum, edule,
expanſum, pomeridianum, tortuoſum.

FRUTICOSA, CAULE LIGNOSO DURO—SHRUBBY, WITH A HARD WOODY STALK:
Calamiforme, noctiflorum, ſplendens, umbellatum—barbatum,
deltoide, emarginatum, falcatum, glomeratum, hiſpidum,
ſpinoſum, ſcabrum, ſtipulaceum, tuberoſum, villoſum,
uncinatum—bicolor, glaucum, micans, pugi-
oniforme, ſerratum, verruculatum.

ALTERNIFOLIA——ALTERNATE-LEAVED:
Cryſtallinum, nodiflorum, Tripolium—pugioniforme.

LATIFOLIA——BROAD-LEAVED:
Cryſtallinum, nodiflorum, Tripolium, pugioniforme.

TETRAGYNA——TETRAGYNEOUS:
Geniculiflorum, noctiflorum—tortuoſum.

DECAGYNA——DECAGYNEOUS:
Linguiforme, pomeridianum, pugioniforme.

121. MORÆA.

MORÆA.

L. G. Pl. 60. Triandria Monogynia. Cl. 15. Ord. 1.
1. vegeta. Channelled-leaved Moræa.

122. MYRICA.

CANDLEBERRY MYRTLE.

L. G. Pl. 1107. Dioecia Pentandria. Cl. 22. Ord. 5.
1. cordifolia. Kermes-Oak-leaved Myrica.
2. quercifolia - - 1. Oak-leaved Myrica.
3. *quercifolia hirfuta* - 2. Hairy Oak-leaved Myrica.

123. MYRSINE.

MYRSINE.

L. G. Pl. 269. Pentandria Monogynia· Cl. 5: Ord. 1.
1. africana. African Myrfine.

124. MYRTUS.

MYRTLE-TREE——(Fr.)—Mirte.

L. G. Pl. 628. Icofandria Monogynia· Cl. 12. Ord. 1.
1. latifolia * - *(romana)* 1. Broad-leaved Roman Myrtle.
2. *latifolia notata* - - 2. Gold-tipped Broad-leaved Ro. Myr.
3. *trilatifolia* - - - 3. Three-leaved, or Jews Myrtle.
4. aurantiifolia. (*bœtica*) Orange-leaved Spanifh Myrtle.
5. plena - - - *(plena)* Double-flowering Myrtle.
6. belgica - - - - - Dutch Myrtle.
7. lufitanica - - - - ' Portugal acute-pointed Myrtle.
8. mofchata - - - 1. Nutmeg Myrtle.
9. *mofch. argenteo ftriata* 2. Silver-ftriped Nutmeg Myrtle.
10. *mofch. argenteo var.* - 3. Blotched-leaved Nutmeg Myrtle.
11. criftata (*criftata*) 1. Bird's-neft, or Cockscomb Myrtle.
12. *crift. aureo punctata* 2. Gold-dotted Cockscomb Myrtle.
13. *crift. argenteo varieg.* 3. Silver-ftriped Cockscomb Myrtle.
14. erecta * - *(italica)* · 1· Upright Italian Myrtle.
15. *erec. argenteo varieg.* 2. Silver-ftriped Italian Myrtle.
16. *erec. aureo varieg.* - 3. Gold-ftriped Italian Myrtle.
17. *erec. rufcifolia* - - 4. Butchers-broom leaved Italian Myr.
18. buxifolia *(tarentina)* 1. Box-leaved Myrtle.

19. *buxifolia aureo-var.* 2.   Gold-ftriped Box-leaved Myrtle.
20. thymif. (*mucronata*) 1.   Thyme-leaved Myrtle.
21. *thymif. arg. varieg.* 2.   Striped Thyme-leaved Myrtle.

The word in the parenthefis is the Trivial name of Linnæus; four of which I have changed, to make them correfpond better with the defcription of the Plant, and have arranged the above according to the fize of the Leaves.

125. NERIUM.

OLEANDER, or ROSE-BAY——(Fr.)—Laurier-Rofe.

L. G. Pl. 297.   Pentandria Monogynia.   Cl. 5. Ord. 1.

1. divaricatum.   White fweet-fcented Oleander.
2. latifolium - - - 1.   Double Oleander.
3. *lativariegatifolium* - 2.   Striped-leaved Double Oleander.
4. Oleander - - - 1.   Red Oleander.
5. *Oleander album* - - 2.   White Oleander.

126. OLEA.

OLIVE-TREE——(Fr.)—Olivier.

L. G. Pl. 20.   Diandria Monogynia.   Cl. 2. Ord. 1.

1. africana.   African Olive.
2. americana.   American Olive.
3. buxifolia.   *   Box-leaved African Olive.
4. gallo-provincialis. *   Provence Olive.
5. hifpanica.   *   Spanifh Olive.

127. ONONIS.

REST-HARROW——(Fr.)—Arrete Boeuf.

L. G. Pl. 863.   Diadelphia Decandria.   Cl. 17. Ord. 3.

1. crifpa.   Curled-leaved Reft-harrow.
2. Natrix.   Yellow Reft-harrow.
3. rotundifolia.   Round-leaved Reft-harrow.

128. ORIGANUM.

MARJORAM.

L. G. Pl. 726.   Didynamia Gymnofpermia.   Cl. 14. Ord. 1.

1. ægyptiacum.   Ægyptian Marjoram.
2. Dictamnus.   Cretan Dittany.

M 3

3. Majorana.   Sweet Marjoram.
4. Sipyleum - - - 1.   Marjoram of Mount Sipylus.
5. *Sipyleum hirfutum* - 2.   Hairy Marjoram of Mount Sipylus.

124. OSTEOSPERMUM.

HARD-SEEDED CHRYSANTHEMUM.

L. G. Pl. 992.   Syngenefia Polygamia Neceffaria.   Cl. 19. Ord. 4.

1. moniliferum.   Poplar-leaved Ofteofpermum.
2. pififerum.   Cape Ofteofpermum.

130. OTHONNA.

RAGWORT:

L. G. Pl. 993.   Syngenefia Polygamia Neceffaria.   Cl. 19 Ord. 4.

1. abrotanifolia.   Southernwood-leaved Ragwort.
2. arborefcens.   Tree Ragwort.
3. bulbofa.   Wedged-fhaped-leaved Ragwort,
4. coronopifolia.   Sea Ragwort.
5. pectinata.   Winged-leaved Ragwort.

131. OXALIS.

OXALIS, or WOOD-SORREL.

L. G. Pl. 582,   Decandria Pentandria.   Cl. 1c. Ord. 4.

1. flava.   Yellow Wood-Sorrel,
2. incarnata.   Flefh-coloured Wood-Sorrel.
3. Pes Capræ.   Umbelliferous Wood-Sorrel.
4. trifoliata purpurea - 1.   Three-leaved Purple Wood-Sorrel.
5. *trifoliata alba* - 2.   Three-leaved White Wood-Sorrel.
6. *trifoliata kermefina* - 3.   Three-leaved Crimfon Wood-Sor.

132. PASSERINA.

SPARROW-WORT.

L. G. Pl. 489.   Octandria Monogynia.   Cl. 10. Ord. 1.

1. filiformis.   Linear-leaved White Pafferina,

133. PERIPLOCA.
VIRGINIAN SILK.

L. G. Pl. 303.   Pentandria Digynia.   Cl. 5. Ord. 2.
1. africana.   African Periploca.
2. fruticofa.   Shrubby Periploca.

134. PHLOMIS.
SAGE-TREE.

L. G. Pl. 723.   Didynamia Gymnofpermia.   Cl. 14. Ord. 1
1. Leonurus.   African Lion's-tail.
2. nepetæfolia.   Cat-mint-leaved Lion's-tail.
3. purpurea.   Purple Phlomis.

135. PHYLICA.
BASTARD ALATERNUS, or AFRICAN HEATH.

L. G. Pl. 266.   Pentandria Monogynia.   Cl. 5. Ord. 1.
1. buxifolia.   Box-leaved Phylica.
2. ericoides.   Heath-leaved Phylica.

136. PHYLLIS.
BASTARD HARE'S-EAR.

L. G. Pl. 323.   Pentandria Digynia.   Cl. 5. Ord. 2.
1. Nobla.   Canary Phyllis.

137. PHYSALIS.
WINTER CHERRY.

L. G. Pl. 250.   Pentandria Monogynia.   Cl. 5. Ord. 1.
1. fomnifera.   Somniferous Winter Cherry.

138. PISTACIA.
PISTACHIA NUT, or TURPENTINE-TREE.

L. G. Pl. 1108.   Dioecia Tetrandria.   Cl. 22. Ord. 4.
1. Lentifcus.   Maftich-tree.
2. Terebinthus. *   Turpentine-tree.
3. trifolia. *   Three-leaved Turpentine-tree.
4. vera. *   Piftachia-Nut-tree.

M 4

139. POLEMONIUM.
GREEK VALERIAN.

L. G. Pl. 217.   Pentandria Monogynia.   Cl. 5. Ord. 1.
1. rubrum.   Red Greek Valerian.

140. POLYGALA.
MILKWORT.

L. G. Pl. 851.   Diadelphia Octandria.   Cl. 17. Ord. 2.
1. myrtifolia.   Myrtle-leaved African Milkwort.

141. POLYPODIUM.
POLYPODY.

L. G. Pl. 1179.   Crytogamia Filix.   Cl. 24. Ord. 1.
1. lusitanicum.   Portugal Polypody.

142. POTERIUM.
GARDEN BURNET.

L. G. Pl. 1069.   Monoecia Polyandria.   Cl. 21. Ord. 8.
1. spinosum.   Shrubby Cretan Burnet.

143. PRASIUM.
HEDGE-NETTLE.

L. G. Pl. 737.   Didynamia Gymnospermia.   Cl. 14. Ord. 1.
1. majus.   Cretan Hedge Nettle.

144. PRINOS.
WINTER BERRY.

L. G. Pl. 441.   Hexandria Monogynia.   Cl. 6. Ord. 1.
1. glaber.   Winter Berry.

145. PROTEA.
SILVER-TREE.

L. G. Pl. 111.   Tetrandria Monogynia.   Cl. 4. Ord. 1.
1. argentea.   Broad-leaved Silver-tree.
2. conifera.   Narrow-leaved Silver-tree.

146. PSORALEA.
PSORALEA.

L. G. Pl. 894.   Diadelphia Decandria.   Cl. 17. Ord. 3.
1. aculeata.   Prickly-leaved blue Pforalea.
2. bituminofa.   Three-leaved Pforalea.
3. cytifoides.   Red-fpiked Cape Pforalea.
4. pinnata.   Pinnated Pforalea.

147. PUNICA.
POMEGRANATE-TREE——(Fr.)—Grenadier.

L. G. Pl. 618.   Icofandria Monogynia.   Cl. 12. Ord. 1.
1. nana. *   Dwarf Pomegranate-tree.

148. RANDIA.

L. G. Pl. 111.   Pentandria Monogynia.   Cl. 5. Ord. 1.
1. aculeata.   Prickly Randia.

149. RHUS.
SUMAC——(Fr.)—Sumac.

L. G. Pl. 369.   Pentandria Digynia.   Cl. 5. Ord. 1.
1. anguftifolium.   Narrow-leaved Sumach.
2. incanum.   Hoary-leaved Sumach.
3. lucidum - - - 1.   Shining-leaved Sumach.
4. *lucidum minus* - - 2.   Small Shining-leaved Sumach.
5. tomentofum.   Downy-leaved Sumach.

150. ROSA.
ROSE-TREE——(Fr.)—Rofier.

L. G. Pl. 631.   Icofandria Polygynia.   Cl. 12. Ord. 5.
1. chinenfis. *   Chinefe Rofe-tree.

151. ROSMARINUS.

ROSEMARY——(Fr.)—Romarin.

L. G. Pl. 38.   Diandria Monogynia.   Cl. 2. Ord. 1.

1. argenteo variegata * 1.   Silver-ftriped Rofemary.
2. *aureo variegata* * - 2.   Gold-ftriped Rofemary.

152. ROYENA.

ROYENA, or AFRICAN BLADDER-NUT-TREE.

L. G. Pl. 355.   Decandria Digynia.   Cl. 10. Ord. 2.

1. glabra.   Smooth-leaved Royena.
2. hirfuta.   Hairy-leaved Royena.
3. lucida.   Shining-leaved Royena.

153. RUSCUS.

BUTCHER'S-BROOM.

L. G. Pl. 1139.   Dioecia Syngenefia.   Cl. 22. Ord. 13.

1. Androgynus.   *   Broad-leaved Alexandrian Laurel.
2. Hypophyllum. *   Broad-leaved Butcher's-Broom.

154. SALVIA.

SAGE——(Fr.)—Sauge.

L. G. Pl. 39.   Octandria Monogynia.   Cl. 8. Ord. 1.

1. ægyptiaca.   Ægyptian Sage.
2. africana.   African Sage.
3. aurea.   Gold-flowered Sage.
4. canarienfis.   Canary Sage.
5. mexicana.   Mexican Sage.

155. SAPINDUS.

SOAP-BERRY-TREE.

L. G. Pl. 499.   Octandria Trigynia.   Cl. 8. Ord. 3.

1. Saponaria.   American Soap-berry-tree.

156. SCABIOSA.

SCABIOUS——(Fr.)—Scabieufe,

L. G. Pl. 115.   Tetrandria Monogynia.   Cl. 4. Ord. 1,

1. africana.   African Scabious.
2. argentea.   Silvery Scabious.
3. cretica.   Cretan Scabious.
4. rigida.   Stiff-leaved Scabious,

157. SCHINUS.

INDIAN MASTICK.

L. G. Pl. 1130.   Dioecia Decandria,   Cl. 22. Ord. 9.

1. Areira.   Brafilian Maftick.
2. Molle.   Peruvian Maftick.

158. SCROPHULARIA.

FIGWORT——(Fr.)—Scrofulaire.

L. G. Pl. 756.   Didynamia Angiofpermia.   Cl. 14. Ord. 2.

1. fambucifolia,   Elder-leaved Figwort.

159. SELAGO.

SELAGO.

L. G. Pl. 769.   Didynamia Angiofpermia.   Cl. 14. Ord. 2.

1. corymbofa.   Linear-leaved Selago.
2. fpuria.   Thread-leaved Selago,

160. SEMPERVIVUM.

HOUSELEEK, or SEDUM.

L. G. Pl. 612.   Dodecandria Polygynia.   Cl. 11. Ord. 1.

1. arachnoideum.   Cobweb Sedum.
2. arboreum - - - - 1.   Tree Houfeleek.
3. *arbor. argenteo-var.* - 2.   Silver-ftriped Tree Houfeleek.
4. *arbor. aureo-var.* - - 3.   Gold-ftriped Tree Houfeleek.
5. canarienfe.   Canary Sedum,

161. SIDEROXYLON.

IRON-WOOD.

L. G. Pl. 264.	Pentandria Monogynia,	Cl. 5. Ord. 1.
1. inerme.	Broad-leaved Ironwood.	
2. oppofitifolium.	Oppofite-leaved Ironwood.	

162. SILENE.

VISCOUS CAMPION.

L. G. Pl. 567.	Decandria Trigynia.	Cl. 10. Ord. 3.
1. fruticofa.	Myrtle-leaved Vifcous Campion.	

163. SMILAX.

ROUGH BINDWEED.

L. G. Pl. 1120.	Dioecia Hexandria.	Cl. 22. Ord. 6.
1. afpera. *	Rough Bindweed.	
2. excelfa.	Oriental Climber.	

164. SOLANUM.

NIGHTSHADE.

L. G. Pl. 251.	Pentandria Monogynia.	Cl. 5. Ord. 1.
1. guinenfe.	Black Nightfhade.	
2. Pfeudocapficum.	White Cherry, or Amomum Plinii,	
3. quercifolium.	Oak-leaved Nightfhade.	
4. fodomeum.		
5. tomentofum.	Hoary-leaved Nightfhade.	
6. verbafcifolium.	Moth-Mullein-leaved Nightfhade.	

165. SOLDANELLA.

SOLDANEL.

L. G. Pl. 199.	Pentandria Monogynia.	Cl. 5. Ord. 1.
1. alpina.	Alpine Soldanel.	

166. SPARTIUM.

BROOM.

L. G. Pl. 853.   Diadelphia Decandria.   Cl. 17. Ord. 3.
1. radiatum. *   Starry Broom.
2. spinosum.   Thorny Broom.

167. STAPELIA.

STAPELIA.

L. G. Pl. 307.   Decandria Digynia.   Cl. 10. Ord. 2.
1. hirsuta.   Hairy Stapelia.
2. variegata.   Variegated Stapelia.

168. STATICE.

THRIFT, or SEA PINK.

L. G. Pl. 388.   Pentandria Pentagynia.   Cl. 5. Ord. 5.
1. monopetala.   Plantain-leaved Sea-Lavender.
2. speciosa.   Broad-leaved Sea-Lavender.
3. suffruticosa.   Shrubby Sea-Lavender.
4. tatarica.   Tartarian Sea-Lavender.

169. STYRAX.

STORAX-TREE.

L. G. Pl. 595.   Dodecandria Monogynia.   Cl. 11. Ord. 1.
1. officinale.   Storax-tree.

170. TANACETUM.

TANSEY——(Fr.)—Tanesie.

L. G. Pl. 944.   Syngenesia Polygamia Superflua.   Cl. 19. Ord. 2.
1. fruticosum.   Lavender-leaved Shrubby Tansey.
2. suffruticosum.

171. TARCHONANTHUS.

SHRUBBY AFRICAN FLEABANE.

L. G. Pl. 940.   Syngenesia Polygamia Æqualis.   Cl. 19. Ord. 1.
1. camphoratus.   Shrubby African Fleabane.

172. TETRAGONIA.

TETRAGONIA.

L. G. Pl. 627.   Icofandria Pentagynia.   Cl. 12. Ord. 4.
1. fruticofa.   Shrubby Tetragonia.
2. herbacea.   Herbaceous Tetragonia.

173. TEUCRIUM.

TREE GERMANDER.

L. G. Pl. 706.   Didynamia Gymnofpermia.   Cl. 14. Ord. 1.
1. fruticans.   Tree Germander.
2. latifolium.   Broad-leaved Tree Germander.
3. Marum.   Syrian Maftick, or Marum.
4. Polium.   Shrubby Mountain Poley.

174. THYMBRA.

MOUNTAIN HYSSOP.

L. G. Pl. 708.   Didynamia Gymnofpermia.   Cl. 14. Ord. 1.
1. fpicata.   Spiked Mountain Hyffop.
2. verticillata.   Verticillated Mountain Hyffop.

175. THYMUS.

THYME——(Fr.)—Thim.

L. G. Pl. 727.   Didynamia Gymnofpermia.   Cl. 14. Ord. 1.
1. maftichinus.   Maftick Thyme.
2. Zygis.   Narrow-leaved Upright Thyme.

176. TRACHELIUM.

THROATWORT.

L. G. Pl. 221.   Pentandria Monogynia.   Cl. 5. Ord. 1.
1. cœruleum.   Blue Throatwort.

177. TRICHOMANES.

MAIDENHAIR.

L. G. Pl. 1181.   Cryptogamia Filix.   Cl. 24. Ord. 1.
1. canarienfis.   Canary Maidenhair.

178. TRIOPTERIS.

TRIOPTERIS.

L. G. Pl. 574. Decandria Trigynia. Cl. 10. Ord. 3.
1. jamaicenſis. Jamaica Triopteris.

179. TROPÆOLUM.

INDIAN CRESS, or NASTURTIUM.

L. G. Pl. 466. Octandria Monogynia. Cl. 8. Ord. 1.
1. majus plenum. Indian Creſs, or Double Naſturtium.

180. VERBENA.

VERVAIN.

L. G. Pl. 32. Diandria Monogynia. Cl. 2. Ord. 1.
1. bonarienſis. Tall Buenos-Ayres Vervain.

181. VIBURNUM.

WAYFARING-TREE——(Fr.)—Viorne.

L. G. Pl. 370. Pentandria Trigynia. Cl. 5. Ord. 5.
1. glabrum. Smooth Wayfaring-tree.

182. VITEX.

CHASTE-TREE.

L. G. Pl. 790. Didynamia Angioſpermia. Cl. 14. Ord. 2.
1. Negundo. Chineſe Chaſte-tree.
2. trifoliata. Three-leaved Chaſte-tree.

183. WACHENDORFIA.

WACHENDORFIA.

L. G. Pl. 61. Triandria Monogynia. Cl. 3. Ord. 1.
1. thyrſiflora. Single-ſtalked Wachendorfia.

184. XERANTHEMUM.

ETERNAL FLOWER.

L. G. Pl. 947. Syngeneſia Polygamia Superflua. Cl. 19. Ord. 2.
1. reflexum. Reflexed Everlaſting Flower.

185. YUCCA.

Yucca, or Adam's Needle.

L. G. Pl. 429.   Hexandria Monogynia.   Cl. 6. Ord. 1.

1. aloifolia.   *   Aloe-leaved Adam's Needle.
2. draconis.   Dragon-leaved Yucca.
3. filamentofa.   *   Virginian thready-leaved Yucca.
4. gloriofa.   *   Adam's Needle.

186. ZANTHOXYLON.

Tooth-ach-tree.

L. G. Pl. 1109.   Dioecia Pentandria.   Cl. 22. Ord. 5.

1. fempervirens.   Evergreen Tooth-ach-tree.

187. ZYGOPHYLLON.

Bean Caper.

L. G. Pl. 530.   Decandria Monogynia.   Cl. 10. Ord. 1.

1. Morgfana.   Four-leaved Bean Caper.
2. feffilifolium.   Seffile-leaved Bean Caper.

As feveral Plants, commonly preferved in Greenhoufes, thrive better when planted in the open Ground, and will live in mild Winters, it was neceffary to infert them here, as well as in the Catalogue of Hardy plants, which are marked with an Afterifm.

CHAP.

CHAP. IV.

STOVE PLANTS.

1. ACHYRANTHES.
ACHYRANTHES.

L. G. Pl. 288.	Pentandria Monogynia.	Cl. 5. Ord. 1.
1. aspera.	Rough Upright Achyranthes.	
2. lappacea.	Climbing Achyranthes.	

2. ADANSONIA.
BAHOBOB, or SOUR-GOURD.

L. G. Pl. 836.	Monadelphia Polyandria.	Cl. 16. Ord. 5.
1. Bahobab.	Æthiopian Sour-gourd.	

3. ÆSCHYNOMENE.
BASTARD SENSITIVE PLANT.

L. G. Pl. 888.	Diadelphia Decandria.	Cl. 17. Ord. 3.
1. grandiflora.	Bastard Sensitive Plant.	

4. AGAVE.
AMERICAN ALOE, or AGAVE.

L. G. Pl. 431.	Hexandria Monogynia.	Cl. 6. Ord. 1.
1. Karatto.	Karatto Agave.	
2. vivipara.	Childing Agave.	

5. ALETRIS.
ALETRIS.

L. G. Pl. 428.	Hexandria Monogynia.	Cl. 6. Ord. 1.
1. capensis.	Cape Aletris.	
2. fragrans.	Sweet-scented Aletris.	

N

3. guinenfis.	Guinea Aletris.
4. hyacinthoides.	Hyacinth Aletris.
5. zeylanica.	Ceylon Aletris.

6. AMARYLLIS.

AMARYLLIS, or LILY-DAFFODIL,——(Fr.)—Lis-Narciffe.

L. G. Pl. 400.　　　　Hexandria Monogynia.　　　Cl. 6. Ord. 1.

1. Belladonna.	Mexican Lily.
2. capenfis.	Cape Lily.
3. ciliaris.	African Scarlet Lily.
4. formofiffima.	Jacobea Lily.
5. longifolia.	Cape Coaft Lily.
6. orientalis.	Oriental Lily, or Brunfwigia.
7. zeylanica.	Ceylon Lily.

7. AMOMUM.

GINGER,———(Fr.)—Gingembre.

L. G. Pl. 2.　　　　Monandria Monogynia.　　　Cl. 1. Ord. 1.

1. Zenziber.	Ginger.
1. Zerumbet.	Wild Ginger.

8. ANNONA.

CUSTARD APPLE.

L. G. Pl. 693.　　　　Polyandria Polygynia.　　　Cl. 13. Ord. 7.

1. afiatica.	Afiatic Cuftard Apple.
2. muricata.	Sour Cuftard Apple.
3. reticulata.	Netted Cuftard Apple.
4. fquamofa.	Sweet Cuftard Apple.

9. APOCYNUM.

DOGSBANE,———(Fr.)—Apocin.

L. G. Pl. 305.　　　　Pentandria Digynia.　　　Cl. 5. Ord. 2.

1. frutefcens.	Shrubby Dogsbane.
2. reticulatum.	Veined-leaved Dogsbane.

10. ARETIA.

ARETIA.

L. G. Pl. 195.　　　　Pentandria Monogynia.　　　Cl. 5. Ord. 1.

1. alpina.	Alpine Aretia.

11. ARUM.

ARUM, or WAKE-ROBIN.

L. G. Pl. 1028.	Gynandria Polyandria.	Cl. 20. Ord. 2.
1. arborefcens.	Tree Arum.	
2. Colocafia.	Greater Arum.	
3. efculentum.	Eatable Arum.	
4. minor.	Leffer Arum.	
5. peregrinum.	Heart-leaved Arum.	
6. trilobatum.	Ceylon Arum.	

12. ARUNDO.

REED,——(Fr.)—Rofeau.

L. G. Pl. 93.	Triandria Digynia.	Cl. 3. Ord. 2.
1. Bombos.	Bambu Cane.	

13. ASCLEPIAS.

SWALLOW-WORT.

L. G. Pl. 306.	Pentandria Digynia.	Cl. 5. Ord. 2.
1. curaffavica.	Orange Apocynum, or Swallow-W.	

14. BARLERIA.

BARLERIA.

L. G. Pl. 785.	Didynamia Angiofpermia.	Cl. 14. Ord. 2.
1. Prionitis.	Jamaica Four-fpined Barleria.	

15. BASELLA.

MALABAR NIGHTSHADE.

L. G. Pl. 382.	Pentandria Trigynia.	Cl. 5. Ord. 3.
1. alba.	White Malabar Nightfhade.	
2. rubra.	Red Malabar Nightfhade.	

16. BAUHINIA.

MOUNTAIN EBONY.

L. G. Pl. 511.	Decandria Monogynia.	Cl. 10. Ord. 1.
1. undulata.	Mountain Ebony.	

17. BELLONIA.

BELLONIA.

L. G. Pl. 226.	Pentandria Monogynia.	Cl. 6. Ord. 1.
1. afpera.	American Shrubby Bellonia.	

N 2

18. BESLERIA.

BESLERIA,——(Fr.)—

L. G. Pl. 755.   Didynamia Angiofpermia.   Cl. 14. Ord. 2.
1. melittifolia.   American Ovate-leaved Befleria.

19. BIGNONIA.

BIGNONIA, or TRUMPET-FLOWER,——(Fr.)—

L. G. Pl. 759.   Didynamia Angiofpermia.   Cl. 14. Ord. 1.
1. Leucoxylon.   Rofe-coloured-flowered Bignonia.
2. pentaphylla.   Five-leaved Bignonia.
3. triphylla.   Three-leaved Bignonia.

20. BIXA.

ARNOTTO,——(Fr.)—Roefu.

L. G. Pl. 654.   Polyandria Monogynia.   Cl. 13. Ord. 1.
1. Orellana.   Arnotto.

21. BOCCONIA.

BOCCONIA, or GREATER TREE CELANDINE.

L. G. Pl. 591.   Polyandria Monogynia.   Cl. 13. Ord. 1.
1. frutefcens.   American Bocconia.

22. BOMBAX.

SILK COTTON-TREE.

L. G. Pl. 835.   Monadelphia Polyandria.   Cl. 16. Ord. 5.
1. Ceiba.   Five-leaved Silk Cotton-tree.
2. villofum.   Hairy-leaved Silk Cotton-tree.

23. BONTIA.

BARBADOES WILD OLIVE.

L. G. Pl. 791.   Didynamia Angiofpermia.   Cl. 14. Ord. 2.
1. daphnoides.   Barbadoes Wild Olive-tree.

24. BORASSUS.

PALM-TREE.

L. G. Pl. 1220.   Cryptogamia Filix.   Cl. 24. Ord. 1.
1. flabellifer.   Fan Palm-tree.

25. BRABEJUM.

AFRICAN ALMOND-TREE.

L. G. Pl. 169.   Tetrandria Monogynia,   Cl. 4. Ord. 1.
    1. ftellatifolium.   African Almond-tree.

26. BROMELIA.

PINE-APPLE,——(Fr.)—Anane.

L. G. Pl. 395.   Hexandria Monogynia.   Cl. 6. Ord. 1.
    1. anguſtifolia.   Long narrow-leaved Pine.
    2. braſilienſis.   Braſilian or black Pippin.
    3. grenadenſis.   Grenade marbled-leaved Pine.
    4. lucida.   Shining green-leaved Pine.
    5. montſerratenſis.   Montſerrat Pine.
    6. nigra.   Black Antigua, or Ripley Pine.
    7. regina.   Queen Pine.
    8. rex.   King Pine.
    9. rubra.   Red-fruited Pine.
    10. ſerotina.   Late Olive-coloured Pine.
    11. argenteo-variegata.   Silver-ſtriped Pine.
    12. aureo-variegata.   Gold-ſtriped Pine.
    13. Pinguin.   Wild Pine.

All the above may be found in the Nurſeries near London, with ſome other Varieties.

27. BRUNIA.

L. G. Pl. 274.   Pentandria Monogynia.   Cl. 5. Ord. 1.
    1. nodiflora.   Imbricated-leaved Brunia.

28. BRUNSFELSIA.

BRUNSFELSIA.

L. G. Pl. 260.   Pentandria Monogynia.   Cl. 5. Ord. 1.
    1. americana.   American Brunsfelſia.

29. CÆSALPINA.

BRASILETTO-TREE.

L. G. Pl. 516.   Decandria Monogynia.   Cl. 10. Ord. 1.
    1. braſilienſis.   Braſilian Braſiletto.

N 3

30. CANNA.
INDIAN FLOWERING REED, or INDIAN SHOT.
(Fr.)—Balifier.

L. G. Pl. 1.   Monandria Monogynia.   Cl. 1. Ord. 1.
1. glauca.   Smooth green Indian Shot.
2. indica.   Red Indian Shot.
3. lutea.   Yellow Indian Shot.

31. CAPSICUM.
CAPSICUM, INDIAN or GUINEA PEPPER,—(Fr.)—Poivre d'Inde.

L. G. Pl. 252.   Pentandria Monogynia.   Cl. 5. Ord. 1.
1. conoide.   Hen Pepper.
2. frutefcens.   Berberry Pepper.
3. minimum.   Bird, or Cayenne Pepper.
4. pyramidale.   Yellow Pepper.

32. CARICA.
PAPAW-TREE.

L. G. Pl. 1127.   Dioecia Decandria.   Cl. 22. Ord. 9.
1. Papaya.   Papaw-tree.

33. CASSIA.
CASSIA, or WILD SENA.

L. G. Pl. 514.   Decandria Monogynia.   Cl. 10. Ord. 1.
1. biflora.   Two-flowered Caffia.
2. Finula.   Alexandrian Purging Caffia.
3. liguftrina.   Privet-leaved Caffia.

34. CASSYTHA.
CASSYTHA.

L. G. Pl. 505.   Enneandria Monogynia.   Cl. 19. Ord. 1.
1. filiformis.   Berry-bearing Caffytha.

35. CATESBÆA.
LILY-THORN.

L. G. Pl. 130.   Tetrandria Monogynia.   Cl. 4. Ord. 1.
1. fpinofa.   Lily-Thorn.

36. CEDRELA.
BARBADOES CEDAR-TREE.

1. odorata.   Sweet-fcented Barbadoes Cedar-tree.

37. CELASTRUS.
CELASTRUS, or STAFF-TREE.

L. G. Pl. 270. Pentandria Monogynia. Cl. 5. Ord. 1.
1. Pyracantha. Æthiopian Celaſtrus.

38. CERBERA.
AHOUAI.

L. G. Pl. 294. Pentandria, Monogynia. Cl. 5. Ord. 1.
1. Ahouai. Ovate-leaved Ahouai.

39. CESTRUM.
CESTRUM, or BASTARD JASMIN.

L. G. Pl. 261. Pentandria Monogynia. Cl. 5. Ord. 1.
1. diurnum. Day-ſmelling Ceſtrum.
2. latifolium. Broad-leaved Ceſtrum.
3. montanum. Mountain Ceſtrum.
4. noctiflorum. Night-ſmelling Ceſtrum.

40. CHAMÆROPS.
DWARF PALM, or PALMETTO.

L. G. Pl. 1219. Palma flabellifolia. Cl. 25. Appendix.
Poiygamia Dioecia.
1. humilis. Dwarf Palm, or Palmetto.

41. CHRYSOPHYLLUM.
STAR-APPLE.

L. G. Pl. 263. Pentandria Monogynia. Cl. 5. Ord. 1.
1. Cainito. Gold-coloured-leaved Star-apple.
2. glabrum. Smooth-leaved Star-apple.

42. CITHAREXYLON.
FIDDLE-WOOD-TREE,——(Fr.)—Fidelle-bois.

L. G. Pl. 760. Didynamia Angiofpermia. Cl. 14. Ord. 1.
1. caudatum. Oval-leaved Fiddle-wood-tree.
2. cinereum. Fiddle-wood-tree.

43. COCOS.
COCOA-NUT-TREE.

L. G. Pl. 1223. Palma pennatifolia. Cl. 25. Appendix.
Monoecia Hexandria.
1. nucifera. Cocoa-nut-tree.

N 4

44. COCCOLOBA.
SEA-SIDE GRAPE.

L. G. Pl. 496. Octandria Trigynia. Cl. 8. Ord. 3.
1. punctata.   Veined-leaved Sea-side Grape.
2. rubescens.   Downy-leaved Sea-side Grape.
3. Uvifera.   Shining-leaved Sea-side Grape.

45. COFFEA.
COFFEE-TREE,——(Fr.)—

L. G. Pl. 230. Pentandria Monogynia. Cl. 5. Ord. 1.
1. arabica.   Arabian Coffee-tree.

46. COMMELINA.
COMMELINA.

L. G. Pl. 62. Triandria Monogynia. Cl 3. Ord. 1.
1. africana.   African Commelina.

47. COPAIFERA.
BALSAM OF CAPEVI-TREE.

L. G. Pl. 543. Decandria Monogynia. Cl. 10. Ord. 1.
1. officinalis.   Balsam of Capevi-tree.

48. CORDIA.
CORDIA, or SEBASTEN.

L. G. Pl. 256. Pentandria Monogynia. Cl. 5. Ord. 1.
1. Sebestena.   Scarlet-flowered Cordia.

49. CORYPHA.
CORYPHA.

L. G. Pl. 1221. Palma flabellifolia. Cl. 25. Appendix.
1. umbraculifera. Dwarf prickly Palm.

50. COSTUS.
ZEDOARY.

L. G. Pl. 3. Monandria Monogynia. Cl. 1. Ord. 1.
1. arabicus.   Arabian Costus.

51. CRESCENTIA.
CALABASH-TREE.

L. G. Pl. 762. Didynamia Angiospermia. Cl. 14. Ord. 2.
1. Cujette.   Calabash-tree.

52. CRINUM.
CRINUM, or LILY ASPHODEL.

L. G. Pl. 405.　　Hexandria Monogynia.　　Cl. 6. Ord. 1.
1. africanum.　　　　African Blue Crinum.
2. amboinenfe.　　　Amboynan.
3. americanum.　　　American.
4. afiaticum.　　　　Afiatic.
5. latifolium.　　　　Broad-leaved.

53. CROTALARIA.
CROTALARIA,——(Fr.)—Crotalaire.

L. G. Pl. 862.　　Diadelphia Decandria.　　Cl. 17. Ord. 3.
1. latifolia.　　　　Broad-leaved Crotalaria.

54. CURCUMA.
TURMERIC.

L. G. Pl. 6.　　Monandria Monogynia.　　Cl. 1. Ord. 1.
1. longa.　　　　Long-rooted Turmeric.

55. CYCAS.
SAGOE-TREE.

L. G. Pl. 1222.　　Palma pennatifolia.　　Cl. 25. Appendix.
1. circinalis.　　　Sagoe-tree.

56. DIOSCOREA.
DIOSCOREA.

L. G. Pl. 1122.　　Dioecia Hexandria.　　Cl. 22. Ord 9.
1. bulbifera.　　　Yams.
2. fativa.　　　　Diofcorea.

57. DRACONTIUM.
DRAGON,——(Fr.)—Serpentaire.

L. G. Pl. 1029.　　Gynandria Polyandria.　　Cl. 20. Ord. 7.
1. pertufum.　　　Perforated-leaved Dragon.
2. fpinofum.　　　Prickly Dragon.

58. DURANTA.
DURANTA.

L. G. Pl. 786.　　Didynamia Angiofpermia.　　Cl. 14. Ord. 2.
1. Ellifia.　　　　Yellow-berried Duranta.
2. Plumieri.　　　Prickly Duranta.

59. EHRETIA.
BASTARD CHERRY-TREE, or EHRETIA.

L. G. Pl. 257.   Pentandria Monogynia.   Cl. 5. Ord. 1.
1. tinifolia.   Ehretia.

60. ELÆOCARPUS.
ELÆOCARPUS.

L. G. Pl. 693.   Polyandria Monogynia.   Cl. 13. Ord. 1.
1. ferrata.   Serrated-leaved Elæocarpus.

61. ELEPHANTOPUS.
ELEPHANT's-FOOT.

L. G. Pl. 997.   Syngenesia Polygamia Segregata.   Cl. 19. Ord. 5.
1. scaber.   Rough-leaved Elephant's-foot.

62. ERYTHRINA.
CORAL-TREE.

L. G. Pl. 855.   Diadelphia Decandria.   Cl. 17. Ord. 3.
1. Corallodendron.   Coral-tree.
2. herbacea.   Herbaceous Coral-tree.
3. picta.   Painted Coral-tree.

63. EUGENIA.
EUGENIA.

L. G. Pl. 616.   Icosandria Monogynia.   Cl. 12. Ord. 1.
1. malaccensis.   Malacca Eugenia.

64. EUPHORBIA.
SPURGE,——Fr.—Titimale.

L. G. Pl. 609.   Dodecandria Trigynia.   Cl. 11. Ord. 3.
1. antiquorum.   Triangular Spurge.
2. canariensis.   Canary Spurge.
3. cotinifolia.   Venice Sumach-leaved Spurge.
4. neriifolia.   Oleander-leaved Spurge.
5. officinalis.   Officinal Spurge.
6. pedifolia.   Laurel-leaved Spurge.

65. FAGARA.
IRONWOOD-TREE.

L. G. Pl. 150.   Tetrandria Monogynia.   Cl. 4. Ord. 1.
1. Pterota.   American Fagara.
2. Tragodes.   Prickly-leaved American Fagara.

66. FICUS.

FIG-TREE,——(Fr.)—Figuier.

L. G. Pl. 1168. Polygamia Trioecia. Cl. 23. Ord. 3.
1. benghalenfis. Bengal Fig-tree.
2. indica. Indian Fig-tree.
3. maxima. Long-leaved Fig-tree.
4. nymphæifolia. Water Lily-leaved Fig-tree.
5. pumila. Dwarf Fig-tree.
6. racemofa. Clufter-fruited Fig-tree.
·7. religiofa. Malabar Fig, or Indian God-tree.

67. GENIPA.

GENIPA.

L. G. Pl. 240. Pentandria Monogynia. Cl. 5. Ord. 1.
1. americana. American Genipa.

68. GLORIOSA.

GLORIOSA, or SUPERB LILY.

L. G. Pl. 413. Hexandria Monogynia. Cl. 6. Ord. 1.
1. fuperba. Malabarian Gloriofa, or Superb Lily.

69. GLYCINE.

GLYCINE.   .I

L. G. Pl. 868. Diadelphia Decandria. Cl. 17. Ord. 3.
1. Abrus. Weft Indian Wild Liquorice.

70. GREWIA.

GREWIA.

L. G. Pl. 1026. Gynandria Polyandria. Cl. 20. Ord. 7.
1. orientalis. Spear-fhaped-leaved Grewia.

71. GUAJACUM.

LIGNUM VITÆ, or POCKWOOD.

L. G. Pl. 518. Decandria Monogynia. Cl. 10. Ord. 1.
1. officinale. Lignum Vitæ, or Pockwood.

72. GUETTARDA.

GUETTARDA.

L. G. Pl. 1064. Monoecia Heptandria. Cl. 21. Ord. 7.
1. fpeciofa. Jamaica Guettarda.

73. GUILANDINA.
BONDUC, or NICKAR-TREE.

L. G. Pl. 517. Decandria Monogynia. Cl. 10. Ord. 1.
1. Bonduc.   Nickar-tree.

74. HÆMATOXYLON.
LOGWOOD, or CAMPEACHY WOOD.

L. G. Pl. 525. Decandria Monogynia. Cl. 10. Ord. 1.
1. campechianum. Logwood, or Campeachy Wood.

75. HEDYSARUM.
FRENCH HONEYSUCKLE.

L. G. Pl. 887. Diadelphia Decandria. Cl. 17. Ord. 3.
1. Styracifolium. Storax-leaved Hedyfarum.

76. HELICTERES.
SCREW-TREE.

L. G. Pl. 1024. Gynandria Decandria. Cl. 20. Ord. 6.
1. Ifora.   Screw-tree.

77. HELIOCARPUS.
HELIOCARPUS.

L. G. Pl. 606. Dodecandria Digynia. Cl. 11. Ord. 2.
1. americana. Veracrucian Heliocarpus.

78. HERNANDIA.
HERNANDIA, or JACK-IN-A-BOX.

L. G. Pl. 1049. Monoecia Triandria. Cl. 21. Ord. 3.
1. fonora.   Hernandia, or Jack-in-a-box.

79. HIBISCUS.

L. G. Pl. 846 Monadelphia Polyandria. Cl. 16. Ord. 3.
1. Abelmofchus. Mufk.
2. ficulneus. Ceylon Fig-leaved Hibifcus.
3. malvavifcus. Mallow-leaved Hibifcus.
4. mutabilis. Changeable Hibifcus.
5. populneus. Poplar-leaved Hibifcus.
6. Rofa finenfis - - 1. China Rofe.
7. *Rofa fin. plena* - - 2. Double China Rofe.
8. Sabdariffa. Cotton-leaved Hibifcus.
9. tiliaceus. Jamaica Lime-tree-leaved Hibifcus.

80. HIPPOMANE.

MANCHINEEL-TREE.

L. G. Pl. 1088.   Monoecia Monadelphia.   Cl. 21. Ord. 9.
  1. Mancinella.   Manchineel-tree.

81. HURA.

HURA, or SANDBOX-TREE.

L. G. Pl. 1087.   Monoecia Monadelphia.   Cl. 21. Ord. 9.
  1. crepitans.   American Hura, or Sandbox-tree.

82. HYMENÆA.

LOCUST-TREE.

L. G. Pl. 512.   Decandria Monogynia.   Cl. 10. Ord. 1.
  1. Courbaril.   Locuft-tree, or Gum Elemi-tree.

83. HYPOXIS.

HYPOXIS.

L. G. Pl. 417.   Hexandria Monogynia.   Cl. 6. Ord. 1.
  1. decumbens.   Trailing Jamaican Hypoxis.

84. JATROPHA.

CASSADA, or CASSAVA,——(Fr.)—Caffave.

L. G. Pl. 1084.   Monoecia Monadelphia.   Cl. 21. Ord. 9.
  1. Curcas.   Angular-leaved Phyfic-Nut.
  2. goffypifolia.   Cotton-leaved Phyfic-Nut.
  3. multifida.   Scarlet-flowered Phyfic-Nut.
  4. urens.   Stinging Phyfic-Nut.

85. JUSSIÆA.

JUSSIÆA.

L. G. Pl. 538.   Decandria Monogynia.   Cl. 10. Ord. 1.
  1. repens.   Creeping Juffiæa.

86. JUSTICIA.

JUSTICIA, or MALABAR NUT.

L. G. Pl. 27.   Diandria Monogynia.   Cl. 2. Ord. 1.
  1. Ecbolium.   Reflexed-flowered Malabar Nut.
  2. byffopifolia.   Hyffop-leaved Snap-tree.
  3. picta.   Painted-leaved Malabar Nut.

87. IXORA.

IXORA.

L. G. Pl. 131. Tetrandria Monogynia. Cl. 4. Ord. 1.
1. americana. American Ixora, or Wild Jafmin.

88. KÆMPFERIA.

KÆMPFERIA.

L. G. Pl. 7. Monandria Monogynia. Cl. 1. Ord. 1.
1. Galanga. Galangale.

89. LANTANA.

LANTANA, or AMERICAN VIBURNUM.

L. G. Pl. 765. Didynamia Angiofpermia. Cl. 14. Ord. 2.
1. aculeata. Prickly Nettle-leaved Lantana.
2. Camara. Balm-leaved Lantana.
3. involucrata. Round-leaved Lantana.
4. odorata. Sweet-fcented Lantana.

90. LAURUS.

BAY-TREE.

L. G. Pl. 503. Enneandria Monogynia. Cl. 19. Ord. 1.
1. Caffia. Caffia, or Baftard Cinnamon.
2. Cinnamomum. Cinnamon-tree.

91. LEEA.

LEEA.

L. G. Pl. 1276. Monoecia Tetrandria. Cl. 21. Ord. 4.
1. crifpa. Curled-leaved Leea.

92. LIMODORUM.

LIMODORUM, or BASTARD HELLEBORE.

L. G. Pl. 458. Heptandria Digynia. Cl. 7. Ord. 2.
1. tuberofum. Baftard Hellebore.

93. LOBELIA.

LOBELIA, or CARDINAL-FLOWER.

L. G. Pl. 1006. Syngenefia Monogamia. Cl. 19. Ord. 6.
1. longiflora. Long-flowered Cardinal-flower.

94. MALPIGHIA.
BARBADOES CHERRY-TREE.

L. G. Pl. 572.   Decandria Trigynia.   Cl. 10. Ord. 2.
1. glabra.   Smooth-leaved Barbadoes Cherry.
2. longifolia.   Long-leaved Barbadoes Cherry.
3. nitida.   Shining-leaved Barbadoes Cherry.
4. urens.   Stinging-leaved Barbadoes Cherry.

95. MAMMEA.
MAMMEE-TREE.

L. G. Pl. 656.   Polyandria Monogynia.   Cl. 13. Ord. 1.
1. americana.   American Mammee-tree.

96. MANGIFERA.
MANGO-TREE.

L. G. Pl. 278.   Pentandria Monogynia.   Cl. 5. Ord. 1.
1. indica.   Indian Mango-tree.

97. MARANTA.
INDIAN ARROW-ROOT.

L. G. Pl. 5.   Monandria Monogynia.   Cl. 1. Ord. 1.
1. arundinacea.   Indian Arrow-Root.

98. MARTYNIA.
MARTYNIA.

L. G. Pl. 753.   Didynamia Angiospermia.   Cl. 14. Ord. 2.
1. perennis.   Perennial Martynia.

99. MELASTOMA.
AMERICAN GOOSEBERRY.

L. G. Pl. 544.   Decandria Monogynia.   Cl. 10. Ord. 1.
1. holofericea.   Satten-leaved Melastoma.

100. MIMOSA.
ACACIA and SENSITIVE PLANT,——(Fr.)—Sensitive.

L. G. Pl. 1158.   Polygamia Monoecia.   Cl. 23. Ord. 1.
1. arborea.   Tree Acacia.
2. cornigera.   Mexican Horned Acacia.

3. farnefiana.   Italian Yellow Acacia, or Gazia.
4. latifolia.   Broad-leaved Acacia.
5. latifiliqua.   Broad-podded Acacia.
6. pernambucana.   Pernambucan Acacia.
7. perfica.   Silk-flowering Acacia.
8. pudica.   Humble Plant.
9. fenfitiva.   Senfitive Plant.
10. tamarindifolia.   Tamarind-leaved Acacia.

101. MUSA.

PLANTAIN-TREE.

L. G. Pl. 1141.   Polygamia Monoecia.   Cl. 23. Ord. 1.

1. paradifiaca.   Plantain-tree.
2. fapientum.   Banana.

102. MYRTUS.

MYRTLE-TREE,——Fr.—Mirte.

L. G. Pl. 628.   Icofandria Monogynia.   Cl. 12. Ord. 1.

1. dioica.   Dioicous Myrtle.
2. Pimenta.   Pimento, Jamaica Pepper or Allfpice.
3. zeylanica.   Ceylon Myrtle.

103. NYCTANCHES.

ARABIAN JASMIN.

L. G. Pl. 16.   Diandria Monogynia.   Cl. 2. Ord. 1.

1. Sambac - - - 1. Arabian Jafmin.
2. *Sambac plena* - - 2. Double-flowered Arabian Jafmin.

104. PANCRATIUM.

PANCRATIUM, or SEA DAFFODIL.

L. G. Pl. 404.   Hexandria Monogynia.   Cl. 6. Ord. 1.

1. amboinenfe.   Amboyna Pancratium.
2. caribæum.   Caribbean Pancratium.
3. latifolium.   Broad-leaved Pancratium.
4. mexicanum.   Mexican Pancratium.
5. zeylanicum.   Ceylon Pancratium.

105. PASSIFLORA.

PASSION-FLOWER,——(Fr.)—Fleur de Paffion.

L. G. Pl. 1021.   Gynandria Pentandria.   Cl. 20. Ord. 4.

1. holoferica.   Silky three-leaved Paffion Flower.
2. laurifolia.   Bay-leaved Paffion Flower.

3. maliformis,	Apple-shaped-fruited Passion-Flower.
4. minima.	Least-flowered Passion-Flower.
5. minuta.	Minute Passion-Flower.
6. Murucuja.	Two-lobed Moon-shapedleav'd P. Fl.
7. quadrangularis.	Square-stalked Passion-Flower.
8. rubra.	Two-lobed scarlet-fruited P. Fl.
9. ferratifolia.	Sawed-leaved Passion-Flower.
10. suberosa.	Cork-barked Passion-Flower.

106. PENTAPETES.
PENTAPETES.

| L. G. Pl. 834. | Monadelphia Dodecandria. | Cl. 16. Ord. 4. |
| 1. phœnicia. | Scarlet Pentapetes. | |

107. PETIVERIA.
GUINEA HENWEED.

| L. G. Pl. 459. | Hexandria Tetragynia. | Cl. 6. Ord. 4. |
| 1. alliacea. | Guinea Henweed. | |

108. PHOENIX.
PALM, or DATE-TREE.

L. G. Pl. 1224.	Palma pennatifolia.	Appendix. Cl. 25.
	Dioecia Triandria.	
1. dactylifera - -	1. Male Palm, or Date-tree.	
2. dactylifera fœminea	2. Female Palm, or Date-tree.	

109. PHYLLANTHUS.
SEA-SIDE LAUREL.

L. G. Pl. 1050.	Monoecia Triandria.	Cl. 21. Ord. 3.
1. Emblica.	Pinnated Indian Phyllanthus.	
2. Epiphyllanthus.	Serrated-leaved Phyllanthus.	
3. grandifolia.	Great-leaved Phyllantbus.	
4. Niruri.	Trailing-branched Phyllanthus.	

110. PHYSALIS.
WINTER CHERRY.

| L. G. Pl. 250. | Pentandria Monogynia. | Cl. 5. Ord. 1. |
| 1. curaffavica. | Curaffavian Winter-Cherry. | |

111. PIPER.
PEPPER,——(Fr.)—Poivre.

| L. G. Pl. 43. | Diandria Trigynia. | Cl. 2. Ord. 3. |
| 1. Amalago. | Jamaica long Pepper-tree. | |

O

2. obtusifolium.   Obtuse-leaved Pepper.
3. reticulatum.   Nettle-leaved Brasilian Pepper-tree.

112. PISCIDIA.

PISCIDIA.

L. G. Pl. 856.   Diadelphia Decandria.   Cl. 17. Ord. 3.
1. Erythrina.   Jamaica Piscidia.

113. PISONIA.

FINGRIGO.

L. G. Pl. 1162.   Polygamia Dioecia.   Cl. 23. Ord. 2.
1. aculeata.   Prickly Fingrigo.

114. PLUMBAGO.

LEADWORT.

L. G. Pl. 213.   Pentandria Monogynia.   Cl. 5. Ord. 1.
1. zeylanica.   Ceylon Leadwort.

115. PLUMERIA.

PLUMERIA, or RED JASMIN.

L. G. Pl. 298.   Pentandria Monogynia.   Cl. 5. Ord. 1.
1. alba.   White-flowered Plumeria.
2. obtusa.   Obtuse-leaved Plumeria.
3. rubra.   Red-flowered Plumeria.

116. POINCIANA.

BARBADOES FLOWER-FENCE, or SPANISH CARNATIONS.
(Fr.)—Poincillade.

1. pulcherrima.   Barbadoes Flower-fence.

117. POLYPODIUM.

FERN. POLYPODY.

L. G. Pl. 1179.   Cryptogamia Filix.   Cl. 24. Ord. 1.
1. aureum.   Golden Polypody.
2. auriculatum.   Auriculated Polypody.

118. PORTLANDIA.

PORTLANDIA.

L. G. Pl. 227.   Pentandria Monogynia.   Cl. 5. Ord. 1.
1. grandiflora.   Large-flowered Portlandia.

119. PSIDIUM.
GUAVA, or BAY-PLUM.
L. G. Pl. 615.   Icofandria Monogynia,   Cl. 12. Ord. 1
 1. pomiferum.   Red Apple-fhaped Guava.
 2. pyriferum.   White Pear-fhaped Guava.

120. RANDIA.
RANDIA.
L. G. Pl. 211.   Pentandria Monogynia.   Cl. 5. Ord. 1.
 1. mitis.   Jamaica Randia.

121. RIVINIA.
RIVINIA.
L. G. Pl. 162.   Tetrandria Monogynia.   Cl. 4. Ord. 1.
 1. canefcens.   Downy-leaved Rivinia.
 2. capenfis.   Cape Rivinia.
 3. humilis.   Dwarf Rivinia.

122. RONDELETIA.
RONDELETIA.
L. G. Pl. 224.   Pentandria Monogynia.   Cl. 5. Ord. 1.
 1. americana.   American Rondeletia

123. SACCHARUM.
SUGAR CANE.
L. G. Pl. 73.   Triandria Digynia.   Cl. 3. Ord. 2.
 1. officinarum.   Sugar Cane.

124. SAPINDUS.
SOAP-BERRY-TREE.
L. G. Pl. 499.   Octandria Trigynia.   Cl. 8. Ord. 3.
 1. Saponaria.   Soap-berry-tree.
 2. fpinofa.   Thorny Soap-berry-tree.

125. SIDEROXYLON.
IRON-WOOD-TREE.
L. G. Pl. 264.   Pentandria Monogynia.   Cl. 5. Ord. 1.
 1. inerme.   Æthiopian Ironwood.

O 2

126. SOLANUM,

NIGHTSHADE,——(Fr.)—Morelle.

L. G. Pl. 251. Pentandria Monogynia. Cl. 5. Ord. 1.
1. guinense. Guinea Nightshade.
2. igneum. Red-thorned Nightshade.
3. tomentosum. Woolly Nightshade.

127. SOPHORA.

SOPHORA.

L. G. Pl. 508. Decandria Monogynia. Cl. 10. Ord. 1.
1. microphylla. Small-leaved Otaheite Sophora.
2. tomentosa. Silvery Ceylon Sophora.

128. SWIETENIA.

MAHOGANY-TREE.

L. G. Pl. 521. Decandria Monogynia. Cl. 10. Ord. 1.
1. Mahagoni. Mahogany-tree.

129. TAMARINDUS.

TAMARIND-TREE.

L. G. Pl. 46. Triandria Monogynia. Cl. 3. Ord. 1.
1. indicus. Tamarind-tree.

130. THEOBROMA.

CHOCOLATE-NUT-TREE, and BASTARD CEDAR.

L. G. Pl. 900. Polyadelphia Pentandria. Cl. 18. Ord. 1.
1. Cacao. Chocolate-nut-tree.
2. Guazuma. Jamaica Theobroma, or Bast. Cedar.

131. TOURNEFORTIA.

TOURNEFORTIA.

L. G. Pl. 192. Pentandria Monogynia. Cl. 5. Ord. 1.
1. cymosa. Cymose-flowered Tournefortia.
2. foetidissima. Stinking Tournefortia.
3. serrata. Sawed-leaved Tournefortia.
4. suffruticosa. Upright Woolly-leaved Tournefort.
5. volubilis. Climbing Tournefortia.

132. TRIUMFETTA.

TRIUMFETTA.

L. G. Pl. 600. Dodecandria Monogynia. Cl. 11. Ord. 1.
1. Lappula. Jamaica Triumfetta.

133. TURNERA.

TURNERA.

L. G. Pl. 376.　　　Pentandria Trigynia.　　　Cl. 5. Ord. 3.
1. ulmifolia.　　　　Elm-leaved Turnera.

134. VERBESINA.

VERBESINA.

L. G. Pl. 975.　Syngenefia Polygamia Superflua.　Cl. 19. Ord. 2.
1. alata.　　　　Winged-ftalked Verbefina.

135. VINCA.

PERIWINKLE,——(Fr.)—Pervence.

L. G. Pl. 295.　　Pentandria Monogynia.　　Cl· 5. Ord. 1.
1. rofea.　　　Madagafcar Rofe Periwinkle.

136. VITIS.

VINE,——(Fr.)—Vigne.

L. G. Pl. 284.　　Decandria Monogynia.　　Cl. 5. Ord. 1.
1. indica.　　　Indian Vine.
2. trifolia.　　Three-leaved Indian Vine.

137. VOLKAMERIA.

VOLKAMERIA.

L. G. Pl. 788.　Didynamia Angiofpermia.　Cl. 14. Ord. 2.
1. aculeata.　　Prickly Volkameria.
2. inermis.　　Smooth Volkameria.

138. WINTERANA.

WILD CINNAMON.

L. G. Pl. 598.　Dodecandria Monogynia.　Cl. 11. Ord. 1.
1. canella.　　Wild Cinnamon-tree.

139. ZAMIA.

ZAMIA.

L. G. Pl. 1227.　Palma pennatifolia.　Appendix. Cl. 25.
1. pumila.　　Dwarf Palm-tree.

O 3

CHAP. V.

ANNUAL, BIENNIAL, AND PERENNIAL FLOWER SEEDS.

The following three Marks denote the Duration of each Plant, whether

| ⊙ Annual. | ♂ Biennial. | ♃ Perennial. |

English Name.	*Botanical Latin Generic, and Trivial Name.*	*Class and Order.*
⊙ Adonis Flower	Adonis, annua	Polyand. Polygynia
⊙ African Marygold	Tagetes, erecta	Syng. Polyg. Super.
⊙ ———Orange	———— erec. aurantiaca	
⊙ ——Yellow	——erec. lutea.	
⊙ ——Brimstone-colour'd	——erec. sulphurea	
⊙ ——Sweet-scented	—— erec. odorata	
Alkekengi	Physalis	Pentand. Monogyn.
⊙ ——Blue	——maxima	
⊙ ——White	——	
Alysson	Alyssum	Tetradyn. Angiosp.
♃ ——White	——	
♃ ——Sweet	——	
Amaranth	Amaranthus	Monoecia Pentand.
⊙ ——Three-colour'd	——tricolor	
⊙ ——Two colour'd	——melancholicus	
⊙ ——Love lies ableeding	—— caudatus	
⊙ ——Tree	——maximus	
⊙ ——Princess Feather	——lividus	
⊙ ——Cockscomb	Celosia, cristata	Pentand. Monogyn
⊙ ——Red	——crist. rubra	
⊙ ——Yellow	——crist. lutea	
⊙ ——Dwarf	——crist. pumila	

O 4

—— Globe Amaranth	Gomphrena, globofa	Pentandria Digynia.
⊙ ——Purple	——globofa purpurea	
⊙ ——White	——glob. alba	
⊙ —— Variegated	—— glob. variegata	
⊙ ——Spiked	——interrupta	
♃ Anemone	Anemone, coronaria	Polyandria Polyg.
♃ Antirrhinum, fee	Snap-dragon	
♃ Apocynum	Apocynum, venetum	Pentandria Digynia.
After, Chinefe	After, chinenfis	Syn. Polyg. Superfl.
⊙ ——Double white	——chin. albus	
⊙ ——Double purple	——chin. purpureus	
⊙ ——Double red	——chin. ruber	
⊙ ——Striped of each colour	——chin. variegatus	
♃ Aftragalus, Purple	Aftragalus	Diadel. Decandria.
♃ Auricula	Primula-Auricula	Pentandria Monog.
⊙ Balm, Moldavian	Dracocephalum, Moldavica	Didynam. Gymnof.
Balfam	Impatiens, Balfamina	Syng. Monogamia.
⊙ ——Double Purple	——Balf. purpurea	
⊙ ——Double Scarlet	——Balf. coccinea	
⊙ ——Double White	——Balf. alba	
⊙ ——Yellow, or Touch me not	——noli me tangere	
Bee Larkfpur	Delphinium	Polyand. Trigynia.
♃ ——Great-flowering	——grandiflorum	
♃ ——Siberian	——elatum	
⊙ Belvidere	Chenopodium Scoparia	Pentandria Digyn.
Campanula	Campanula, Trachelium	Pentandria Monog.
♃ —White Nettle-leaved	——Trach. album	
♃ —Blue Nettle-leaved	——Trach. cœruleum	
Candy-tuft, white	Iberis, umbellata	Tetradyn. Siliful.
⊙ ——Large white	——umbell. major	
⊙ ——Purple	——umbell. purpurea	
Canterbury Bell	Campanula, Medium	Pentandria Monog.
♂ ——White	——Medium album	
♂ ——Blue	——Medium cœruleum	

Capficum	Capficum	Pentandria Monog.
☉ ——Long-podded	——propendens	
☉ ——Heart-fhaped	——cordiforme	
☉ ——Bell-fhaped	——tetragonum	
☉ ——Cherry fhaped	——cerafiforme	
♃ Carnation	Dianthus, Caryophyllus	Decandria Digynia
☉ Caterpillar	Medicago, polymorpha	Diadel. Decandria.
Chryfanthemum	Chryfanthemum	Syn. Polyg. Super.
☉ ——White	——*album*	
☉ ——Yellow	——*luteum*	
☉ ——Quilled	——*fiftulofum*	
Clary	Salvia Sclarea	Octandria Monog.
♂ ——Purple-topped		
♂ ——Red-topped		
Columbine	Aquilegia	Polyandria Pentag.
♃ ——Canadian	——canadenfis	
♃ ——Double	——hortenfis plena	
Convolvulus	Convolvulus	Pentandria Monog.
☉ —— Great blue	——hederaceus	
☉ ——Great blue ftriped	——*hederaceus variegatus*	
☉ ——Great white	——*hederaceus albus*	
☉ ——Small blue	——tricolor	
☉ ——Small blue ftriped	——*tricolor variegatus*	
☉ ——Small white	——*albus*	
☉ ——Scarlet	——coccineus	
Cornbottle	Centaurea, Cyanus	Syng. Polyg. Fruft.
☉ ——Blue	——Cyan. cœruleus	
☉ ——White	——*Cyan. albus*	
☉ —— Red	——*Cyan. ruber*	
☉ ——Purple	——*Cyan. purpureus*	
☉ ——Striped	——*Cyan. variegatus*	
☉ Cucumber, Spurting	Momordica, Elaterium	Monoecia Syngen.
☉ Cyanus, *fee* Cornbottle	Centaurea, Cyanus	Syn. Polyg. Fraftr.
Cyclamen	Cyclamen	Pentandria Monog.
♃ ——European	——europæum	
♃ ——Perfian	——perficum	
☉ Devil in a bufh, *fee*	Nigella	Polyandria Pentag.

Egg-plant	Solanum, Melongena	Pentandria Monog.
⊙ ——purple	——Melong. purpurea	
⊙ ——white	——Melong. alba	
♃ Flax, perennial	Linum, perenne	Pentandria Pentag.
Foxglove	Digitalis	Didynamia Angiofp.
♂ ——Purple	——purpurea	
♃ ——White	——alba	
♃ ——Iron-coloured	——ferruginea	
Fraxinella	Dictamnus	Decandria Monog.
♃ ————White	——albus	
♃ ————Red	——ruber	
French Honeyfuckle	Hedyfarum, coronarium	Diadelph. Decan.
♂ ——White	——coron. album	
♂ ——Red	——coron. rubrum	
⊙ French Marygold	Tagetes, patula	Syng. Polyg. Super.
⊙ ——Sweet-fcented	——pat. odorata	
⊙ ——Striped	——pat. firiata	
⊙ Globe Amaranth, fee	Amaranth	
⊙ Globe Thiftle	Echinops Sphærocephalus	Syng. Polyg. Segr.
♁ Gourd	Cucurbita	Monoecia Syngen.
Hawkweed	Hieracium	Syng. Polyg. Æq.
♃ ——Purple	——aurantiacum	
♃ ——Spanifh	——umbellatum	
♃ ——Yellow	——fabaudum	
⊙ Hedgehog Trefoil	Medicago, intertexta	Diadelphia Decand.
♃ Hollyhock, Double	Alcea, rofea	Monadelphia Poly.
♂ Honefty	Lunaria, rediviva	Tetradyn. Silicul.
⊙ Humble Plant	Mimofa, pudica	Polygam. Monoecia
⊙ Ice Plant, or Diamond Ficoides	Mefembryanthemum ——cryftallinum	Icofandria Pentag.
⊙ Indian Corn, or Maize	Zea, vulgaris	Monoecia Triandr.
⊙ Ketmia, Bladder	Hibifcus, Trionum	Monad. Polyandria
Larkfpur	Delphinium	Polyand. Trigynia.
⊙ ——Branching	——Confolida	
⊙ ——Varieg. Branch.	——Conf. variegata	
⊙ ——Double Upright	——Ajacis plenum	
⊙ ——Double Rofe-col.	——Ajacis variegatum	
Lavatera	Lavatera	Monadelph. Polyan.
⊙ ——White	——cretica alba	
⊙ ——Red	——cretica rubra	

Lobel's Catchfly,	Silene, Armeria	Decand. Trigynia.
⊙ ——White	———Armeria alba	
⊙ ——Purple	———Arm. purpurea	
⊙ ——Red	———Arm. rubra	
Love-apple	Solanum, Lycoperficon	Pentandria Monog.
⊙ ——Red	——— Lyc. rubrum	
⊙ ——White	———Lyc. album	
Lupine	Lupinus	Diadel. Decandria.
⊙ —Yellow	———luteus	
⊙ —White	———albus	
⊙ —Narrow-leav'd Blue	———anguftifolius	
⊙ —Great hairy Blue	———hirtutus	
⊙ —Hairy Rofe-coloured	——— birf. incarnatus	
⊙ —Leffer Blue	———varius	
Mallow	Malva	Monadelphia Poly.
⊙ ———oriental	———orientalis	
⊙ ———Curled	——— crifpa	
⊙ Marvel of Peru	Mirabilis, Jalapa	Pentandria Monog.
⊙ ———ftriped	——— Jal. varieg.	
Mignonette	Refeda	Dodecandria Trig.
⊙ —fweet-fcented	———odorata	
⊙ ——upright		
Nafturtium	Tropæolum	Octandria Monog.
⊙ ———Large	———majus	
⊙ ———Dwarf	———humile	
⊙ Nettle, Roman	Urtica, pilulifera	Monoecia Tetrand.
Nigella	Nigella	Polyandria Polyg.
⊙ ——Roman White	———damafcena	
⊙ —— Spanifh Blue	———hifpanica	
⊙ Nolana (Peruvian)	Nolana proftrata	Pentandria Monog.
Ox-eye Daify	Chryfanthemum	Syng. Polyg. Super.
4 Great Ox-eye Daify	———Leucanthemum	
⊙ Palma Chrifti	Ricinus vulgaris	Monoecia Monad.
⊙ Panfey, or Heart's-eafe	Viola tricolor	Syng. Monogamia.
Pea	Lathyrus	Diad. Decandria.
⊙ -——Purple, Sweet	———odoratus	
⊙ —— White	———odoratusalbus	

☉ Pea, Painted Lady	——odoratus zeylanicus	Diadel Decand.
☉ ——Tangier	——tingitanus	
♃ ——Everlafting	——latifolius	
☉ ——Winged	Lotus, tetragonolobus	
☉ Perficaria	Polygonum, Perficaria	Octandria Trigynia
♃ Pink	Dianthus deltoides	Decandria Digynia.
♃ Polyanthus	Primula, Polyanthus	Pentandria Monog·
Poppy	Papaver	Polyandria Monog.
☉ —Double Dwarf	——Rhæas plenum	
☉ —Double Carnation	——fomniferum plenum	
♃ —Yellow Welfh	——cambricum	
☉ —Yell. Horned Poppy	Chelodonium, Glaucium	
Ranunculus	Ranunculus	Polyandria Polyg.
♃ ——Perfian	——afiaticus	
♃ ——Scarlet	————fanguineus	
Reed	Canna	Monandria Monog.
♃ ——Scarlet-flowered	——coccinea	
♃ ——Yellow-flowered	——lutea	
Rhubarb	Rheum	Enneandria Trigy.
♃ ——Palmated Rhubarb	——palmatum	
Rocket	Hefperis	Tetradynam. Siliq·
♂ ——Double White	——inodora alba	
♂ ——Double Purple	————*inodora purpurea*	
Rofe-Campion	Agroftemma, Coronaria	Decandria Pentag.
♃ ——White	——Coronaria alba	
♃ ——Red	——*Coronaria rubra*	
♃ ——Red and White	——*Coronaria bicolor*	
Scabious	Scabiofa	Tetrandia Monog.
☉ ——Sweet-fcented	————atropurpurea	
☉ Senfitive Plant	Mimofa, fenfitiva	Polyg. Monoecia.
☉ Snail-Trefoil	Medicago fcutellata	Diad. Decandria.
♃ Snap-dragon	Antirrhinum majus	Didyn. Angiofper.
——Purple	——majus purpureum	
——Red	——*majus rubrum*	
——Yellow	——*majus luteum*	
——Striped-leaved	——*majus variegatum*	
☉ Annual	——ficulum	

Stock-July-flower	Cheiranthus	Tetradyn. Siliquof.
☉ —Purple Ten-weeks	——annuus purpureus	
☉ —White	——annuus albus	
☉ —Red	——annuus rofeus	
☉ —Wall-flower-leaved	—— an. leucojifolius	
☉ —White Ditto	—— an. leucojif. albus	
☉ —Dwarf Annual Virg.	——maritimus	
♂ —Brompton Stock	——incanus coccineus	
♂ —Queen's Stock	——incanus ruber	
Stramonium	Datura, faftuofa	Pentand. Monog.
☉ ——Double Purple	——faftuofa purpurea	
☉ ——Double White	——faftuofa alba	
☉ Strawberry Spinage	Blitum, capitatum	Monand. Digynia.
Sunflower.	Helianthus, annuus.	Syn. Polyg. Fruf.
☉ ——Annual Peruvian.	——annuus	
☉ ——Annual Dwarf	——annuus pumilus	
Sweet Sultan	Centaurea	Syn. Polyg. Fruf.
☉ ——Purple	—mofchata purpurea	
☉ ——Red	—mofchata incarnata	
☉ ——White	—mofchata alba	
☉ ——Yellow	—Amberboi	
Sweet William	Dianthus, barbatus	Decand. Digynia.
♂ ——Red	——barbatus ruber	
♂ ——Variegated	——barbatus variegatus	
Tobacco	Nicotiana	Pentand. Monogya.
☉ ——Virginian	——Tabacum	
☉ ——Englifh	——ruftica	
Tree Primrofe	Oenothera	Octand. Monogya.
♂ Biennial Tree Primrofe	——biennis	
☉ Tricolor, fu	Amaranth	
Valerian	Valeriana	Triand. Monogya.
♃ ——Valerian	——Phu	
♃ ——Red	—— rubra	
♃ ——White	——alba	
♂ ——Yellow	——fibirica	
Valerian, (Greek)	Polemonium	Pentand. Monogya.
♃ ——Blue	——cœruleum	
♃ ——White	——cœruleum lanatum	

Venus's Looking-glafs	Campanula, Speculum	Pentand. Monogyn.
☉ ———Purple	—Speculum purpureum	
☉ ———White	—*Speculum album*	
☉ ———Small	—hybrida	
☉ Venus's Navel-wort	Cynogloffum, linifolium	Pentand. Monogyn.
Veronica, or Speedwell	Veronica	Diandr. Monogyn.
♃ ———Auftrian	———auftriaca	
♃ ———Welfh	———hybrida	
♃ ———Sea	———maritima	
♃ ———Spiked	———fpiacta	
Wall-flower	Cheiranthus Cheiri.	Tetrad. Siliquofa.
♂ ———Yellow	—Cheiri	
♂ ———Bloody	—Cheiri ferrugineus	
♂ ———White	—Cheiri albus	
Xeranthemum	Xeranthemum annuum.	Syng. Polyg. Sup.
☉ ———Red	———annuum rubrum	
☉ ———White	———*annuum album*	
Zinnia	Zinnia	Syng. Polyg. Sup.
☉ ———Red	———pauciflora	
☉ ———Yellow	———multiflora.	

CHAP.

CHAP. VI.

SEEDS, ACORNS, BERRIES, CONES, &c.

OF

Foreſt-trees, Evergreens, American Trees,

AND

FLOWERING SHRUBS.

ACACIA.
GLEDITSIA.
Triple-thorned   ſpinoſa

ACACIA, (the Falſe)
ROBINIA.
Falſe Acacia   Pſeudo Acacia
Scarlet   coccinea

ALLSPICE.
CALYCANTHUS.
Carolinian   florida.

ANDROMEDA,
ANDROMEDA.
Calyculated   calyculata
Ovate-leaved   mariana
Crenated-leaved   paniculata
Roſemary-leaved   Polifolia

ANNONA.
ANNONA.
Annona or Papaw   triloba

ARBOR-VITÆ.
THUJA.
Common   occidentalis
Sweet-ſcented   occid. odorata
Chineſe   orientalis

ASH-TREE.
FRAXINUS.
Engliſh   excelſior
Virginian   paniculata
Carolinian   americana
New-England   alba
Black   nigra
Penſylvanian.   penſylvanica

AZALEA.
AZALEA.
Red   nudiflora
White   viſcoſa

BAY-TREE.
LAURUS.
Common   nobilis

BEECH-TREE.
FAGUS.

English	sylvatica
American purple	purpurea

BIRCH-TREE.
BETULA.

English	alba
Canadian	lenta
Black Virginian	nigra
Poplar-leaved	populifolia

BIRD-CHERRY-TREE.
PRUNUS-CERASUS.

Canadian	canadensis
Virginian	virginiana

BLADDER-NUT-TREE.
STAPHYLÆA.

Three-leaved	trifoliata
English	pinnata

BLADDER-SENA.
COLUTEA.

Common	arborescens
Oriental	orientalis

BROOM.
SPARTIUM.

English	scoparium.
Spanish	junceum.
White-flowered	monospermum

BROOM.
GENISTA.

Portugal	lusitanica
Lucca	tinctoria italica

BUTTON-WOOD-TREE.
CEPHALANTHUS.

American	occidentalis

CANDLEBERRY-MYRTLE
MYRICA.

Candleberry Myrtle	cerifera
Broad-leaved	carolinensis

CEDAR-TREE.
JUNIPERUS.

White	caroliniana
Red	virginiana
Bermudian	bermudiana

CEDAR of LIBANUS.
PINUS-LARIX.

Cedar of Libanus	Cedrus

CHESNUT-TREE.
FAGUS-CASTANEA.

Spanish	Castanea
American	dentata
Dwarf	pumila

CISTUS, or ROCK-ROSE.
CISTUS.

Labdanum-bearing	ladaniferus
Montpelier	monspeliensis
Portugal	lusitanicus
Spanish	hispanicus

CLETHRA.
CLETHRA.

Ash-leaved	alnifolia

CORK-TREE.
QUERCUS-SUBER.

Cork-tree	Suber

CYPRESS-TREE.
CUPRESSUS.

Dwarf Maryland	Thyoides
Deciduous	disticha
Portugal	lusitanica
Spreading	horizontalia
Upright	sempervirens

CYTISUS.
CYTISUS.

Evergreen hairy	hirsutus

DAHOON HOLLY.
ILEX.

Carolinian or Dahoon Holly	Cassine

DOGWOOD.
CORNUS.

Virginian	florida
Narrow-leaved	anguftifolia
Blue-berried	Amomum

ELDER-TREE.
SAMBUCUS.

Canadian	canadienfis
Scarlet-berried	racemofa

FIR-TREE.
PINUS-ABIES.

Yew-leaved Silver	alba
Hemlock Spruce	americana
Balm of Gilead	Balfamea
Newfoundl. white	canadenfis
Newfoundl. black	can. nigricans
Newfoundl. Red	can. rubefcens
Norway Spruce	Picea
Long-coned Cornifh Pic. longa	

HAWTHORN-TREE.
CRATÆGUS.

Hawthorn	Oxyacantha
Yellow-berried	Oxy. bacciflava

HICKERY-NUT-TREE.
JUGLANS.

White	alba
Small	minor
Shag-barked	ovata
Pignut	minima

HORNBEAM-TREE.
CARPINUS.

Common	Betulus
Hop	Oftrya
Virginian	virginiana

HORSE-CHESNUT-TREE.
ÆSCULUS.

Common	Hippocaftanum
Scarlet-flowered	Pavia

JUNIPER-TREE.
JUNIPERUS.

Common	communis
Swedifh	fuecica

JUDAS-TREE.
CERCIS.

Canadian	canadenfis
European	Siliquaftrum
White European	Siliq. album

KALMIA.
KALMIA.

Narrow-leaved	anguftifolia
Broad-leaved	latifolia

LABURNUM.
CYTISUS-LABURNUM.

Broad-leaved	latifolium
Narrow-leaved	anguftifolium

LARCH-TREE.
PINUS-LARIX.

Common	Larix

LAUREL-TREE.
PRUNUS-LAURO-CERASUS.

Common	Lauro-Cerafus
Portugal	lufitanica

LILAC.
SYRINGA.

White	vulgaris alba
Blue	vulg. cærulea
Purple	vulg. purpurea

LIME-TREE.
TILIA.

Common	europæa
American	americana
Carolinian	caroliniana

P

LIQUIDAMBER, or STORAX-TREE.
LIQUIDAMBAR.

Virginian	Styraciflua
Canadian	afplenifolia

MAGNOLIA, or LAUREL-LEAVED TULIP-TREE.
MAGNOLIA.

Blue Deciduous	acuminata
Small-leaved	glauca
Evergreen	grandiflora
Umbrella-tree	tripetala

MAPLE-TREE.
ACER.

Small Maple	campeftre
Virginian	Negundo
Penfylvanian	penfylvanicum
Norway	Platanoides
Sycamore	Pfeudo-Platan.
Scarlet	rubrum
Sugar	faccharinum

MEDLAR-TREE.
MESPILUS.

Canadian	canadenfis

MEZEREON.
DAPHNE.

Purple	Mezereum
White	Mez. album
Red	Mez rubrum
Autumnal	Mez.autumnale

MOUNTAIN ASH-TREE.
SORBUS.

Mountain Afh	Aucuparia

NETTLE-TREE.
CELTIS.

American	occidentalis

MULBERRY-TREE.
MORUS.

Virginian	rubra

OAK-TREE.
QUERCUS.

Englifh	Robur
White Virginian	alba
Black Virginian	nigra
Chefnut-leaved	Prinus
Scarlet Virginian	rubra
Willow-leaved	Phellos
Red Mountain	montana

OAK-TREE, (EVERGREEN)
QUERCUS-ILEX.

Ilex	Ilex

PINE-TREE.

Aphernoufli	Cembra.
Prickly-coned	echinata
Swamp	paluftris
Stone	Pinea
Virginian 3-leaved	rigida
Scotch	rubra
Weymouth	Strobus
Pineafter	fylveftris
Frankincenfe	Tæda
Virginian 2-leaved	virginiana

PLANE-TREE.
PLATANUS.

Virginian	occidentalis

POPLAR-TREE.
POPULUS.

Carolinian	balfamifera
Virginian	heterophylla

ROSE-BAY.
RHODODENDRON.

Large Rofe-Bay	maximum

ROBINIA, or FALSE ACACIA.
ROBINIA.

Falfe Acacia	Pfeudo-Acacia
Scarlet	coccinea

SASSAFRAS-TREE.
LAURUS.

S.ffafras-tree	Saffafras

SNOWDROP, or FRINGE-TR.
CHIONANTHUS.
Virginian   virginica

SPINDLE-TREE.
EUONYMUS.
Evergreen americ. americanus.
Long-leaved   longifolius

STAFF-TREE.
CELASTRUS.
Canadian   scandens
Virginian   bullatus

STRAWBERRY-TREE.
ARBUTUS.
Common   Unedo

SUMACH-TREE.
RHUS.
Carolinian   typhinum
Lentiscus-leaved copallinum
Scarlet   glabrum

TOOTHACH-TREE.
ZANTHOXYLON.
Toothach-tree   Clava Herculis
Ash-leaved   fraxinifolium

TULIP-TREE.
LIRIODENDRON.
Virginian   Tulipifera

VIBURNUM.
VIBURNUM.
Common   Lantana
Plum-leaved   prunifolium
Pear-leaved   pyrifolium

WALNUT-TREE.
JUGLANS.
Pensylvanian   cinerea
Black Virginian   nigra
Oblong Black   oblonga nigra
Oblong White   oblonga alba

WINTER-BERRY.
PRINOS.
Virginian   verticillatus

YEW-TREE.
TAXUS.
Common   baccata

CHAP. VII.

SEEDS and PLANTS

FOR THE

KITCHEN-GARDEN.

With the Botanical Latin, and Common Englifh Names.

ANGELICA.
ANGELICA. ♃
Common   fativa

ARTICHOKE.
CYNARA. ♃
Green   Scolymus
Globe   hortenfis

ASPARAGUS.
ASPARAGUS. ♃
Afparagus   , altilis

BALM.
MELISSA. ♃
Common   officinalis
Striped-leaved   offic. variegata

BASIL.
OCYMUM. ☉
Sweet Bafil   Bafilicum
Bufh   minimum

BEAN.
VICIA-FABA. ☉
Mazagan
Portugal
Small Spanifh
Broad Spanifh
White-bloffomed
Red-bloffomed
Non-pareil
Fan, or Clufter
Toker
Windfor

BEET.
BETA. ♂
White   vulgaris alba
Green   vulg. viridis
Red   vulg. rubra

BOORCOLE, or SCOTCH KALE.
BRASSICA-SABELLICA. ♂
Green	fabellica viridis
Purple	fabel. purpurea
Variegated	fabel. variegata

BORAGE.
BORAGE. ☉
Borage	officinalis

BROCCOLI.
BRASSICA, ITALICA. ☉
Purple	italica purpur.
Early Purple	italica præcox
Cauliflower	italica alba

BURNET.
POTERIUM-SANGUISORBA. 24
Burnet	Sanguisorba

CABBAGE.
BRASSICA-OLERACEA. ♂
Early Yorkfhire	eboracenfis
Early Ruffian	mufcovitica
Sugar-loaf	pyramidalis
Early Sugar-loaf	pyr. præcox
Flat-fided	compreffa
Red	rubra
Milan	
Green Savoy	fabauda
White Savoy	fabauda alba
Yellow Savoy	fabauda flava
Bruffels Sprouts	bruxellenfis

CABBAGE.
FOR FEEDING OF CATTLE.
White Scotch	fcotica
Turnep-rooted	Napobraffica
Cabbage-Turnep	Caulorapa
Anjou	algarvenfis
American	americana

CAMOMILE.
ANTHEMIS 24
Camomile	nobilis
Double-flowered	nobilis plena

CARROT.
DAUCUS-CAROTA.
Early Horn	præcox
White	alba
Orange	aurantiaca

CAULIFLOWER.
BRASSICA-BOTRYTIS. ☉
Early	Botrytis præc.
Late	Botr. ferotina

CELERY.
APIUM. ♂
Upright	dulce
Solid-ftalked	folidum
Celeriac	rapaceum

CHERVIL.
CHÆROPHYLLUM. ☉
Chervil	aromaticum

CHARDON.
CYNARA-CARDUNCULUS. ☉.
Chardon	Cardunculus

CIVE.
ALLIUM-CEPA, 24
Cive	Schænoprafum

CLARY.
SALVIA-SCLAREA.
Clary	vulgaris

COLE-SEED.
BRASSICA-NAPUS. ☉
Cole-feed	fylveftris

CORN-SALLAD.
VALERIANA. ☉
Corn-Sallad	Locufta

CRESS.
LEPIDIUM. ☉
Garden Crefs	fativum
Curled-leaved	fativum crifp.
Broad-leaved	fativ. latifol.

CUCUMBER,
CUCUMIS. ☉
Early Prickly	fativus præcox
Long Prickly	fativus longus

Cluftered   fat. corymbofus.
White Turkey   fativus albus
Green Turkey   fativus viridis

DILL.
ANETHUM. ☉.
Dill   graveolens

ENDIVE.
CICHORIUM-ENDIVIA. ☉
Green-curled   Endivia viridis
White-curled   Endivia alba
Broad-leaved   Endivia latif.

ESCHALOT.
ALLIUM-CEPA. ♃
Efchalot   afcalonica

FENNEL.
ANETHUM-FOENICULUM. ☉
Fennel   vulgare

FINOCHIO.
ANETHUM-FOENICULUM. ☉
Finochio   azoricum

FRENCH-BEAN.
PHASEOLUS, NANUS. ☉
DWARFS.
Early yellow
Early white
Speckled
Canterbury
Batterfea
Speckled Amber
Cream-coloured
Sparrow-Egg

RUNNERS.
PHASEOLUS, VULGARIS. ☉
Scarlet-flowered
White-flowered
Negroe
Large Dutch
Batterfea
Variable

GARLIC.
ALLIUM. ♃
Garlic   fativum

HORSE-RADISH.
COCHLEARIA-ARMORACIA. ☉
Horfe-Radifh   Armoracia

HYSSOP.
HYSSOPUS. ♃
Hyffop   officinalis

JERUSALEM ARTICHOKE
HELIANTHUS. ♃
Jeruf. Artichoke   tuberofus

LAVENDER.
LAVANDULA.
Narrow-leaved   anguftifolia

LEEK.
ALLIUM-PORRUM. ♂
Narrow-leaved   anguftifolium
Broad-leaved   latifolium

LETTUCE.
LACTUCA, SATIVA. ☉
Cabbage
Brown Dutch
Cilicia
Spotted Aleppo
Admirable
Imperial
Roman
Honey
Red Capuchin
Green Capuchin
Black Cos
Green Cos
White Cos
Royal

MARYGOLD.
CALENDULA. ☉
Single   officinalis
Double   officinal. plena

MARJORAM.
ORIGANUM. ♃

Pot	vulgare
Winter	heracleoticum
Knotted	Majorana

MELON.
CUCUMIS-MELO. ☉

Musk
Small Portugal
Romana
Cantaleupe

MINT.
MENTHA. ♃

| Spear Mint | spicata |
| Pepper Mint | piperita |

MUSHROOM.
FUNGUS, ESCULENTUS.

| Mushroom | esculentus |

MUSTARD.
SINAPIS. ⊖

| White | alba |
| Black | nigra |

ONION.
ALLIUM-CEPA. ♂

Strasburg	vulgaris
Silver-skinned	argentea
Spanish	hispanica
Portugal	lusitanica
Welsh	cambrica
Scallion	ascalonica

PARSLEY.
APIUM-PETROSELINUM. ♂

Common	Petroselinum
Curled-leaved	Petrosel.crispum
Large-rooted	latifolium

PARSNEP.
PASTINACA. ♂

| Parsnep | sativa |

PEA.
PISUM, SATIVUM. ☉

Small Dwarf
Sugar Dwarf
Ledman's Dwarf
Nicholas's Early
Early Golden
Charlton
Early Hessian
Early Grey Cluster
Masters's Hotspur
Reading Hotspur
Essex Hotspur
Early White Dwarf
Early Tall White
Blue Union
Nonpareil
Green Nonpareil
Rouncival
Large Grey
Egg Pea
Lord Anson's
Crown Pea
Frame Pea for Hotbeds

PENNYROYAL.
MENTHA-PULEGIUM. ♃

| Pennyroyal | Pulegium |

POTATOE.
SOLANUM, ESCULENTUM. ♃

Early	escul. præcox
Purple	escul. purpur.
White	escul. album
Kidney-shaped	escul. reniforme
Clustered	esc. conglomeratum

PURSLANE.
PORTULACA. ☉

| Green | oleracea viridis |
| Golden | oleracea aurea |

RADISH.
RAPHANUS, SATIVUS. ♂

Short-topped	fat. brevifolius
Deep Red	fat. ruber
Salmon	fat. roseus
Long-topped	fat. longifolius
Black Spanish	niger
Turnep-rooted	orbiculatus

RAMPION.
CAMPANULA-RAPUNCULUS. ♂

Rampion	Rapunculus

RAPE.
BRASSICA-NAPUS. ☉

Rape	sylvestris

ROCAMBOLE.
ALLIUM-SCORODOPRASUM. ♃

Rocambole	Scorodoprasum

ROSEMARY.
ROSMARINUS. ♄

Narrow-leaved	angustifolius

RUE.
RUTÆ. ♄

Rue	graveolens

SAGE.
SALVIA. ♄

Green	officinalis
Red	offic. rubra
Tea, or Balsamic	off. tomentosa

SALSAFY.
TRAGOPOGON. ♄

Salsafy	porrifolium

SAVORY
SATUREJA. ☉ ♃

Summer	hortensis
Winter	montana

SCORZONERA.
SCORZONERA. ♂

Scorzonera	hispanica

SKIRRET.
SIUM-SISARUM. ♂

Skirret	Sisarum

SCOTCH-KALE.
See BOORCOLE.

SORREL.
RUMEX-ACETOSA.

Sorrel	pratensis
Roman	scutata

SPINACH.
SPINACIA. ☉

Smooth-seeded	glabra
Prickly-seeded	oleracea

TANSEY.
TANACETUM. ♃

Tansey	vulgare

TARRAGON.
ARTEMISIA-DRACUNCULUS. ♃

Tarragon	Dracunculus

THYME.
THYMUS.

Broad-leaved	vulgaris

TURNEP.
BRASSICA-RAPA. ☉

Early Dutch	præcox
Yellow	flavescens
Green-topped	viridis
White	candida
Long-rooted	oblonga
Purple-rooted	punicea

TURNEP. (French.)
BRASSICA-NAPUS.

White-rooted	albus

WATER-CRESS.
SISYMBRIUM. ☉

Water-Cress	Nasturtium aquaticum

CHAP. VIII.

SEEDS, PLANTS, AND ROOTS,

FOR THE

Improving of LAND, for MANUFACTURES,

FEEDING of CATTLE, &c.

Barley	Hordeum	Triandria Trigynia
☉ —Spring Barley	——vulgare	
☉ —Sprat, or Battledore	——diftichon	
☉ —Long-eared	——Zeocriton	
☉ —Siberian	——fibiricum	
Bean	Vicia-Faba	Diadelphia Decand·
☉ ——Horfe Bean	——minor	
Buckwheat, or Brank	Polygonum-Helxine	Octandria Trigynia
☉ ——Buckwheat	—— Fagopyrum	
Burnet	Poterium-Sanguisorba	Monoecia Polyand.
♃ ——Burnet	——Sanguisorba	
Cabbage	Braffica	Tetradynam. Siliq.
♂ ——White Scotch	——fcotica	
♂ ——American	——americana	
♂ ——Anjou	——algarvenfis	
♂ ——Turnep-rooted	—— Napobraffica	
♂ ——Cabbage Turn.	——Caulorapa	
Canary-grafs	Phalaris	Triandria Digynia·
♀ ——Canary-feed	——canarienfis	

Carrot		Daucus-Carota	Pentandria Digynia
♂	—Orange, or Sandwich	———aurantiaca	
	Clover	Trifolium	Diadelph. Decandr.
♂	——Red, or Dutch	———pratenfe	
♂	——Hop	———agrarium	
♃	——White Dutch, or Honeyfuckle Grafs	———repens	
	Cole-feed	Braffica-Napus	Tetradynam. Siliq·
	Flax	Linum	Pentandria Monog.
☉	——Flax, or Linfeed	——ufitatiffimum	
♄	Furze, Whins, or Gorfe	Ulex	Diadelphia Decand.
	—Furze	——europæus	
	Hemp	Cannabis	Dioecia Pentandria.
☉	——Hemp-feed	——fativa	
	Indian Corn	Zea	Monoecia Triandria
☉	———Indian Corn	——vulgaris	
	Madder	Rubia	Tetrandria Monog.
♃	—Madder	——tinctorum	
	Maw feed	Papaver	Polyandria Monog.
☉	——Maw-feed	——fomniferum	
	Millet	Milium	Triandria Digynia.
☉	——Millet	———lendigerum	
	Oat	Avena	Triandria Digynia.
☉	——White	——alba	
☉	——Black	——nigra	
☉	——Red	——rubra	
☉	——Naked	——nuda	
	Parfley	Apium	Pentandria Digynia
♂	——Parfley	———Petrofelinum	
	Parfnep	Paftinaca	Pentandria Digynia
♂	——Parfnep	——fativa	
	Pea	Pifum	Diadelph. Decand.
☉	——Grey Pea		
	Potatoe	Solanum	Pentandria Monog·
♃	—Cluftered American	——efculentum conglomeratum	
	Rape	Braffica-Napus	Tetradynam. Siliq.
☉	——Rape feed	——fylveftris	

Rye	Secale	Diandria Digynia.
⊙ ——Winter		
⊙ ——Summer		
Rye, or Ray-grafs	Hordeum	Triandria Trigynia.
♃ —— Rye-grafs		
Safflower, or	Carthamus	Syngen. Polyg.Æq.
⊙ ——Baſtard Saffron	——tinctorius	
Saffron	Crocus	Triandria Monog.
♃ ——Saffron	——officinalis	
Saintfoin	Hedyſatum	Diadelph. Decand.
♃ ——Saintfoin	—— Onobrychis	
Tare	Ervum	Diadelph. Decand.
⊙ ——Spring	——ſolonienſe	
⊙ ——Winter		
⊙.——Lentil	——Lens	
Teaſel	Dipſacus	Tetrandria Monog.
♂ ——Teaſel	——Fullonum	
Timothy-grafs	Phleum	Triandria Digynia.
♃ ——Timothy-grafs	——pratenſe	
Trefoil	Trifolium	Diadelph. Decand.
♃ ——Trefoil	——ochroleucum	
♃ ——Strawberry Tref.	——fragiferum	
♃ ——Hop Trefoil, or		
Noneſuch	——filiforme	
Turnep	Braſſica-Rapa	Tetradynam. Siliq.
♂ ——Green-topped	——viridis	
♂ ——White	——candida	
Vetch	Lathyrus	Diadelph. Decand.
⊙ ——Chichling Vetch	——Cicera	
Weld	Reſeda	Dodecand.Trigynia
♂ ——Weld	——Seſamoides	
Woad	Iſatis	Tetradyn. Siliquoſa
♂ ——Woad	——tinctoria	
Wheat	Triticum	Triandria Trigynia
⊙ ——Spring, or Sum.	——æſtivum	
⊙ ——Winter	——hybernum	
⊙ —-Poland	——pol nicum	
⊙ ——White-coned	——qu dratum album	
⊙ ——Red-coned	——quadratum rubrum	
⊙ ——Grey Pollard, or		
Duckbill	——turgidum	
⊙ ——Siberian Wheat,		
or Barley	——ſibiricum	

CHAP. IX.

A

CATALOGUE of FRUITS

CULTIVATED in ENGLAND.

ALMOND-TREE.
AMYGDALUS.

1	Bitter	communis
2	Sweet	dulcis

APPLE-TREE.
PYRUS-MALUS.

1 Juneating
2 Englifh Codlin
3 Dutch Codlin
4 Margaret
5 Summer Pearmain
6 Kentifh Fill-bafket
7 Nonefuch
8 Red Colvil
9 White Colvil
10 French Pippin
11 Golden Pippin
12 Aromatic Pippin
13 Embroidered
14 Black Pippin
15 Stone Pippin
16 Spencer's Pippin
17 Golden Rennet
18 Herefordfhire Pearmain
19 Loan's Pearmain
20 Royal Pearmain
21 Scarlet Pearmain
22 Chefter Pearmain
23 Kentifh Pippin
24 Kitchen Rennette
25 Pipy Ruffet
26 Acklam's Ruffet
27 Quince Apple
28 Lemon Pippin
29 Monftrous Rennette
30 Winter Pearmain
31 Holland Pippin
32 Kentifh Wilding
33 Norfolk Storing
34 Royal Ruffet
35 Wheeler's Ruffet
36 Pile's Ruffet
37 Norfolk Paradife
38 Cat's-head
39 Barnard's Baker
40 Nonpareil

APPLES FOR CYDER.
1 Redſtreak
2 Devonſhire Royal Wilding
3 John Apple
4 Herefordſhire Under-leaf
5 White Sour
6 Gennet Moyle
7 Everlaſting Hanger

APRICOT-TREE.
ARMENIACA.
1 Early Maſculine
2 Orange
3 Algier
4 Roman
5 Turkey
6 Breda
7 Blotched-leaved
8 Lord Dunmore's Breda
9 Temple
10 Bruſſels

BERBERRIS.
BERBERRY.
1 Common
2 Stoneleſs
3 White-fruited
4 Canadian

CHERRY-TREE,
PRUNUS-CERASUS.
1 Early May
2 May Duke
3 Spaniſh
4 White Heart
5 Red Heart
6 Amber Heart
7 Ox Heart
8 Tradeſcants
9 Harriſon's Heart
10 Bleeding Heart
11 Yellow Spaniſh
12 Late, or Arch-Duke
13 Lukeward
14 Kentiſh
15 Black Coronne

16 Large Mazard
17 Black
18 Carnation
19 Morello
20 Double-flowering

CHESNUT-TREE.
FAGUS-CASTANEA.
1 Spaniſh

CURRANT-TREE.
RIBES.
1 White Dutch
2 Red Dutch
3 Engliſh Red
4 Engliſh White
5 Champaign
6 Black

FIG-TREE.
FICUS.
1 Early Long Blue
2 Early White Marſeilles
3 Brown Iſchia
4 Small Brown Iſchia
5 Black Iſchia
6 Green Iſchia
7 Yellow Iſchia
8 Small Brown Iſchia
9 Black Genoa
10 Large White Genoa
11 Malta
12 Brown Naples
13 Brunſwick or Madonna
14 Large Blue or Purple
15 Large Brown
16 Black Provence

FILBERT.
CORYLUS.
1 Red Filbert
2 White Filbert
3 Hazle Nut
4 Byzantine
5 Tranſylvanian
6 Spaniſh

GOOSEBERRY.
RIBES-GROSSULARIA.

1 Hairy Green
2 Hairy Red
3 White Dutch
4 Amber
5 Hunt's Early Amber
6 Yellow-leaved Amber
7 Great Amber
8 Large Oval Yellow
9 Large Ironmonger
10 Smooth Green
11 Smooth Red
12 Red Rafpberry
13 Damfon
14 Hairy Globe
15 Rombullion
16 Deep Red
17 Late Hairy Red
18 Large White
19 Large Tawney
20 Champaign
21 Afton's Red

GRAPE.
VITIS.

1 July
2 White Sweet-water
3 Black Sweet-water
4 White Mufcadine
5 Black Mufcadine
6 Royal Mufcadine
7 Black Clufter
8 Burgundy
9 Corinth, or Currant
10 Black Hamburgh, or Warner
11 Red Hamburgh, or Warner
12 Claret
13 Parfley-leaved
14 Frankindal
15 Tokay
16 White Frontiniac
17 Black Frontiniac
18 Grifley Frontiniac

19 Raifin
20 Party-coloured, or Striped
21 Alexandrian Mufcat
22 Saint Peter's

MEDLAR-TREE.
MESPILUS.

1 Dutch
2 Nottingham

MULBERRY-TREE.
MORUS.

1 Black
2 Red
3 White

NECTARINE-TREE.
AMYGDALUS-PERSICA.

1 Fairchild's Early
2 Elruge
3 Newington
4 Scarlet
5 Italian
6 Roman
7 Murry
8 Golden
9 Temple
10 Peterborough

NUT-TREE.
CORYLUS.

1 Hazel Nut
2 Byzantine
3 Barcelona
4 Spanifh

PEACH-TREE.
AMYGDALUS-PERSICA.

1 White Nutmeg
2 Red Nutmeg
3 Early Ann
4 Small Mignon
5 Yellow Alberge
6 White Magdalen

7 Early Purple
8 Early Newington
9 French Mignon
10 Chevreuse
11 Red Magdalen
12 Montauban
13 Malta
14 Vanguard
15 Swalih
16 Nobleffe
17 Chancellor
18 Bellegarde
19 Lifle
20 Bourdine
21 Rofanna
22 Admirable
23 Old Newington
24 Carlile
25 Rambouillet
26 Belle de Vitri
27 Eaton
28 Portugal
29 Royal George
30 Venus's Breaft
31 Late Purple
32 Sion
33 Nivette
34 Royal
35 Perlique
36 Late Admirable
37 Monltrous Pavy
38 Catharine
39 Bloody
40 Double-flowering
41 Dwarf Orleans

PEAR-TREE.
PYRUS.
SUMMER PEARS.
1 Little Mufk
2 Little Baftard Mufk
3 Mufcadel
4 Jargonelle
5 Windfor
6 Orange Mufcat
7 Gros Blanquet

8 Summer Bergamot
9 Orange Bergamot
10 Rofe
11 Long-ftalked Blanquette
12 Summer Boncretien
13 Rofe-water
14 Prince
15 Great Ruffelet
16 Summer Bergamot

AUTUMN PEARS.
17 Autumn Bergamot
18 Swifs Bergamot
19 Red Buerrè
20 Grey Buerrè
21 Dean
22 Long Green
23 Monfieur John
24 Green Sugar
25 Marquifs
26 Burnt Cat
27 Crafan
28 Dauphin
29 Rouffeline
30 Swan's Egg

WINTER PEARS.
31 Colmar
32 Echafferie
33 Virgoleufe
34 Ambrette
35 Winter Thorn
36 Spanifh Boncretien
37 Winter's Wonder
38 Saint Germain
39 Winter Ruffelet
40 Winter Boncretien
41 German Mufcat
42 Saint Martial
43 Befi of Chaumontelle
44 Eafter Bergamot
45 Holland Bergamot

BAKING PEARS.
46 Parkinfon's Warden
47 Cadillac
48 Winter Citron

49 Uvedale's St. Germain
50 Franc-real
51 Double-flowering

A more numerous Catalogue could have been given of French Pears, but those have been selected as some of the best.

PLUM-TREE.

1 Primordian
2 Morocco
3 Early Damask
3 Early Tours
5 Orleans
6 White Orleans
7 Fotheringham
8 Black Perdigron
9 Violet Perdigron
10 White Perdigron
11 Imperial
12 Red Bonum Magnum
13 White Bonum Magnum
14 Cheston
15 Apricot Plum
16 Maitre Claude
17 Diaper
18 Little Queen Claude
19 Damson
20 Myrobalan
21 Green Gage
22 Large Queen Claude
23 Cloth of Gold
24 Saint Catharine
25 Royal
26 Mirabelle
27 Brignole
28 Empress
29 Cherry Plum
30 White Pear
31 Muscle
32 St. Julian
33 Black Bullace
34 White Bullace
35 Black-thorn, or Sloe

QUINCE-TREE.
PYRUS-CYDONIA.

1 Apple Quince
2 Pear Quince
3 Portugal Quince

RASPBERRY.
RUBUS.

1 White
2 Red
3 Twice-bearing

SERVICE-TREE.
CRATÆGUS.

1 Service
2 Azarole

STRAWBERRY.
FRAGARIA.

1 Red Wood
2 White Wood
3 Montreuil, or Dutch Wood
4 Alpine
5 White Alpine
6 Green Wood
7 Female Hautboy
8 Male Hautboy
9 Globe Hautboy
10 Virginian, or Scarlet
11 Female Chili
12 Bath Chili
13 Devonshire Chili
14 Dutch Chili
15 Carolinian
16 White Carolinian

For a larger Collection, see Page 82—84

WALNUT-TREE.
JUGLANS.

1 Common
2 Large
3 Thin-shelled
4 French

CATA-

A

CATALOGUE of FRUITS,

NATIVES of GREAT BRITAIN and IRELAND.

BERBERRY.
BERBERIS.
Red.
White.
Stoneless.

BILBERRY.
VACCINIUM, MYRTILLUS.
Bilberry, or Black Whort.
Great Bilberry   uliginosum.

BLACKBERRY.
RUBUS, FRUTICOSUS.
Blackberry, or Bramble.

BULLACE-TREE.
PRUNUS, INSITITIA.
White.
Black.

CHESNUT-TREE.
FAGUS-CASTANEA.
Chesnut.

CHERRY-TREE.
PRUNUS-CERASUS.
Wild Black.

CLOUDBERRY.
RUBUS-CHAMOEMORUS.
Cloudberry, or Dwarf Mulberry.

CRAB-TREE.
PYRUS-MALUS.
Crab.

CRANBERRY.
VACCINIUM-OXYCOCCOS.
Cranberry, Moss or Moorberry.

CROWBERRY.
EMPETRUM, NIGRUM.
Crowberry.

CURRANT.
RIBES.
Red.
White.

DEWBERRY.
RUBUS, CÆSIUS.
Dewberry.

ELDER-TREE.
SAMBUCUS.
Black.

Q

PEAR-TREE.
PYRUS.
Wild Pear.

NUT-TREE.
CORYLUS.
Hazel-Nut.

RASPBERRY.
RUBUS, IDÆUS.
Red.
White.

SERVICE-TREE.
CRATÆGUS,
Service.

SLOE-TREE.
PRUNUS.
Sloe.   ſpinoſa.

STRAWBERRY.
FRAGARIA.
Red Wood.   ſylveſtris.
White Wood.   ſylv. alba.
Green Wood.   viridis.
Hautboy.   moſchata.

WHORTLE-BERRY,
or RED WHORTS.
VACCINIUM, VITIS IDÆA,
Red Whorts.

AN
ENGLISH INDEX,
REFERRING TO THE
LATIN NAMES OF THE PLANTS.

Q 2

INDEX.

INDEX.

Q 3

INDEX.

I N D E X.

Q 4

INDEX.

INDEX.

INDEX.

I N D E X.

INDEX.

I N D E X.

I N D E X.

INDEX.

R

INDEX.

INDEX.

R 2

INDEX.

INDEX.

INDEX.

INDEX.

INDEX.

INDEX.

I N D E X.

INDEX.

V.

THE END.

HARDY TREES AND SHRUBS.

69. ILEX. p. 17.
34 Americana   Amer. Holly.

114. RIBES. p. 31.
5 Cynosbati   Prickly-fruited.
6 Grossularifolium Goose-berry-
             leav'd Currant.

116. RUBUS. p. 37.
12 Chamæmorus Cloudberry, or
            Dwarf Mulberry.

121. SALVIA. p. 39.
9 tomentosa - Tea Sage.

140. THYMUS. p. 43.
7 glaber   Great Mother
           of Thyme.

HERBACEOUS PLANTS.

6. ADONIS. p. 48.
2 annua   1 Red Adonis flo. ☉
3 an. lutea   2 Yel. Adonis flo. ☉

15. ALLIUM-CEPA. p. 51.
8 arborea   Tree Onion.

AMARANTHUS. p. 51.
L. G. Pl. 1060. Cl. 21. Ord. 5.
For the Varieties, see p. 199.

AMETHYSTEA. p. 52.
L. G. Pl. 34. Cl. 2. Ord. 1.
1   Amethystea. ☉

45. ASTER. p. 58.
chinensis   Chinese Starwort.
For the Varieties, see p. 200.

AVENA. p. 60.
L. G. Pl. 91. Cl. 3. Ord. 2.
For the Varieties, see p. 218.
           S

55. BORAGO. p. 61.
2 officinalis Borage. ☉

61. CALENDULA. p. 63.
5   Purple and white
          Dwarf Marygold.

64. CAMPANULA. p. 64.
1 Spec. alb. 1. Venus's Looking-
            glass.
2 Spec. purp. 2 Purple.
3 Spec. hybr. Small

CHENOPODIUM, p. 69.
L. G. Pl. 309. Cl. 5. Ord. 2.
1 Scoparia Belvidere, or Sum-
         mer Cypress.

98. CROCUS. p. 73.
9 variegatus Striped or Scotch
          Crocus.

101. CUCURBITA. p. 74.
2 pyriformis Pear-shaped Gourd
3 aurantiiform. Orange shaped G.

104. CYNOGLOSSUM. p. 75.
2 linifolium   Venus's Navelwort.

120. DRACOCEPHALUM. p. 78.
5 Moldavica   Moldavian Balm.

155. HEDYSARUM. p. 89.
7 coronarium alb. White French
              Honey Suckle. ♂
8 cor. rubr.   Red Fr. Honeyf. ♂

163. HIBISCUS. p. 90.
2 Trionum   Bladder Ketmia.

185. LATHYRUS. p. 96.
4 odoratus   Sweet Pea.

189. LEPIDIUM. p. 97.
2 fativum   Garden Crefs.
3 fat. crifp.   Curled-leaved Gar-
            den Crefs.
4 fat. latifol. Broad-leaved Gar-
            den Crefs.

LINUM. p. 98.
2 ufitatiffimum   Flax.

196. LOTUS. p. 93.
2 tetragonolobus Winged Pea. ☉

203. MALVA. p. 100,
12 orientalis   Oriental Mallow.

206. MEDICAGO. p. 101.
4 intertexta   Hedgehog Trefoil.
5 fcutellata   Snail Trefoil.

250. PHYSALIS. p. 111.
2. maxima   Blue Alkekengl.
3.   White.

271. RANUNCULUS. p. 116.
14. fanguineus Scarlet Ranunculus.

273. RESEDA. p. 117.
3.   Upright Refeda.

RICINUS. p. 118.
L. G. Pl. 1085. Cl. 21. Ord. 9.
1. vulgaris   Palma Chrifti. ☉

314. SOLANUM. p. 126.
1. Lycoperficon Red Love Apple.
2. Lycop. alb.   White Love Apple.
1. Melongena   Purple Egg-plant.
2. Mel. alb,   White Egg-plant.

336. TRAGOPOGON. p. 131.
3. porrifolium.   Salfafy.

TROPÆOLUM. p. 175.
L. G. Pl. 466. Cl. 8. Ord. 1.
1. majus   1. Large Nafturtium. ☉
2. minus   2. Dwarf Nafturt. ☉

348. VALERIANA. p. 133.
9. Locufta   Corn Sallad. ☉

353. VICIA. p. 135.
5. Faba   Bean.
For the Varieties, fee p. 212.

355. URTICA. p. 136.
4. pilulifera   Roman Nettle.

GREENHOUSE PLANTS.

55. CITRUS-AURANTIUM.
       p. 148.
17.   Bergamot Orange.

126. OLEA. p. 165.
6. odoratiffima Chinefe fweet-fcent-
            ed Olive-tree.

OMITTED.

KITCHEN-GARDEN SEEDS.

In Page 212, to 216.

ALEXANDER.
SMYRNIUM. ♃
Common   Olufatrum.

BEAN.
Long-podded.
Dwarf Red-bloffomed.
Dwarf White-bloffomed.
Mumford.
Turkey.

BOORCOLE.
Green variegated.
Purple variegated.
Sea Kale.

BROCCOLI.
Late Dwarf Purple.

CABBAGE.
Early Batterfea.
Hollow.

COLEWORT.
Hardy Green.

CUCUMBER.
White Dutch.

LETTUCES.
Forcing, or black-feeded Cabbage.
Hammerfmith Green.
Spotted Cos.
Forcing Cos.

ONION.
Deptford.
Red Spanifh.
Tree Onion.

PEA.
Dwarf Marrowfat.
Tall Marrowfat.
Spanifh Morotto.
Green Rouncival.
White Rouncival.
Grey Rouncival.
Crooked Sugar.

POTATOE.
Wifeman's Early.

RADISH.
Red Turnep-rooted.
Yellow Short-topped.

SPINACH.
Red-leaved.
French.

In the English Index.

Tarragon   Artemifia-Abfinthium Dracunculus   56, 216

9 781120 031518